Reshaping Social Work Series

Series Editors: **Robert Adams, Lena Dominelli and Malcolm Payne**

The **Reshaping Social Work** series aims to develop the knowledge base for critical, reflective practitioners. Each book is designed to support students on qualifying social work programmes and update practitioners on crucial issues in today's social work, strengthening research knowledge, critical analysis and skilled practice to shape social work to meet future challenges.

Published titles

Social Work and Power Roger Smith
Social Work Research for Social Justice Beth Humphries

Forthcoming titles

Anti-Racist Practice in Social Work Kish Bhatti-Sinclair
Social Care Practice in Context Malcolm Payne
Critical Issues in Social Work with Older People Mo Ray, Judith Phillips and
    Miriam Bernard
Social Work and Spirituality Margaret Holloway and Bernard Moss

Invitation to authors
The Series Editors welcome proposals for new books within the *Reshaping Social Work* series. Please contact one of the series editors for an initial discussion:

- Robert Adams at rvadams@rvadams.karoo.co.uk
- Lena Dominelli at lena.dominelli@durham.ac.uk
- Malcolm Payne at M.Payne@stchristophers.org.uk

Reshaping Social Work
Series Editors: **Robert Adams, Lena Dominelli and Malcolm Payne**
Series Standing Order ISBN 1–4039–4878–X
(outside North America only)

You can receive future titles in this series as they are published by placing a standing
order. Please contact your bookseller or, in the case of difficulty, write to us at the address
below with your name and address, the title of the series and the ISBN quoted above.

Customer Services Department
Macmillan Distribution Ltd
Houndmills
Basingstoke
Hampshire
RG21 6XS
England

Social Work Research for Social Justice

Beth Humphries

palgrave
macmillan

Published by
PALGRAVE MACMILLAN
Houndmills, Basingstoke, Hampshire RG21 6XS and
175 Fifth Avenue, New York, N.Y. 10010
Companies and representatives throughout the world

PALGRAVE MACMILLAN is the global academic imprint of the Palgrave Macmillan division of St. Martin's Press, LLC and of Palgrave Macmillan Ltd. Macmillan® is a registered trademark in the United States, United Kingdom and other countries. Palgrave is a registered trademark in the European Union and other countries.

ISBN-13: 978–1–4039–4935–6
ISBN-10: 1–4039–4935–2

This book is printed on paper suitable for recycling and made from fully managed and sustained forest sources. Logging, pulping and manufacturing processes are expected to conform to the environmental regulations of the country of origin.

A catalogue record for this book is available from the British Library.

A catalog record for this book is available from the Library of Congress.

10	9	8	7	6	5	4	3	2	1
17	16	15	14	13	12	11	10	09	08

Printed in China

Contents

Tables

Abbreviations

BASW	British Association of Social Workers
BJSW	*British Journal of Social Work*
CA	conversation analysis
CDA	critical discourse analysis
DELTA	Development Leadership Teams in Action
ESRC	Economic and Social Research Council
HGC	Healthy Gay City
PAR	participative or participatory action research
PR	participatory research
PRA	Participatory Rural Appraisal
QAA	Quality Assurance Agency
RCT	randomized control trial
SCIE	Social Care Institute for Excellence
SPSS	Statistical Package for the Social Sciences
SSD	social services department
WHO	World Health Organization
WILF	Wiltshire Independent Living Fund

Acknowledgements

My thanks go to the general editors of the series, Robert Adams, Lena Dominelli and Malcolm Payne, for inviting me to write this book and for giving me the opportunity to bring together germinating ideas about social work research and social justice.

Sage Publications and Palgrave Macmillan gave permission to reproduce extracts from books, for which I owe thanks. These are acknowledged in the text where they appear.

I also appreciate the advice, understanding and patience of Catherine Gray, Mari Shullaw and Sheree Keep at Palgrave Macmillan, particularly when there were unannounced changes to the manuscript.

Over the years numerous students have challenged my thinking about social work, about research and about social justice, and any contribution the book will make is in no small way due to their enthusiasm and effort.

Last, but definitely first, I appreciate the unfailing support of Marion and our dogs, Sally, little Lligwy who visited us briefly and left us far too soon, and that lovable rascal, Bramble.

chapter 1 Introduction: research as contentious

Introduction

This is a book about research methods for social work and social care practice. The emphasis on the need for students to understand research approaches and for practitioners to be 'research-minded' is an important development for the profession and one to be welcomed. The book is intended as a practical contribution both in enhancing awareness of studies that inform practice and in offering tools to those who conduct their own studies. There are a number of good books on research methods that are used widely on training courses (see, for example, Bell, 1993; Denscombe, 2003; Mark, 1996; Royse, 2003; Sheppard, 2004) and that offer detailed practical instructions for conducting research projects. I have resisted the temptation to write another text that is solely a 'how-to-do-it' manual, because no human activity is uninfluenced by particular ways of viewing the world, and research no less than any other activity is always in the interests of some social group or other. It is as well to acknowledge that at the outset, and to declare what this means for the rest of the book.

In constructing the content therefore, it has been my aim to set the book firmly in a framework of social justice and thus to take a position which sees social research not solely as a range of neutral approaches to the examination of social problems, but as itself a profoundly political exercise, and as having potential to contribute to social change for good or ill. In describing a range of methodologies available to social workers and social work researchers, I offer a critique of them in relation to their use towards transformation in the conditions of poverty and oppression experienced by many of those who find themselves in the system of welfare.

The book is aimed at qualifying students who are required to demonstrate that they understand the methods and debates advocated for practitioner-researchers, at practitioners who are increasingly urged to evaluate their practice and to pursue continuing professional development, at academics who are responsible for teaching and research in social work and social care, at managers who are accountable for the work they supervise and at policy makers who often set the terms of research undertaken. It is also an appeal to service user groups who increasingly carry out their own research, or demand a say in that of dominant institutions, or for whom an informed critique of research affecting them is crucial to their future. Although the content of the book is written from the UK social work and social care context, many of the themes – epistemological and methodological debates, 'evaluation', 'evidence-based practice', 'research-mindedness', for example – as well as the methods presented, will be relevant to concerns in the social and health professions in the wider global economy, and I hope will contribute to a critical rethinking of practice in this field.

This introductory chapter and the following chapter are used to set the context of research in social work, and to address some of the key themes readers will need to appreciate in the effort to grasp the implications of the methods and approaches described later. For this reason it is important for readers not to skip these chapters, but to persevere in the intellectual effort to understand the complexities of the notion of research-mindedness, the concept of evidence-based practice, competing research paradigms and generally the politics of social research, as these form the building blocks for what comes later.

Research-mindedness

In recent years social workers and other professionals have been encouraged to develop 'research-mindedness', both informing themselves of research findings and applying them to their practice, and undertaking their own research where appropriate, though the tradition of research in social work has a long history. Dominelli (2005) offers a full discussion of this and of the background to the contemporary interest in research. Briefly, in the UK the government has insisted on this in a number of ways, notably through the Quality Assurance Agency statement about expectations of standards of degrees in social work (QAA, 2000), within National Occupational Standards, the requirements for the degree in social work and in post-qualifying training. The remit of the Social Care Institute for Excellence (SCIE) is to promote 'useful and relevant knowledge' (Walter et al., 2004, Preface). Along with this have been established a number of government-supported organizations, and the Economic and Social Research Council (ESRC) has brought universities into a UK Network for Evidence-based Policy and Practice. But research-mindedness is not a straightforward notion, and is caught up with competing definitions of the nature of 'knowledge', what counts as 'research', whose interests are served by it, and so on. This debate about what counts as research and knowledge, and who decides on what is acceptable as methods and data, is at the heart of concerns of social researchers. There are many kinds of knowledge, and in our society some are regarded as more acceptable than others, in research as in other aspects of life. In the hierarchy of knowledge, certain per-spectives are privileged over others, and it is important for social work and health professionals not to be naïve about the politics of social research that affects their practice. For example, managerial and gov-ernment priorities are focused on urgent answers to practical problems – what will work in changing behaviour? What resources are needed? What are the costs involved? (see Butler and Pugh, 2004) – often to the exclusion of explanations as to why the issue became a problem in the first place, or the meaning of behaviour to individuals and groups. In this scenario 'best-practice' research-mindedness is concerned with targets, budgets, resources. On the other hand some have argued that research-mindedness is 'best practice' when it inquires into inequali-ties and injustices that result in problematic behaviour, and indeed when it questions why such behaviour is regarded as problematic (Webb, 2001). Here research-mindedness requires a commitment – even a passion – on the part of practitioners and researchers, which will lead them towards thinking that is beyond common-sense, taken-for-granted and instrumental knowledge, where they explore perspec-tives on social issues that they care deeply about.

Research-mindedness in social work is meant to refer to the need for practitioners to be aware of research findings and to apply these in their daily practice. It also entails social workers involving them-selves in evaluating their own practice and in making appropriate changes to it. However with regard to the first of these, a complica-tion is that research findings are seldom clear or straightforward and indeed can be conflicting, so 'application' is a matter of interpreta-tion within organizations, which will have their own priorities and interests. Practitioners should not accept these interpretations uncrit-ically. In situations where practitioners or students are engaged in their own research or evaluation of practice it is important to be aware that there will always be a number of ways of defining the problem to be researched, even where one is apparently collecting statistics about client need and services. Therefore a key ingredient of research-mindedness is a questioning attitude that asks why, and to what purpose. Jo Campling, in the foreword to Everitt et al. (1992) offers a vision of research-mindedness that widens the official defini-tions of it to include dimensions linked to ethics and justice. Her three principles are:

- a participatory/developmental model of social work, as opposed to a social control model;
- anti-oppressive values;
- striving towards a genuine partnership between practitioners and those whom they serve. (p. vii)

In Campling's view, research-mindedness should be explored in an holistic way:

> Problem formulation, data collection, data analysis and evaluation are not treated as discrete stages in the supposedly linear process of research. Instead each of these is addressed using the same framework: values, purposes, ethics, communication, roles and skills. Anti-oppressive practices and developmental principles also anchor the process from beginning to end. (p. vii)

For the research-minded practitioner, the taken-for-granted is opened up to critical scrutiny. Always in mind is the way in which values and interests pervade research studies, the knowledge produced by them and the policies that are implemented as a result of them.

Evidence-based practice

Evidence-based practice is a dimension of research-mindedness, refer-ring to the application of research findings to practice, instead of practitioners operating simply on what is common sense, or their own whimsical or preferred methods of intervention. Increasingly official statements about helping professions assume evidence-based criteria as a building block of practice (e.g. Audit Commission, 1996; ESRC, 2001). Research that takes place in health and social care, and indeed in all other settings, should be credible, rigorous and method-ologically sound, and should provide a basis that can guide and underpin practice. Across the professional and political spectrum the model is applied, 'evidence-based medicine, evidence-based educa-tion, evidence-based social work, evidence-based policy making and evidence-based practice ... evidence-based everything' (Oakley, 2000, p. 308). This seems desirable and straightforward, but as with 'research-mindedness', there are complexities. It needs to be said that (i) what 'evidence' is, is not straightforward and (ii) 'evidence' is seldom if ever clear, definitive and unambiguous. This means there are different views about what it is legitimate to call evidence (e.g. expert observations? Research participants' experiences and under-standings?). Evidence is also open to a range of interpretations that can result in very different action being taken. In social care research a debate is going on about what kinds of research are appropriate and

legitimate. There is a view that the government and social care organizations prefer a scientific approach, conducted by experts and
based on experiments as used in the physical sciences, and on 'hard'
data. This is set in opposition to the 'soft' data that result from qualitative interviewing and include the meanings, opinions and stories of
the people who are being researched (see Butler and Pugh, 2004). The
following definition was developed in the field of health, but contains the key ingredients of this scientific approach:

> Evidence-based practice is the conscientious, explicit and
> judicious use of current best evidence in making decisions
> about the care of individual patients, based on skills which
> allow the doctor to evaluate both personal experience and
> external evidence in a systematic and objective manner.
> (Sackett et al., 1997, p. 2)

Newman et al. (2005, p. 4) spell out what they understand by 'consci-
entious' (governed by a sense of duty where professionals can justify
their claims to knowledge); 'explicit' (distinctly expressing all that is
meant, by making clear on what basis decisions about interventions
are made); and 'judicious' (exercising sound judgement grounded in
experience). Few people would argue with the view that available evidence helps us in decision-making in the best interests of service users
(although there are always questions about what it is actually telling
us). However, there have been concerns that the model of research
that currently dominates social work and social care is the scientific
model that meets managerial priorities to find urgent answers to practical problems, mainly concerned with what works in regulating
people's behaviour with the expectation of identifying definitive
interventions in the attempt to measure change and productivity. As
a result a more qualitative approach that produces evidence about the
context in which problems arise, as well as the views of those who are
most affected by them are dismissed as too subjective. Nevertheless
one criticism of scientific approaches to evidence-based practice is
that they are biased because they are unable to take account of the
wider socio-economic and cultural contexts that have relevance for
behaviour. They therefore distort the evidence by presenting only a
partial view. Thus this advocacy of a very limited definition of social
need and social research is seen as political because it poses questions
and engages methods that exclude an examination of both the messiness of practice and the social structures that form the context for all
our lives (see Humphries, 2003 for a fuller discussion).

A second criticism of the dominant model of evidence-based practice is as I have noted above: there is often conflicting evidence and
little by way of 'proof' or certainty that allows a smooth process from

'clear findings' to application to practice. This leads to misleading beliefs that it is possible to produce reliable evidence in a way that will guide practice. This approach emphasizes the application of scientific models of measurement, normally used in controlled laboratory-type conditions, and that are not universally accepted as appropriate for research with people. The approach rests on a belief that (i) changing behaviour is a priority in the social care professions and that (ii) the best tools for understanding what works in achieving this are experiments – 'scientific observations taken in carefully controlled conditions' (Webb, 2001, p. 62). Thus if a programme of behaviour change is found to 'work' in one setting, it can be replicated and can achieve similar results elsewhere. Yet there is no certainty that successful interventions with, for example, girls thought to be at risk of delinquency in a particular housing estate will 'work' in another housing estate (see Oakley, 2000 for other examples). Later in the chapter I discuss the controversies surrounding the philosophical assumptions inherent in this model (see the section on research paradigms), but here suffice to say that it is criticized for ignoring the complex processes involved in social work and other professional interventions that are not dependent only on rational decisions. Nevertheless the view that evidence-based practice is scientific and its methods objective is a 'value-laden belief which is being constantly fostered in social work practice and government policy' (Webb, 2001, p. 74), leading to a technical view of practice that excludes professional discretion. Yet there are many factors at play in any decision about policy or intervention. For example, the belief that 'prison works' has resulted in an increase in the numbers of 18–21-year-old men imprisoned, and ignores research that suggests locking up young offenders increases the risk of youth crime (NACRO, 2001; Ramsbotham, 2001). This suggests that other influences such as political expediency are influential in the process. We also know that attempts to impose change are unlikely to work unless they have the co-operation of the people upon whom they are focused. Evidence-based practice is at risk of leaving human agency and will out of the equation. Webb's very useful critique claims that social work simply does not and cannot work in the way evidence-based practice suggests, that the methods involved are too mechanistic and that what is required are models that recognize complexity and instability in the dynamic processes of interconnections between human beings. This is an argument for keeping research options open, and for placing greater value on a range of approaches to studying human beings.

This debate is at the heart of the discussion of research models considered in this book. They are each underpinned by philosophical assumptions that make different claims as to their effectiveness in conveying a 'true' picture of human activity, and this will be addressed as the book proceeds. So the question of whether to use qualitative or quantitative methods is not solely one of which is appropriate for a particular study. Different researchers hold strong views about the appropriateness, the effectiveness and the legitimacy of each of them and the philosophical assumptions that inform them.

The qualitative–quantitative divide

Much of the debate about competing methods centres on which are best – quantitative or qualitative methods. Since at least the 1970s researchers have argued about their beliefs in the predominance of either qualitative or quantitative approaches. Sarantakos (2005, p. 46) sets out the comparisons (see Table 1.1).

The main perceived differences are that

- Qualitative methods claim to be 'subjective' (i.e. they are concerned with the perspectives of the research subjects) and bring the researcher close to the subjects; they are flexible and can be adapted according to the context; and they see data as mutually constructed between the research subjects and the researcher.
- Quantitative methods claim to be 'objective' (they attempt to remove the researcher's views and values from the study); they emphasize cause-effect linkages; they are based on a model of the physical sciences and on strict, inflexible rules; they distance the researcher from the research subjects.

Quantitative and qualitative methods are not only different approaches to research, in the controversies around them they are

Table 1.1 Qualitative versus quantitative approaches

Quantitative	Qualitative
Sets researchers apart from reality	Sets researchers close to reality
Studies reality from the outside	Studies reality from the inside
Uses closed questions	Uses open methods of data collection
Employs a fixed research design	Employs a flexible research design
Captures a still picture of the world	Captures the world in action
Employs scientific/statistical methods	Employs naturalistic methods
Analyses data only after collection	Analyses data during and after
Chooses methods before the study	collection
Produces most useful quantitative	Chooses methods before/during study
data	Produces most useful qualitative data

Source: S Sarantakos, *Social Research*, 2005, 3rd edn. Reproduced with permission of Palgrave Macmillan.

valued differently, with each camp dismissive of the other (see Butler and Pugh, 2004; Sarantakos, 2005; Webb, 2001). The heated debate involves qualitative researchers criticizing quantitative methods as inadequate and inappropriate for research with human beings; and quantitative researchers seeing qualitative methods as 'a soft option', unsystematic and without rigour. It must be said however, that quantitative research designs appear to be those that are most favoured by governments because of their apparent potential to deliver statistically reliable answers quickly and relatively cheaply. When we speak of 'quantitative' and 'qualitative', we are not solely discussing methods, but are invoking deeper questions of what philosophical paradigms or what sets of assumptions about the social world are appropriate for the social sciences. I address these questions later under a heading of 'research paradigms'.

Meanwhile, in fact both methodologies may be used within any single research study. For example in a study of school, community and family influences on successful pathways through middle childhood, Kreider and Mayer used a mixed-method approach that included (quantitative) questionnaire surveys of the children's primary caregivers and teachers, as well as in-depth (qualitative) case studies of a sample of the children (Greene, Kreider and Mayer 2005). In spite of this, very often the ways mixed-method studies are written up reveals that the writers regard one as superior to the other, usually in the form of using qualitative studies as preliminary work to the 'real' quantitative substance of the research. Sheldon's (2001) riposte to Webb's (2001) critique of evidence-based research in social work reveals this attitude. Sheldon, while conceding that some qualitative approaches may 'have a place' (p. 806), is clear that these are no substitute for the scientific basis of the quantitative evidence-based approaches he espouses. This attempted assimilation of qualitative approaches is not a satisfactory resolution to the debate.

These debates arise because in the world of science and social science, traditional definitions of what knowledge is have lain in the domain of 'experts'. They have in general been suspicious of and have excluded from legitimate knowledge forms of knowing not originating from the quantitative domain, such as autobiography, oral history, fiction and storytelling – accounts that focus on the quality and meaning of individual experiences.

Nevertheless some writers who may lean towards one approach recognize the contribution of the other. Oakley, a feminist researcher who has advocated qualitative methods to capture women's experiences of oppression, and indeed remains suspicious about *experimental* methods, says:

> As to quantitative methods more generally, the very charting of women's oppression required quantification surely: we needed figures for women's schooling and education *vis-à-vis* that of men, the distribution and work of women in the paid and unpaid labour markets, women's earnings, the burden of health problems and so forth, in order to say to what extent the situations of men and women were (are) structurally differentiated. (2000, p. 19)

In other words, if it had not been for the large-scale quantitative studies, the reality of women's oppression (and that of other groups) might have remained at a level of individual women and might easily have been dismissed as not a common experience. The availability of data on the bigger picture makes such dismissal less likely. The goal, she argues, is for 'a democratization of ways of knowing . . . and also a synthesis of these, so that the focus is on choosing the right method for the research question' (p. 21).

Nevertheless, as is clear in the discussion about the evidence-based practice movement, there is a long way to go to reach this goal. Officially there continues to be approval of and preference for quantitative, particularly experimental or quasi-experimental, approaches and for the production of 'hard' data about 'what works'. In social work, as elsewhere, this has provoked much antagonism and debate in the literature (see, for example, Butler and Pugh, 2004; Humphries, 2003; Humphries, 2004a; Sheldon, 2001; Webb, 2001), a debate that is not new in the wider social research community, indeed has raged over decades, and is likely to go on and on.

The paradigm debate

The debate about methodology is incomplete if it is pitched only in terms of the qualitative/quantitative divide. It is symptomatic of the deeper quarrel about research paradigms.

The notion of paradigms in social research has been discussed in a variety of ways (see, for example, Hammersley, 1995). Here, for simplicity, I have identified two broad paradigms and categorized them as 'constructivist' and 'realist', though 'positivist' is used frequently, with a similar meaning to 'realist', and 'phenomenological' or 'post-positivist' have broadly similar meanings to 'constructivist'.

Thomas Kuhn defines a paradigm as a general conceptual framework that reflects a set of scientific and metaphysical beliefs within which theories are tested, evaluated and revised if necessary (see Audi, 1995). A paradigm guides people within a discipline in formulating questions deemed to be legitimate, identifying appropriate techniques and instruments and building explanatory schemes for the phenomena under consideration. It offers a framework within which individuals or groups choose certain research directions and approaches to accomplish their research ends.

Central to the concept is the notion of belief – people's choices of paradigm depend on their values and convictions, and are influenced by historical context. The debate revolves around the incompatibility of realist and constructivist paradigms. The belief that research should aim as far as possible to exclude personal and other influences and to strive only towards the pursuit of (quantitative) knowledge is based on the realist or positivist (see Hammersley, 1995) view that the physical sciences provide the ideal model to be adopted by the social sciences. This model holds that social reality is external to the researcher, to be grasped and understood through appropriate methods that are rigorously examined and applied to remove all kinds of bias, including the prejudices of the researcher. Its 'gold standard' method is the experiment, which entails controlling the environment so that intervening variables do not contaminate the research.

This approach has been challenged by constructivists on a number of grounds. First, it is argued that research models based on the physical sciences are not appropriate for the study of human beings, who cannot be controlled in laboratory settings in the same way, and as sentient, thinking people bring their own meanings and interpretation to events. Methods that are appropriate to capture this reality must be naturalistic – that is, they must observe people going about their daily lives rather than in laboratory-type conditions, and discuss their understandings in some depth and in different settings. Moreover, it is argued that researchers are also thinking, interpreting humans contributing to the construction of reality, which may vary at different times and in different contexts. Their actions, words and understanding of events are also regarded as phenomena to be studied in detail in their own right, but are not to be removed from their environment and its influence on behaviour. Reality is not 'out there' but is actively and inevitably being constructed by both research participants and the researcher. The researcher's location in all this is as important as that of those being researched, and needs to be made available for examination and interrogation.

A constructivist paradigm recognizes the existence of multiple perceptions and plurality of world-views that can best be represented as an intricate network of human constructs. In contrast, a realist paradigm contends that there is only one independent and ordered reality, whose elements are governed by immutable natural laws of cause and effect, and which is the ultimate focus of all research activities (see Guba, 1990). In summary, what we have are two contrasting accounts of how it is that people 'know':

> While researchers in one camp think they are studying the real world, which consists of things that it is feasible to try to find out about, those in the other dispute the idea that there is a single reality to be known, and regard the pursuit of 'hard data' as impracticable and unachievable. What for one side is a set of 'facts' is for the other a complex and impenetrable kaleidoscope of heavily constructed social meanings. Researchers in one paradigm leap in with all the faith derived from (something called) logical positivism that they will (providing they specify and measure and count enough) indeed be able to establish the truth; whereas their counterparts in the other paradigm walk much more lightly, aware of the shifting ground of human social interaction and identity, and doggedly bound to the apparently more modest goal of reproducing faithfully and democratically whatever it is they think they may have found. (Oakley, 2000, p. 25)

I have included this long quote from Oakley because it describes succinctly the opposing positions. What is signified is not so much a disagreement about techniques (e.g. quantitative and qualitative), but more *a divergence about theories of what knowledge is – ways of framing knowledge as well as means of obtaining it.* Constructivists believe that the people who are the subjects of research have knowledge about their situation, and the task of the researcher is to find ways of making that knowledge available. Realists see research subjects simply as providers of information that is analysed by the researcher and interpreted against a pre-selected set of theories – a dichotomy of 'expert' knowledge and 'lay' knowledge (this exaggerates the difference to make the point. The role of the constructivist researcher in interpretation is not as clear as this characterization suggests).

So is there no convergence between these positions? The associated question is whether the favoured methods associated with these approaches are incommensurable (having no common measure and therefore incompatible). Gendron (2001) explores this question by delineating the two paradigms according to four interconnected axes – ontological (concerned with the nature and essence of things), epistemological (the study of theories of knowledge), methodological (systems of methods and rules) and teleological (concerning the end or purpose) – in order to examine the incompatibility argument, and to help researchers to clarify and articulate their paradigmatic assumptions. Gendron argues that a paradigm's coherence results from the interdependence of the four axes and the overlapping of their respective domains. I have adapted Gendron's model to formulate Table 1.2.

Gendron's depiction does suggest the incompatibility of constructivist and realist paradigms, and of the qualitative and quantitative methods for the most part identified with them. This raises questions for social work research. On the one hand are government policies that insist on the participation of service users in research and practice, a position that suggests qualitative and participatory research (see Chapter 4) as appropriate for studies in community care, mental health, health promotion and child care, for example. This is explicitly with a view to the transformation of services, to ensure they are relevant, appropriate and what the consumer demands. The implication here is of the active involvement of service users, practitioners and researchers at every stage, and one would expect that appropriate methods would be within a constructivist paradigm. A qualitative approach is more readily adaptable to contemporary policies of transformation in public services.

However, the currently favoured methodological approach to research in all these areas is one that draws on a realist paradigm, with an essentially quantitative approach by a neutral researcher, separate from subjects and their interests, as in the evidence-based model of practice discussed earlier. This is an approach that demands to know 'what works?' so that 'effective practice' can be replicated nationwide (Butler and Drakeford, 2001; Humphries, 2003, 2004b). As Hammersley has noted, increasing social research has focused on

> practical inquiry, geared directly to providing information
> that is needed to deal with some practical problem, so that the
> immediate audience for research reports is people with a
> practical interest in the issue; notably but not exclusively,
> policy makers and occupational practitioners. (2000, p. 224)

Not only so, but the 'practical problems' that are envisaged here are concerned with changing 'deviant' and 'anti-social' behaviour, and focused on individuals rather than social structures. The urgent teleological demand for definitive answers to social problems has led social research and social work research into a situation that ignores ontological (the nature of things) and epistemological (theories of knowledge) inconsistencies, and towards methods exclusively concerned with changes in individual behaviour.

But perhaps the arguments about incommensurability have been over-stated? We saw above an example of mixed-method inquiry,

Table 1.2 Gendron's model

Axis	Description	Constructivist	Realist
Ontological	Nature, constitution and structure of reality	Existence of multiple perceptions of reality	Only one independent and ordered reality
Epistemological	Defining features and limits of legitimate knowledge	Pluralist and subjectivist; knowledge is a constructed representation subject to continual change; researcher is implicated in the construction of knowledge	Knowledge is meant to reflect a world regulated by causal laws; researcher attempts to remain separate from the observed object
Methodological	Methods, procedures and techniques for perceiving the world and that allow the generation of findings and conclusions	Methods based on processes of association and relationships; multiple representations of world-views emerge. Meanings are negotiated with the various actors involved	Focus is on reductive methods in order to describe, predict and control. Observable and measurable facts and their potential replication lead to expressions of natural truth, the single reality postulated by a realist ontology
Teleological	Intentional agents are self-organized to gain their ends. This determines the course along which projects develop, and reveals the interests of adherents	Researchers share responsibility for meanings and interpretations, and are accountable for the use or misuse of knowledge. They thus participate directly in the transformation of world-views	There is no other purpose of a study other than the production of objective knowledge that can be generalized and used by others

Source: Adapted from S Gendron, 'Transformative alliance between qualitative and quantitative approaches in health promotion research', in I Rootman et al. (eds) *Evaluation in Health Promotion: principles and perspectives*, Part 2, *Perspectives*, 2001.

and in social work Sheldon has argued that although his evidence-based research is largely experimental, he has used qualitative methods in the same studies, to supplement quantitative approaches (Sheldon, 2001). Does this simply reflect methodological pluralism? Realists do not deny that social reality may be socially constructed. Neither do all social constructionists deny the existence of an external, independent reality.

In any case, researchers do see themselves as pragmatic, searching for and using a combination of those methods that are most suited to their research aims, whatever their philosophical origins. This is what constitutes the notion of triangulation – the use of a range of different methods in order to gain a holistic view of a research problem (Denzin, 1970). However the use of triangulation has come to be dominated by a realist paradigm in that it is commonly understood as the joint use of qualitative and quantitative methods in order to cancel the errors inherent in each and so ensure greater validity in respect of the object studied and its underlying single reality.

In her discussion of the possibility of complementarity of methods, Gendron (2001) notes that approaches that may be fundamentally different, even antagonistic, may interact to contribute to innovative research, and that such a process should not be suppressed. Lincoln and Guba (1985) call this 'multiparadigm inquiry'. They make the point that while this enables researchers to combine features of qualitative and quantitative approaches, such a combination interweaves the approaches, rather than fusing them. In critical approaches to social research for instance (see Chapter 7), researchers are interested in collecting objective data about social structures and institutions and how these act in the interests of some classes and social groupings, and against the interests of other groups in terms of class, gender and ethnicity (set within a realist paradigm). But they also insist in the legitimacy of the point of view of these oppressed groups and use methods that will make available the meanings to them of their situation (set within a constructivist paradigm). The elements composing each paradigm remain distinct and operational, and researchers have to live with the uncertainty and contingency, and the messiness this brings. Thus the importance of meaning and subjectivity can be asserted, while not denying the authority of realist ways of knowing. The question, what should be the purpose of social work research – the production of knowledge or the transformation of world-views – is answered by 'both, not one or the other'. This position would not be without methodological tensions. Transformation of world-views may require political rather than rational-technical engagement, leading researchers to abandon pretensions of neutrality and to take sides that go far beyond debates about paradigms and methodologies.

Meanwhile the debate between constructivist and realist research paradigms continues, and is reflected in all the methods selected for presentation in this book. Moreover, it is not possible to argue that one paradigm more than the other, *per se*, is suited to research with a concern for social justice. The paradigm argument may be over-stated on a practical and technical level. Nevertheless we should not lose sight of the function of the paradigm war as a metaphor for the powerful and the powerless. In this sense, then, it is a concern in the struggle for social justice.

Conclusion: the contentious nature of social research

One conclusion from the above discussions about research-mindedness, evidence-based practice and competing methods and paradigms must be that research is both contentious and political. Conventional views of research insist that it should be value-free, politically neutral and concerned only with uncovering truth, even if that truth reveals facts and conditions that prove inconvenient to some groups. Nowadays this stance is widely regarded as naïve, and it is acknowledged generally that research never can be 'pure', without inherent presuppositions and external influences. Research is more than a case of 'checking evidence' through systematic inquiry, or concerned with cause and effect or cost-effectiveness. It is a deeply political process where competing agendas and interests are at work. There are two main ways in which research is political.

1 Inherent presuppositions

All research and indeed all human activity, is premised on beliefs or assumptions about the nature of reality. The traditional view of research, embodied in the notion of 'objectivity', is based on the assumption that research in the social sciences is essentially the same as research in the natural sciences, and that the same rules should apply. That means it should aim to be scientific and value-free. As we have seen in the paradigm debate, critics of this approach argue that these goals are impossible. Feminist critique for example, has shown how for many years research was dominated by male views of the world, resulting in findings that have either excluded women and made universal statements about all people based on studies of males only, or have distorted women's experiences to the detriment of their interests (see Humphries, 2004b). In other words it is important to ask questions about where the research is coming from and who is carrying it out, in order to examine the assumptions that impact upon any study. The presence of such presuppositions is inevitable. There is another dimension to this. Even where it is agreed that value-free social research is an unrealistic goal, there is still dispute as to whether research *should* be value-free as demanded by a realist paradigm, whether instead researchers should openly declare whose side they are on, and in whose interests they carry out their work. Some of the approaches considered in the rest of the book are explicitly concerned with social transformation. This leads us to consider external influences.

2 External influences

The other, more obvious way in which research can be regarded as political is where stakeholder interests set its agenda. Stakeholders may be government, organizations, universities, funding bodies, service users and researchers themselves, whose sectional preoccupations compete to control the direction and outcomes of the research. Even the ways research questions are asked reveal the interests of those who ask them. Think for example about the implications of these two questions: 'What are effective ways to change offending behaviour?' and 'How do offenders explain their offending behaviour?' The first is born out of a need for social order and control and thus is tightly framed, the second out of a desire to understand the perspective of the offender and is potentially more open and wide-ranging.

Some versions of research, explicitly designed to be political and to give disadvantaged groups an influence on research design, are clearly partisan. Standpoint feminism for example, holds that women's experiences are potentially more complete and less distorted than those of men, and can be made 'to yield up a truer (or less false) image of social reality' (Harding, 1987, p. 185). This idea is a controversial one, certainly not acceptable to all feminists. The disability movement has also insisted on the appropriation of research for the emancipation of disabled people (Beresford and Croft, 2004), and service users are generally more ready to challenge the expertise and the priorities of researchers, insisting on (and being encouraged by government in this) having a more controlling role.

This is not to say that social research was not political before it was politicized by these groups. There have always been vested interests in the doing of research, with obvious consequences for the autonomy of researchers. Across countries the increasing dependence of universities and social care organizations on the state, and the involvement of business interests and corporate management practices, have brought powerful social interests more centrally into the equation, in the service of national economic goals.

The research approaches considered in this book will not avoid these complexities in the business of doing social work research, but will evaluate the extent to which the interests of those on the margins and the relatively powerless are addressed through this growing dimension of social work. Readers are invited to keep these debates in mind in reading about different approaches and to make use of them in evaluating the methods presented.

Structure of the book

The range of methods included in the book are inevitably a choice from a wider possible selection, and I have tried to include those that are most commonly used in social work, and those that appear to lend themselves to a model of research that is committed to social justice. Chapter 2 examines the moral framework of research, available to us through codes of ethics, and asks whether these are robust enough to be useful towards an aim of social justice in social work research. It also looks at the notion of justice itself and examines the ways it is understood in social work. The chapters that follow consider research based on experimental, participatory, action, case-study, critical, discourse, ethnographic, social-survey and evaluation approaches, offering a critical appraisal of each one. Each chapter is structured around a short introduction, the origins of the particular method of interest, the principles underpinning it, examples of its use in social work and social care, its limitations and its potential to contribute to social justice. The main points are then summarized, readers are asked to 'stop and think' by considering some questions, and are offered annotated suggestions for further reading. At the end of the book I offer a number of useful internet sites for other resources.

Taken altogether the book attempts not only to offer a guide to discrete and unconnected research methods, but also to be a resource for politically committed researchers in a variety of settings struggling to make their research count towards transformation of an unjust society.

- Research-mindedness is increasingly important in social work practice, and it can have many different meanings
- A commitment to social justice is central to social work research
- The 'evidence' informing practice is not straightforward because
  - there is disagreement about what 'evidence' is
  - 'evidence' is seldom clear and unambiguous
  - it is open to a number of interpretations
- Qualitative and quantitative methods are valued differently by different research communities
- Research paradigms reflect our beliefs about the world, and influence researchers' choices about the questions asked, the methods used and the conclusions drawn
- Research is always contentious and political and in the interests of particular groups

stop and think

- What do you understand by 'research-mindedness' and why is it important?
- What values might inform research that aims towards social justice?
- What are some of the problems raised by the idea of 'evidence'?
- What part do research paradigms play in choosing research topics?
- Do you agree that research is always contentious, and if yes, why?

taking it further

- Butler, I and Pugh, R 'The politics of social work research', Chapter 3, in R Lovelock, K Lyons and J Powell (eds) *Reflecting on Social Work – Discipline and Profession* (Aldershot: Ashgate, 2004)
  A major critique of evidence-based practice in social work.
- Humphries, B 'Research mindedness', Chapter 7, in M Lymbery and K Postle (eds) *Social Work: a companion for learning* (London: Sage, 2007)
  Explores a number of dimensions of the idea of research-mindedness for social work research.
- Sarantakos, S *Social Research*, 3rd edn (Basingstoke: Palgrave Macmillan, 2005), Chapter 2
  An introductory and accessible discussion of qualitative and quantitative methods and the concept of paradigms.

2 Ethical research and social justice

Introduction

In the view of this author ethical research practice and social justice are intertwined. This is not a widely held view and will be regarded by some as contradictory, especially those who hold that ethical research strives to be objective, neutral and as far as possible uninfluenced by the views of the researcher. In this opinion, to attempt to set ethical research in a framework of social justice is to impose a particular set of values on research practice, risking distortion of the design, the process and the findings. I take the contrary position that all research (and codes of ethics) is influenced by values of one sort or another, as I discussed in Chapter 1, and what is important is that these are declared and made available for examination. I also argue that a research goal of social justice is a legitimate one, given that social work is universally committed to working towards justice – 'principles of human rights and social justice are fundamental to social work' (IFSW/IASSW, 2005, p. 10) – and it would be rather odd if this applied to all social work activity except research.

In this chapter, then, I examine the ethical guidelines that govern social research, I attempt to delineate some elements of a model of social justice and I try to bring them together in a way that is helpful to social work research practice and in evaluating research reports.

Research ethics for social work

Although there have existed codes of practice for social work for many years (see Briskman and Noble, 1999), it is only comparatively recently that codes of ethics specifically for research practice have developed. This is in response to governments' increasing control and surveillance over what research takes place, by whom, and to what ends. In the UK a national system of research governance for health and social care was published in 2004 (DoH, 2004), aimed at ensuring good practice and at 'protecting participants by ensuring there are clear arrangements to identify and manage any risks associated with a study' (p. 2). This includes an obligation on the part of sponsors of any study to ensure 'a favourable independent opinion on its ethical implications' (p. 8). As a result research ethics committees in institutions in the UK, Europe, Australia and North America have gained a powerful role as gatekeepers. In response professional organizations have begun to build in references to research in their codes of ethics. The British Association of Social Workers adapted its code of professional practice to include research practice (BASW, 2004) and, resulting from a national seminar series sponsored by the ESRC, Butler published a draft code for wider consideration and discussion within social work (Butler, 2002). These are similar to most codes of ethics for social research produced by other professions and disciplines, and are meant to offer clear guidance for the conduct of professional research behaviour.

Codes of ethics

Bulmer's definition of ethical behaviour is typical of the responsibilities considered essential for good research practice:

> the scientific community has responsibilities not only to the ideals of the pursuit of objective truth and the search for knowledge, but also to the subjects of their research . . . the researcher has always to take account of the effects of his [*sic*] actions upon . . . subjects and act in such a way as to preserve their rights and integrity of human beings. Such behaviour is ethical behaviour. (Bulmer, 1982, p. 3)

A point to note here is that, as is clear from the above quote, ethical codes are concerned not only with the protection of the subjects of research, but also with the rights of and protection of institutions in pursuing research. In other words, they are self-interested statements, as described by Friedson (1970) in his study of the profession of medicine. As Truman has pointed out:

> Underpinning the reconstitution of ethical guidelines and research governance are a range of measures which protect institutional interests, without necessarily providing an effective means to address the moral obligations and responsibilities of researchers in relation to the production of social research. (Truman, 2003, abstract)

Another point to make is that the adoption of such codes of ethics for research and professional practice raises problems for social work in the context of social justice. This is because codes of ethics are only concerned with the *individual behaviour of researchers*. The position of the research subject is characterized as passive and dependent and they cannot take account of the *social* structures that are the concern of *social* justice (see also Humphries and Martin, 2000). Moreover, most codes of ethics are framed within a scientific/realist/positivist paradigm (see the discussion on paradigms in Chapter 1) and are focused largely on the methods used to collect data. They are of limited use to researchers operating within constructivist assumptions, where they often meet ethical dilemmas in the process of carrying out research. I return to these points below.

In addition, the assumptions that underpin the main elements of codes of ethics are problematic, and the very general nature of the way they are framed is of little use in grounded situations where ethical dilemmas are experienced.

BASW's version of a code of ethics for social work research is not fundamentally different from other codes, though the familiar social work language of a commitment to 'empowering' subjects can be recognized.

There are a number of interlinked areas that are usually accepted as of key importance in the research process: these are the *social impact* of research; *informed consent*; *privacy;* and *deception*. I shall discuss each of them in turn to illustrate my points.

Social impact

This refers to a warning to researchers not to cause disruption to people's lives during or after the research is concluded, actively protecting participants from 'physical and mental harm, discomfort, danger and unreasonable disruption in their daily lives or unwarranted intrusion into their privacy' (Butler, 2002, p. 245). This is reminiscent of other professional codes that urge researchers to 'do no harm'. Although one can appreciate the intention behind it (even if it is patronizing), the whole tone invokes images of the scientific research we discussed in Chapter 1 – the realist belief that it is possible to control the environment as one might in a laboratory in order to study the effects of an experiment on variables of interest. Is such control possible in studies that involve human beings, where one cannot predict either their responses or the impact of intervention on their lives? Nor can the researcher carefully slice away bits of information, leaving the surrounding ground intact. And who is to arbitrate on 'discomfort' or 'unwarranted intrusion'? Furthermore, in the context of social justice, change in people's lives might be the very purpose of research. As the following chapters will demonstrate, there are a number of models of research that have as one of their goals the transformation of the status quo (see Stanley, 1990; Humphries, 1999). All this raises questions about the appropriateness of the notion of 'social impact' and about its usefulness for the kind of ethical practice that might be compatible with the goals of social work.

Informed consent

This is an ethic that is central to all codes of ethics, and Butler's (2002) draft devotes three paragraphs to it, referring to the 'absolute right' of individuals 'to decline to participate or withdraw' (p. 246). This too is of limited use in real research situations that throw up questions such as: how much and what level of information should be given to someone to allow them to give informed consent? How does one know when informed consent has been obtained (does a nod or a signature necessarily signify understanding)? And what about the circumstances within which consent is sought? Patients in hospital, prison inmates, children in a classroom may feel obliged to take part and may fear punishment if they decline. And what if the research focus changes over time? Once given, is consent to be regarded as given for all time? Who decides when further information should be shared and consent resought? These questions are not addressed in ethical codes. They are questions to do with justice and the possibilities of exploitation, and it seems unsatisfactory that the answers to them are in the control of researchers who, after all, have a vested interest in getting the data they need. In some circumstances the ideal of informed consent turns out to give strictly limited protection to research subjects.

Privacy

Ethical guidelines suggest that privacy should be respected, and warn against methods that invade privacy, such as covert observation (where the person being observed is unaware of being observed) or asking questions that are impertinent or invasive. There are a number of infamous cases of researchers invading privacy such as Humphreys's 1970 study of men's sexual behaviour in public toilets, and there has been debate within feminist research as to whether informal and unstructured interviewing styles in fact invade the privacy of and exploit interviewees (see Humphries, 2002). Researchers defend the invasion of privacy (and the absence of informed consent, and deception) in the interests of gaining knowledge that would not otherwise be available, an argument that is expedient for all circumstances. If the ethical dilemma is resolved in actual situations through the researcher's judgement about the value of the knowledge to be gained, do we really need codes of ethics at all? Again, the power of discretion is in the hands of the researcher, and there is no question of any active part in this by the subjects of the research.

Deception

This refers to the importance of not misleading research subjects or deceiving them as to the presence of the researcher or the purpose of the research. Examples are where a residential care worker is collecting data on practices within a care setting without permission or consent, or where someone leaves a job and then uses information later for research purposes, or where a researcher deliberately joins a group (say, a religious sect) in order to observe and record its practices for research purposes, pretending to be a genuine member. It is closely related to both the issue of informed consent and that of privacy, and the same arguments are advanced when researchers wish to break this element of the code. However in this case, most codes of ethics are quite explicit that deception can be justified in some situations. The draft code for social work says,

> Only in cases where no alternative strategy is feasible, where no harm to the subject is foreseen and where the greater good is self-evidently served, are procedures involving deception or concealment permissible for social work and social care researchers. (Butler, 2002, p. 246)

The use of appeals to methods (no feasible alternative strategy), the subjects' safety (no harm foreseen) and the greater good ('self-evidently served') provides methodological, moral and political justifications for the deception of research subjects. But it goes further in that this very clear permission to deceive at the same time undermines every other element of the code. The same arguments can be (and have been) used for invasion of privacy, for withholding information and its consequence of gaining consent under false pretences. The duty to 'deal open and fairly' is negated. The BASW code insists that social work researchers should 'predicate their work on the perspectives and lived experience of the research subject *except where this is not appropriate*' (BASW, 2004, my emphasis). What does this mean, and who decides when it is not appropriate? As Truman and Humphries (1994) point out, codes of ethics contain such ambiguities and contradictions that the result can be researchers justifying any course of action as 'ethical'. There are a number of observations that can be made as a result of this discussion:
- ethical statements are framed in global terms that are of limited use in real, grounded situations

- ethical codes are regarded as applied by individual researchers as a response to dilemmas they encounter and only discussed occasionally and marginally in research reports
- ethical guidelines take no account of the part played by organizational and other contexts in influencing the ways they are interpreted
- research subjects are not regarded as significant in ethical practice, except in passive ways
- there is no acknowledgement of relations of power in the process

All of this is not necessarily to argue against having guidelines for ethical practice. But research that is genuinely concerned with human rights and social justice will need to accommodate these criticisms of conventional codes of ethics. Later in the chapter I will offer some suggestions as to what elements such guidelines might contain. Here I need to digress to the question begged by the discussion on ethics and social justice – what do we mean by social justice?

The concept of social justice

Across the left and the right of the contemporary spectrum there is agreement that practice based on 'social justice' is a legitimate and worthy aim of policy, though the concept itself remains ambiguous and not clearly articulated. The social work profession internationally has nailed its colours to the mast of social justice (IFSW/IASSW, 2005), and some attempts have been made to spell out what this means. In particular, Ian Shaw has offered some very useful pointers both to how we might consider theories of justice and to how they might be adapted for social work (see Shaw, 2003 for example). In 2002 the *British Journal of Social Work* (*BJSW*, 2002) produced a special issue on the theme, and each of the contributors explores it in the context of social work. For example, Gary Craig (2002, p. 672) sees social justice as:

> - a framework of political objectives, pursued through social, economic, environmental and political policies, based on an acceptance of difference and diversity, and informed by values concerned with achieving fairness and equality of outcomes and treatment;
> - recognizing the dignity and equal worth and encouraging the self-esteem of all;
> - the meeting of basic needs;
> - maximizing the reduction of inequalities in wealth, income and life chances; and
> - the participation of all, including the most advantaged.

Here Craig pitches his understanding of social justice squarely in the public domain, emphasizing the economic and political processes required to achieve it, and underlining diversity, dignity and participation as key values. His guidelines for an ethical practice include:

- *Evidence* – the accumulation and dissemination of evidence that shows the reality of injustice in the lives of the clients of social work, thus giving an explicit role for the collection of research data. Social workers know about injustice because they work closely with its manifestations. They need to be more systematic in making it visible.
- *Voice* – partnership initiatives, including research, remain dominated by partners with power, and there is a need for social workers and researchers to facilitate the voices of those on the margins, and to challenge partnerships that operate on the lowest common denominator (usually targets set by government).
- *Participation* – there is an important role for social workers in becoming more actively engaged in promoting user involvement, and in working more explicitly alongside excluded and deprived people in the collection and use of data.

In the same volume Orme (2002), from a feminist perspective, argues that confining justice to the public domain denies the injustices that operate at the level of the family and the interpersonal. Drawing on Benhabib, she insists on a focus also on the quality of our relations with others in the 'spheres of kinship, love, friendship and sex' (Benhabib, 1992, p. 184). She proposes an 'ethic of care', that is, a notion of justice influenced by the relational – a connectedness, a moral dialogue that brings together justice and care. This perspective regards justice as more than a set of principles but as a process of dialogue: 'a dialogical approach to moral problems would involve discussing and observing from an attitude of caring – that includes attentiveness, responsiveness and a commitment to see issues from different perspectives' (Orme, 2002, p. 810).

Fiona Williams (2000) also tries to extend the ethical vocabulary of welfare through a feminist and socialist analysis that takes account of the intimate dimensions of experience. Her seven principles of recognition and respect include:

- *Interdependence* – we are all mutually dependent, and there is a need to challenge the institutions, structures and social relations which render some groups necessarily dependent.
- *Care* – it is through caring and being cared for that we take account of the needs of others, and recognition is needed of the different needs of both cared-for and carers.
- *Intimacy* – covering relationships grounded in mutual exchange of love based upon parenting, heterosexual relationships, civil partnerships, friendship, kinship ties and paid care relationships,

for example. This also recognizes the potential for the abuse of power in unequal relationships.

- *Bodily integrity* – this can be violated through lack of control in medical examination and treatment, sexual abuse and rape, racial violence, harassment, physical attack, sexual mutilation, slavery, sex trafficking, all of which centre on the right of the individual to protect their body against external or internal risk and abuse.
- *Identity* – a sense of self and belonging through struggles for self-realization and collective struggles against disrespect.
- *Transnational welfare* – national/territorial/geographical boundaries are being redrawn, supra-national boundaries are being created and there has been an increase in people crossing those boundaries as workers, migrants and refugees. The use of nationality as one of the criteria of eligibility to social rights results in denial of social rights, as is their scapegoating as scroungers.
- *Voice* – this final principle runs through the others. It demands a sharing of expert and lay knowledges, and is a version of active citizenship that depends on a notion of democracy that can both account for and address the competing claims of different groups – 'a differential universalism'.

Williams offers these principles as the beginning of a language for a commitment to an equal moral value that challenges structured differentiations that render some groups unequal and excluded. It picks up and expands both Craig's and Orme's notions of justice. If these principles were to be built into an ethical code for professional and research practice they would take us beyond conventional thinking to foster a sensitivity to respect for identity, the quality of relationships and the challenging of boundaries.

Rossiter, Prilleltensky and Walsh-Bowers (2000) expand on another dimension identified by Orme, the concept of dialogue, and discuss the importance of organizational contexts where researchers are located, as well as dialogue between researchers and research subjects. These authors argue that ethics is best protected when researchers perceive as their professional duty the responsibility to create genuine dialogue 'in relations of mutual respect' (p. 98). Rossiter and her colleagues say that researchers' ongoing engagement with their organizations, and the way this relationship shapes their version of ethical practice is forged within power relations that 'condition what is perceived as ethics and how ethical dilemmas can be resolved' (p. 95). Hayes and Humphries (1999) describe an example of this in their research sponsored jointly by a university and a voluntary agency. The researchers' view of what was ethical research was constrained by the values and priorities of the two organizations, their values and their priorities that at times were in conflict with each other.

Briskman and Noble (1999), in a critique of several social work codes of ethics (in Australia, Canada and the USA), address the problem of the emphasis on the individual choice of researchers to engage in ethical practice and on research participants to consent to involvement. They call for a framework that takes account of the diverse interests and plurality of voices involved. Leonard (1997) agrees and argues that guaranteeing disempowered groups a chance to speak asserts responsibility to those who otherwise would have no control over their lives. Instead they should be seen as having dynamic oppositional agency as they engage with their daily lives, and research design and methods should open the researcher to these influences (Cameron et al., 1992).

Some of the debates within social work are reminiscent of discussions in the wider literature where the challenge has been to adopt a notion of social justice that will take account of both the material and the cultural aspects of people's experiences. These include Iris Marion Young's (1990), Nancy Fraser's (1997) and Majid Yar's (2001) models of 'redistribution' (of resources) and 'recognition' (of difference and diversity), which attempt to take account of both material and cultural aspects of oppression and justice.

The discussion so far has led us to consider several factors – the tendency in ethical statements on research to ignore context and organizational structure; the treatment of research subjects as passive and dependent; the absence of any dialogical dimension; the need for some acknowledgement of the 'private' sphere in statements of ethics; international comparisons and changing boundaries; and the parameters of research that might acknowledge material exploitation and the non- or mis-recognition of socially despised groups.

None of the writers considered has argued for the abandonment of codes of ethics (though Briskman and Noble express some ambivalence about this), instead pressing for a move away from individualistic models that do not take account of the context in which ethics operates, and which conceal power relationships where the perspectives and interests of those pursuing research are privileged, resulting in fallacious appeals to impartiality and objectivity. They all appear to be arguing for a concept of 'situated ethics' that is able to take account of the environment of the research, including the organizational determinants of how ethics are defined, the diversity and agency of research subjects, and with a concern for the ethics of intimate relationships and an open dialogue between subjects and researchers.

Reflexivity in research

All of this implies a different understanding of the concept of reflexivity in social work research, away from a view that it relates only to the behaviour of individual researchers. Those trained in the health and social care professions will be familiar with this concept in professional practice, and it is also central to the process of research, discussed widely in the literature. However the literature typically does not examine reflexivity in the context of ethics and social justice:

> Reflexivity combines the process of reflection with self-critical analysis. It is highly valued as a means whereby social science researchers are able to explore their own subjectivity, be more aware of the impact they necessarily have on the research data they collect and increase the sensitivity of their analysis and interpretations of data. (Somekh and Lewin, 2005, p. 348)

In social work research it has been defined by Fook (2000) as 'the ability to locate oneself squarely within a situation, to know and to take into account the influence of personal interpretation, position and action within a specific context' (p. 117). It is a concept beyond reflection, whether it is conceived as reflection-in-action, reflection-on-action or critical reflection (Morrison, 1995), occurring throughout both practice and research. Cohen, Manion and Morrison (2000) suggest that what is being required in the notion of reflexivity is

> a self-conscious awareness of the effects that the participants-as-practitioners-and-researchers are having on the research process, how their values, attitudes, perceptions, opinions, feelings, etc. are feeding into the situation being studied . . . The participants-as-practitioners-and-researchers need to apply to themselves the same critical scrutiny that they are applying to others and to the research. (p. 239)

Hall goes somewhat further in widening the definition beyond the individual to a view in which all research participants are engaged in ensuring that (a) data reflect the experiences of all participants; (b) democratic relations exist between all participants in the research; (c) the researcher's views (which may be theory-laden) do not hold precedence over the views of participants (Hall, 1996, p. 29, cited by Cohen, Manion and Morrison, 2000).

These definitions of reflexivity do move the debate along, but they have two limitations – they do not take account of the organizational context of research and how it influences reflexivity, and they do not locate the obligation to engage in reflexive research practice within an ethical framework. They assume that all participants are free to set up the conditions of democratic research practice, but organizational constraints may be to do with communication systems, hierarchies, bureaucratic structures and so on, conditions that are incompatible with the collegiate, open and collaborative climate assumed. Elliott (1991) does, however, argue that 'self-awareness' brings with it insights into the ways in which the self in action is shaped and constrained by institutional structures. He says that self-awareness and awareness of the institutional context of one's work are not developed by separate cognitive processes: reflexive and objective analysis. They are qualities of the same reflexive process: *'reflexive practice necessarily implies both self-critique and institutional critique. One cannot have one without the other'* (p. 38, my emphasis).

But there are other dimensions of reflexivity where other people beyond the researcher and the research subjects are involved in the research process. For example, interviewing may take place through an interpreter. In an interesting piece Temple and Edwards (2006) focus on a reflexive consideration of working with interpreters. Rather than seeing the role of interpreters as simply translating from one language to another, these authors recognized that their own identities, those of research participants *and* those of the interpreters were invested in and constructed by the research process. Instead of viewing interpreters as 'a neutral party who should not add or subtract from what the primary parties communicate to each other' (Freed, 1988, p. 316), they began to see them as part of the production of the research account, bringing their own assumptions and concerns to the process, identifying what they called 'triple subjectivity' (p. 45). As 'key informants', then, interpreters were interviewed and were asked about aspects of their own life experiences, their relationship to the ethnic groups they worked with, and what issues they regarded as important in relation to the topics being addressed in the interviews and the subject of the research project (Temple and Edwards, 2006, p. 45).

In this way interviews with the interpreters were part of the process of making interpreters visible, and to some extent 'accountable'. Temple and Edwards offer examples from the research that show how the social positioning and the 'intellectual autobiographies' of interpreters had significant implications for the knowledge the research produced. Their insights also render problematic other discussions limited to the technical role of the interpreter and their language proficiency.

This example shows how the concept of reflexivity needs to be broadened to consider not only the impact of the researcher (or practitioner) on the research (or on practice), but to take account of the influence of a number of people who may be involved in the process, as well as the impact of the process on them and their understandings. It also highlights the importance for any researcher to be alert to the context in which their research takes place.

The example also highlights reflexivity as an important dimension of ethical practice, since the impact of not only the researcher but that of her organization, of the research participants, and of others involved such as interpreters, is reflected in both the process and any outcomes of the project.

Putting it all together

There is of course no model of ethical practice that will be a final answer to ethical dilemmas, or any self-complete system to be applied with universal authority. At the same time, any pretence of neutrality is not helpful towards addressing power in research, and what all the writers considered here have been seeking is a different approach to a consideration of ethics in research for social work that can take account of the problematic dimensions of traditional codes. An ethical approach that is informed by social justice will:

- locate researchers in terms of their organizational and political masters, of others who may be involved in the research, as well as of their own biographies, histories and identities;
- take account of the changing national and international context, the ways such boundaries are being challenged and the implications for their research;
- have a commitment to examining injustice and inequality in the intimate sphere as well as in other settings;
- have a desire to uncover hidden articulations of need and a concern to understand frameworks for survival and resistance;
- design research that ensures a plurality of voices is heard;
- encompass a view of research subjects as active, reflexive beings who have insights into their situations and experiences; and
- regard researchers as accountable not only to themselves, their sponsors, the research community, but also to the communities of those they study.

Conclusion: appropriate ethics for social work research

This discussion of ethics and social justice is an attempt to draw ethics in from the margins and to perceive ethical practice as part and parcel of just research practice, as a symbol of the reality that ethics is not concerned only with methods; rather it is fundamental not only at every stage of the research process, but also in taking account of the context in which it takes place. It is an attempt also to embrace an ethical practice that is dynamic and that involves both research subjects and organizational settings in ongoing dialogue about the research.

Unfortunately there is evidence to suggest that social workers are not interested in ethics, and indeed are involved in practices of exclusion that fly in the face of ethical research practice (e.g. Humphries, 2002; Jordan, 2000). There are also suggestions that social workers have become alienated from values of justice and from a sensibility of the oppression of their clients (Jones, 2001; Ferguson and Lavalette, 2004; Lavalette and Mooney, 2000). They are well placed to see the ugliness of an unjust society but, under siege and surveillance, are loaded down with new responsibilities and pressed increasingly into a policing role, and are in danger of losing their commitment to progressive social change. This commitment is at risk of being diluted to a rather vague notion of 'anti-oppressive' practice and an unanalysed notion of 'respecting diversity'. This, it is argued, has weakened the struggle and has 'allowed the problems of society to be recast as due to the moral failings of individuals who need censure and correction from the anti-oppressive social worker' (McLaughlin, 2005, p. 300). As a result the 'evidence base' is preoccupied with evaluations of what works in changing clients' anti-social behaviour.

Ethical social work research that is committed to social justice cannot sustain an unquestioning acceptance of received definitions of social problems, or simply measure the outcomes of social experiments without having an eye to the bigger context, and without asking about the origins, motivations and intended uses of such research. Social work researchers are well placed to accumulate and disseminate direct evidence about the conditions of ordinary people and about the impact of policies on their lives. They can examine the ways structures and institutions reinforce materially and culturally based oppressions, and they can build these understandings into the doing of research and making use of the findings. A research commitment not to be impartial to human suffering, to identify unjust (not just inefficient) processes and make them known, to ensure that subordinated voices are heard and heeded, are entirely compatible with the best traditions of rigorous and systematic research approaches. Social workers have an ethical obligation to act on this knowledge. The rest of this book examines the potential of the research methods available to the social work profession, to offer something towards a moral and just society.

- conventional codes of ethics act to protect institutions
- conventional codes of ethics are limited to the moral behaviour of researchers
- ethical social work research has a concern for social justice in material conditions, intimate relationships and organizational contexts
- an obligation to address an expanded notion of reflexivity should be incorporated into any code of ethics for social work research

stop and think

- Why do you think ethical practice is important in social work research?
- Do you agree that conventional codes of ethics are of limited help in practice?
- If yes, in what ways?
- What dimensions of people's lives should research ethics informed by social justice encompass?
- At what stages of a research study should a researcher consider ethical issues?
- What do you understand by the idea of 'reflexivity for social justice'?

taking it further

- Department of Health *The Research Governance Framework for Health and Social Care: implementation plan for social care* (London: DoH, 2004)
  These are the official government guidelines for good practice in health and social care research. They set up governance arrangements for a social care ethics system.
- Fraser, N *Justice Interruptus: critical reflections on the 'postsocialist' condition* (London: Routledge, 1997), Chapter 8
  A proposed framework for a concept of social justice based on ideas about redistribution of resources and recognition of identities.
- Van Den Hoonaard, W 'Is ethics review a moral panic?' *Canadian Review of Sociology and Anthropology* 38 (1) 19–35
  A critique of the official responses to the need for codes of ethics.
- Young, I M *Justice and the Politics of Difference* (Princeton, NJ: Princeton University Press, 1990), especially Chapter 2.
  A discussion of the concept of social justice. Chapter 2 sets out the basis of Young's 'five faces of oppression'.

3 Experimental ways of knowing

chapter

Introduction

Experimental approaches to research are at the opposite end of the paradigm and methodology spectrum from participatory research, discussed in the next chapter. They are generally considered to be *the* method of the social sciences, and have had a big influence on the evidence-based practice movement and the push towards 'what works?' as discussed in Chapter 1. This chapter introduces the basics of this approach and its influence on research in social work. It considers some of the methods used to evaluate the effectiveness of interventions designed to change behaviour. These methods include both quantitative and qualitative approaches that are derived from the experimental method. Overall there has been a negative reaction towards experimental methods in social work (see, for example, Butler and Pugh, 2004; Humphries, 2003; Jordan, 2000), reflecting a longer critique from the 1960s that questioned their suitability for research with human subjects, particularly from interactionists, phenomenologists and feminists. In addition, the Thatcher government was antagonistic to social science research generally (as was the Reagan administration in the USA), reflecting a shift away from government intervention in social problems (Kirkpatrick, 1984), and research funding was cut. Over the final years of the twentieth century and into the twenty-first, there has been a resurgence of intervention in social issues internationally, and with it the requirement for evaluation and research. The evidence-based practice movement, with its insistence on the superiority of experimental methods has been the favoured instrument to achieve this. The chapter therefore offers a considered examination of experimental approaches, and discusses their potential to contribute to an aim of social justice.

Origins of experimental approaches

Experimental methodology has been attributed to Francis Bacon who in the seventeenth century promoted the method of systematic observation and experiment, which he saw as applicable to all sciences. His work was developed by Descartes, Hobbes and Comte (Turner, 1986), and from this comes a long and authoritative history. Experiments are an everyday practice in the physical sciences, and since the early nineteenth century they have been a major procedure in psychology as a way of discovering knowledge. The rest of the social sciences adopted experimentation and it is now used by researchers within a wide range of disciplines. Derived from the natural sciences, experimental knowing has been and remains a powerful tradition (Krug and Hepworth, 1997). In the modern world with its demand for evidence-based everything, experiments offer what appears to be a useful model for producing objective evidence about the effectiveness of interventions in people's lives. In other words, it promises to inform about 'what works'. It is the preferred approach of government and institutional research. Its method *par excellence* is the randomized control trial (RCT), used not only in clinical research, but also in sociology, criminology, education, health promotion and social work.

However experimental methods have not fulfilled their promise to deliver unequivocal answers to research questions, and conclusions at best are nearly always inconclusive. A number of studies in the USA in the 1950s and 1960s, particularly in education, produced the 'wrong' results in that they failed to identify differences in interventions, or produced results that were statistically not significant. As a result there was a growing disillusionment with experiments from the 1960s onwards. Moreover, in many cases eugenicist assumptions had been built into statistical tests with a view to confirming that some social groups were 'feeble-minded' or inferior to others, or that criminality was inherited, or that pauperism was a biological deficiency rather than caused by economic factors, and that therefore the remedy was restricted breeding (reported in Oakley, 2000). This linked too to recent memories of Nazi experiments on people in concentration camps during the 1939–45 war. There were also notorious, unethical experiments in medicine such as the Tuskegee study (Jones, 1981) where treatment was withheld from poor black men diagnosed with syphilis, and which influenced the growing unpopularity of experimental methods. Needless to say, these studies involved deliberate deception of research subjects. Other epistemological and methodological criticisms, especially from feminists, condemned experiments as 'objectifying', 'alienating' and 'manipulative', a male way of knowing that ignores the meaning and subjectivity of experience (Du Bois, 1983, p.

107). Rose (1994, p. 88) describes such methods as 'controlled violence' and Reinharz (1984) likens them to rape because of their intrusiveness. Feminists have shown that sexist bias can influence each of the stages comprising an experiment (see Reinharz, 1992).

Clearly then, experimental methods arouse strong objections. However it is important to acknowledge that it is the ways they have been used rather than the notion of the experiment itself that have been the issue. Indeed there is a strong argument that such approaches, employed appropriately, are fundamental to the measurement of inequality. Experiments in the area of women's health have revealed weaknesses in systems of breast and cervical screening and cancer, osteoporosis risk, HRT use, over-diagnosis and under-diagnosis (see Oakley, 2000). Nevertheless from the 1960s onwards experimentation became unpopular as a result of its problems and a range of critiques, arguments that are still potent today.

The end of the twentieth century has brought a resurgence of experimental methods, with an emphasis on better design and greater objectivity. In health, social work and social care the well-documented drive towards scientific management and the collection of facts and evidence about administrative efficiency and effectiveness in order to meet government-defined targets (see Humphries, 2003) has neatly facilitated the revival of experimental methods, promising a measure of certainty in offering tested principles for success in practice.

Principles of experimental methods

Experimental studies are firmly rooted in a scientific realist paradigm (Chapter 1) that privileges ways of knowing which assume there is a world 'out there', with facts that the expert knower (the researcher) can apprehend and understand, given the appropriate technical instruments for measuring it. In this view discovering the 'truth' about the social world is a feasible and legitimate pursuit. According to Bryman (1988, pp. 14–15) experimental research has five main themes:

- how social scientists 'know' follows the same rules as how scientists 'know'
- only observable things can be included in valid knowledge
- theory is a compendium of empirically established facts
- knowledge is formed deductively by extracting specific propositions from general accounts
- the act of attempting to know ought to be carried out in such a way that the knower's own value position is removed from the process.

The scope for including other kinds of knowledge such as people's experiences and what they *mean* to individuals, and the legitimacy of interpretive and qualitative approaches to data, are thus restricted and indeed often excluded from the knowledge base. In this way the 'truth' about a phenomenon is reduced to the variables of interest to the researcher. However the issue of what is true and what is not true is a complex one, and what one person claims to be true may be disputed by another. Claims to 'truth' are political, and what counts as knowledge, and how it may be interpreted, is full of difficulty.

Defining characteristics of experiments

Experimental research has a particular language that may not necessarily be used on other approaches. The most important concepts are:
- *Cause and effect* – the process of establishing a causal link between a stimulus and a research outcome, that it was the 'treatment' administered that caused the change.
- *Empiricism* – an emphasis on what the researcher experiences through observation. Data collected must be based solely on what can be observed.
- *Generalizable* – the claim that knowledge generated in a specific context will also be true in all other contexts or for the population that the sample represents.
- *Hypothesis* – a proposition that will be tested in a study.
- *Objectivity* – the removal of the emotions, knowledge, experiences, values and so on of the researcher from the research process, in order to identify the 'truth' of a situation.
- *Population* – all the people or phenomena under study, from whom a sample will be selected for research.
- *Reliability* – research tools or instruments that will produce consistent results across time, across groups of subjects and across the elements being measured.
- *Sample* – the individuals who are chosen for study, selected from the population of interest to the researcher.
- *Validity* – the property of a research instrument that measures what it is supposed to measure, and whether the measurement is accurate and precise.
- *Variables* – characteristics that have more than one value and that can be measured (such as sex or age for example). An *independent* variable is one that is set to cause changes in a *dependent* variable.

From this it will be seen that experiments have a narrow definition of what constitutes knowledge, they use almost entirely quantitative methods, and are employed to test a hypothesis and to develop theory. For example a hypothesis might be 'the provision of leisure activities reduces vandalism in boys aged between 13 and 15'. In other words, having leisure facilities causes a change in the behaviour of these groups. The key concept is one of causation: that is, an association is 'causal' if it is statistically shown (see Chapter 10) to entail a strong and consistent association between two variables ('dependent' variable – that aspect of experience requiring change such as the 'behaviour' of boys aged between 13 and 15; 'independent' variable – the stimulus introduced to achieve the change, such as the provision of leisure facilities). The results of the experiment are only valid if the cause precedes the effect and these are close together in time; if it can be shown that other variables have not caused the effect, and the causality can be explained rationally. Stapf (1995, as cited in Sarantakos, 2005) describes this as the 'Max-Con-Min' rule, in that the researcher must *maximize* the effects of the independent variable on the dependent variable; *control* outside distorting influences; and *minimize* the effects of non-systematic (chance) variables.

Characteristically, experimental designs include at least two groups to be studied, the experimental group (to whom the stimulus will be administered) and the control group (not subjected to the stimulus). So in our example of 13-to-15-year-old boys two groups would be selected, similar in all significant respects, and the sample must be selected in a manner that is free from bias. There are a number of ways this is to be achieved, all of which have their drawbacks, and discussion of them can be found in various textbooks (see, for example, Gomm, 2004; Sarantakos, 2005). The process entails the researcher establishing and controlling the experimental conditions, measuring the dependent variable (characteristics of the behaviour of the boys), introducing the independent variable (the leisure facility), then after an identified period testing the dependent variable again with a view to measuring effects (changes in behaviour). The pre-test and post-test results are analysed and compared, usually by statistical methods, with a view to identifying any causal relationship between the variables that are being studied. If the sample selected is a representative one, the results may be generalized to the wider population of boys aged 13 to 15.

In social situations, of course, the opportunities for such laboratory-like conditions are severely limited, and 'naturalistic' (or field) experiments involve people in the context in which they live their lives, not controlled by the researcher. It is this kind of experimental research that is most commonly used in social work and social care. It is of course this very characteristic (the attempt to control the conditions of the study) and the ethical implications flowing from issues of control and of the ethical dimension of administering or refusing 'treatment' that raises questions about the validity of experiments in the social world, of which more later.

Sarantakos (2005, p. 181) sets out the strengths of experiments:

- *Replication* – experiments are constructed in a manner that allows replication, assuming that repeating the procedure will not lead to different results.
- *Prediction* – their structure and process, and their detailed and rigorous design allow reasonable predictions to a higher degree than many other methods.
- *Causality* – experiments possess all the methodological parameters required for establishing causality.
- *Precision* – rigorous planning and checking of the status of variables, and the validity and reliability of methods allow a high degree of precision in all steps of the research process.
- *Convenience* – the size of the samples, the detailed and accurate preparation of the experimental conditions, and the detailed research design make experiments a most convenient research method.

As can be deduced from the above, experimentation involves a fair degree of manipulation of the research environment in order to rule out factors other than those related to the variable introduced to stimulate change. In the everyday life of human beings this is very difficult to achieve unless people are confined, with all other factors closed off. Even then it is near impossible to achieve the laboratory conditions that exclude distortions and allow the experiment to remain intact. Hypotheses relate to situations, and what is true in one situation may be false in others – 'what works' cannot necessarily be generalized, or taken from one setting and imposed on another. Moreover, the values and interests of the researcher influence the questions asked, the experimental (or any other) design, and the way data are interpreted. The whole process can be viewed as an overly mechanistic way of viewing what is in fact a dynamic interaction of social factors. Nevertheless experimental designs have been employed extensively in social work and social care for the evaluation of interventions.

Examples of experiments in social work and social care

Social science experimental research has covered a wide range of topics to test hypotheses, including whether increasing the police presence on the beat reduces crime, whether watching violence on television increases aggression in viewers, whether intensive social work intervention prevents illness in elderly people and whether targeted educational programmes promote literacy. Vanstone (1999) described a number of effectiveness research studies in different countries on crime reduction, a favourite target for experimental methods, and included in his discussion a list of characteristics that successful programmes tend to have (p. 223). The focus of all the experiments was on changes in behaviour resulting from cognitive-behavioural, skill-oriented interventions with disturbed offenders, drugs users, or others at risk of offending. Statistical analysis of data suggested that in most cases a measure of success was achieved, especially as shown by (short-term) reconviction rates.

Support for elderly people

In the UK Matilda Goldberg carried out one of the first controlled trials of social work intervention, comparing the effects of intensive casework on a group of older people with a similar control group receiving support from non-professional workers (Goldberg, 1970). She and her colleagues were particularly interested in mortality, illness, self-care and social contacts. Most hypotheses about the benefits of social work help were not supported, except those relating to the more qualitative aspects of the experiment – social contacts, attitudes, interests and activities. The results were used by some sceptics to argue that 'nothing works' and that professional social work is no more effective than lay approaches (e.g. Brewer and Lait, 1980). Only a few social scientists raised questions about the value of this kind of systematic experimentation, and indeed the acclaimed policy analyst Richard Titmuss is reported by Oakley (2000, p. 231) to have attached great value to Goldberg's qualitative findings (see also Titmuss, 1970, p. 15). In any case, a question remains regarding the objectives of the experiment – is it a realistic expectation that social workers will delay or prevent the ravages of time on very old and incapacitated people? There are also questions about representativeness and the appropriateness of the methods for research with this group, which I address below.

Children in foster care

Macdonald and Roberts (1995) describe an RCT which aimed to tackle 'decisional drift' of children in foster care, that is those children who had been neglected and who had languished in foster care with no particular plans being made for their future. The researchers wanted to assess whether an intensive, birth-parent-focused service would enhance placement outcomes for children In the study 482 children were randomly assigned to one of two groups, an experimental group and a control group. Parents of children in the experimental group received intensive help from social workers, directed at problems that were identified as preventing rehabilitation. The help included regular visits to the birth parents along with the use of firm contracts with specific goals, and specific help to enable parents to meet these goals. The experiment did not appear to have a particular hypothesis as such, but expected outcomes included: return of child to birth parents, child placed for adoption, appointment of a legal guardian, a positive decision that the child would remain in care. It was reported that there were significant differences between the experimental group and the control group, with, for example, almost half of the experimental group returned home compared with only 11 per cent of the control group. Out of ten problem areas identified, in three of them there was a significant difference in favour of the experimental group.

Macdonald and Roberts say that the large sample size, the detailed description of the interventions undertaken, the careful checks made on the comparability of the two groups, the use of 'hard' outcome measures and appropriate statistical analysis allowed the study to attain 'attributive confidence' (i.e. we can be reasonably sure that it is the help offered that accounts for the improvement in the outcomes of the experimental group). Macdonald and Roberts were able to draw lessons for practice from this example.

Supporting single-parent families

Another example is Humphries's rudimentary and small-scale field experiment in a social work context, inspired by Goldberg's methodology. This involved the evaluation of a project to match volunteers with one-parent families supported by a voluntary agency in Scotland (Humphries, 1976), and aimed to compare the progress of the 32 families allocated a volunteer with a similar group not offered volunteer support. The study took as its starting point research already carried out nationally and locally on one-parent families. This had identified problems faced by such families, in particular financial concerns, planning for the future and social isolation. The research aimed to evaluate the impact of volunteers on these aspects of the life of selected families in comparison with a control group of similar families not offered volunteer help. The hypothesis proposed that families supported by volunteers would decrease social isolation, would be better informed about their financial and career options and would develop plans for the future. The aims of the study were explained to both volunteers and both groups of families, and a structured questionnaire was administered to all the families at the beginning and after a year of the project. The recruitment, selection, training and characteristics of the volunteers were documented and the regular training meetings of volunteers were tape-recorded. An analysis of all this data resulted in a report for the project funders. The selection of the sample was carried out through allocation of alternate appropriate referrals to the experimental group. The decision not to offer a volunteer to the control group was justified on the grounds that there were not enough volunteers to go round in any case, so some would not be offered this support in the normal course of events. It was decided that after the experimental period, members of the control group were to be prioritized for the offer of a volunteer (in the event, all of them declined).

On reflection, although the scheme was adjudged a success, it was impossible to attribute any changes to the volunteer effect. Indeed the most valuable aspects of the exercise were the attempt to document and make transparent the process of mounting a volunteers project, and its role as an early example of systematic evaluation of practice. The report called for a much wider, consistent and systematic evaluation of practice than was regarded as standard at the time.

Drawbacks of experimental research

Sarantakos (2005, p. 182) suggests that the weaknesses of experimental research include:

- *Control* – depending on the circumstances, experiments may not allow the degree of control that is required to exclude unwanted or unintended influences outside the independent variables.
- *Representativeness* – samples are usually too small to produce findings that are representative of the wider group of interest to the researcher.
- *Process* – the research process is too technical and too artificial to allow generalizations.
- *Ethics* – there are cases in which conditions dictate that ethical standards are of secondary importance.

These limitations are reflected in the studies described above. In all of them, any claim that the intervention has caused the change has to be treated with extreme caution.

Control

When we are dealing with human subjects it is impossible to control variables, and change may be the result of the passage of time, improvements may happen spontaneously, situations may become more manageable (e.g. with children growing up), people may be saying what they think is the right thing, other factors may have improved, and so on. These are questions that are typical in any attempt at RCTs, and which raise questions about their suitability in studying human subjects. In addition, the rationale behind control groups is that, all other things being equal, if one group is offered a service and another not, then any difference in outcomes can be attributed to the intervention – 'attributive confidence' – thus establishing a linear cause-effect relationship. What is not taken into account is the *meaning* of the intervention to the recipient, who might believe that the intervention will be helpful however useless it may be, or may respond positively to having been chosen for inclusion and thus feel valued and appreciated. The point is simple. Experimental methods can attempt to isolate the specific effects of a 'treatment' but they cannot evaluate or control the impact of the human mind. In the volunteers and single parents project for instance, the issue of the passage of time is a factor. What happens to a person over the period of the study is outside of the control of the experimenter and might have an influence on the results. Single parents who may have been (in the judgement of social workers) vulnerable in the early stages of contact with a volunteer, may form new and supportive relationships and friendships, may become closer to family and may fare better over time for reasons quite independent of their volunteer visitor. Children mature, grow, go to school, leaving space for a mother to seek further education or work outside the home. There was some evidence that volunteers provided information on jobs and further education opportunities, but these developments might have taken place without their intervention. There were some differences between the experimental and the control groups, but these were not such as to allow definitive conclusions.

In the study of foster children, improved circumstances, including income support, over time may have allowed birth parents to be in an improved situation for the children to be returned to them. They may have felt more able to care for a child who has grown older rather than a child who was a baby or a toddler when s/he was taken into care. Their personal relationships may have been a factor (e.g. living with a different partner or no longer with a partner). Experiments cannot control these aspects.

Another element beyond the control of the researcher is 'interviewer effect'. In the volunteers project, although mothers in the experimental group reported that the volunteers had been helpful and supportive, it is possible that the interviewer effect played a part in this – i.e. the people being interviewed will have known that they were part of an experiment and wanted to give the interviewer what they perceived she wanted to hear – a reminder that we are dealing with the impact on the human mind. Similarly the birth parents in the foster care study may have learned the right things to say in the course of the intervention. Whether those children who were returned home after the experiment, were still at home as time passed, would be of importance in answering this question.

Representativeness

How far is it possible to claim that the group research reflects the characteristics of the wider group of interest to the researcher? The volunteers project was a small-scale field experiment, with a total of 32 families involved. In terms of representativeness, although an attempt was made to include different types of one-parent family, they could not be described as typical of such families, and no father-headed families were included. Furthermore the majority of one-parent families have little or no contact with social work agencies. A much bigger sample would have been required to achieve representativeness and consequently generalizability. Nevertheless most field experiments in social work and related fields rely on small samples, especially where evaluative techniques are involved. The foster children study had a larger sample (241 in each group), but the question arises as to whether it was representative of all children in foster care at the time the study was undertaken. There is an even more serious question here about representativeness. The intervention was aimed at *birth parents* of children in foster care, not at the children themselves, so it may have been more relevant to focus the sample more on the characteristics of the parents than on the children.

Process

This refers to the suitability of the research instruments and their appropriateness for research with human beings. This was also a specific criticism of the Goldberg study of social work intervention with old people. The attempt to administer a kind of treatment to subjects (social workers to old people, social workers to birth parents, social workers to volunteers), broken down into technical elements that can be measured, is indeed an artificial device that is not reflected in real-life situations. The stress on component parts of complex wholes, which is at the heart of experimental methods, risks producing outcomes that are partial and distorted. Where the interest is the service user, the practitioner, the organization or any other dynamic human organism, experiments cannot satisfy the sorts of questions that need to be addressed.

There are also questions about the feasibility of achieving comparability between the experimental and the control groups, and for reducing selection bias. While known and quantifiable factors can be taken into account in attempting to establish comparability, there are numerous unknown, random factors, such as individual psychology, temperament, and so on, that cannot be properly assessed or balanced out. Even with the best matching techniques, individual differences inevitably exist.

Ethics

In experiments the question of ethics tends to be 'secondary', and Sarantakos describes the absence of choice, control and dialogue that characterize experiments. The issue of informed consent, for example, is complicated in all three studies considered here, as declining to take part might be perceived as having consequences in each of them – withdrawal of services in all of them, and in the foster children study the risk that children might never be returned home.

The ethical problems of experiments cannot be avoided. Where there is a control group, regardless of how rigorous the allocation, people are being denied a service that is available and that might make a difference to their situation. There is no question of participation in the sense of respondents having control over the conduct of the research, and choice is out of the question. In many cases it is argued that information about the study should be withheld, otherwise the results would be contaminated. Those involved may in this way be misled about or denied full knowledge of their involvement or lack of it. This duplicity may be essential to the proper conduct of the trial, yet it contravenes a basic right cited in all codes of ethics, that of informed consent, the complexities of which we discussed in Chapter 2. Brown, Crawford and Hicks (2003), discussing health, identify the Catch 22 that this entails:

> to establish a good scientific base of research on which the EBHC (evidence-based health care) culture depends requires random allocation of patients to treatment, yet this disempowers the participating patients from making informed choices about their care – one of the governing principles of the new NHS culture. (p. 129)

One must not ignore ethical issues in relation to experimental groups as well as control groups. The 'treatment' offered may not necessarily be helpful or just, and people may be put at risk as a result (see Polit-O'Hara and Hungler, 1995). In social work research one might raise questions about the ethics of experiments such as tagging, including tagging people who have not been convicted of any crime – powers that are held under asylum rules and included in the 2004 anti-terrorism legislation in the UK. Experimental research is found wanting when it comes to the ethical framework considered in Chapter 2. The opportunities for genuine dialogue with research participants and the acceptance of their knowledge are reduced to a minimum, and the organizational context and influence on the research is excluded from the process.

One of the aims of experiments is to demonstrate that the cause-effect relationship is invariable and will be constant, however many times the study is replicated. But to what extent can a study ever be a true replica of any other study? There is no absolute certainty that the same results will always be achieved (and 'results' are nearly always ambiguous in any case). Where human participants are concerned there will always be differences, however subtle. There may be similarities where the studies use samples that are representative of the groups from which they are drawn, but any generalizations will need to be very cautious indeed. Publications of research can highlight differences and hide similarities among groups, and as Reinharz (1992) has pointed out, overgeneralization that masks differences in 'race', gender, age, education and other factors is inappropriate and possibly dangerous: 'too often studies done on white populations are generalized to all groups, just as studies done on men are generalized to all people, thereby producing distorted results' (p. 107). Given the great cost of undertaking experimental research, the benefits to policy makers are somewhat limited (see Walshe and Rundall 2001).

In summary, there are a number of frequently argued objections to experimental research that raise questions about their appropriateness for studying social interventions and about their ethical underpinnings. Boruch (1975, 1997) has set these out to include:

- their unfeasibility in 'real world' settings;
- their expense and time-consuming character;
- randomization is impossible and/or unethical;
- such designs ignore other useful social data;
- qualitative approaches are regarded as unimportant;
- different people are affected differently by the same intervention;
- they are one-shot affairs and therefore limited in usefulness;
- they give no useful information about how to improve the programme under test;
- their results lack generalizability.

These and the discussion above suggest that much more thought and much less deference need to be given to the experimental method.

Conclusion: experimental methods and social justice

Much more than is legitimate is claimed for the 'gold standard' properties of experiments and other rational-empirical research designs, both in terms of their methodological aspects and in relation to their effectiveness in gaining answers to research questions, though as we have seen, there are some advantages to their use.

However, one of the fundamental principles that has informed social work for decades is the importance of viewing the individual in her/his social environment, and the search continues for a model of practice that will offer an holistic framework for understanding individual social problems, and the discussion of ethics and social justice in Chapter 2 considered this an essential feature of research in social work and social care. Because of the degree of control that is required in experimental approaches to eliminate extraneous variables that may impact on the results of a study, examining holistic problems is rendered meaningless. Most importantly, the kind of experiments predominant in social care and probation where the focus is on individualized cognitive-behavioural changes, serves to exclude socio-economic, political and cultural contexts. They typically aim to reduce offending and social disruption where crime and deviance are seen only in terms of personal aberration (see Vanstone, 1999), with no regard to the influences of unemployment, poverty, racism and other inequalities. Macdonald's (2001) book for example, describes a number of interventions targeted at preventing child abuse and neglect. Macdonald shows herself to be very aware of the socio-economic origins of many social problems, confirmed by 'clients (who) repeatedly testified to the pervasive, deleterious influence of material deprivation on their children' (p. 13), yet the book is concerned primarily with those interventions in the field of child protection aimed at individuals. In a telling paragraph Macdonald says:

> Not included therefore, are a number of important socio-economic interventions that would, if there was sufficient political will, be more likely to impact positively on the lives of thousands of children who come within the remit of the child protection system, than the sum total of effort currently expended by health and social care professionals in this field ... However, in the absence of such political will (and some might argue, economic resources), *it is important to enable practitioners to choose the most effective responses they can, within the systems they operate.* (p. xix, my emphasis)

This illustrates the problems that arise from a more or less exclusive commitment to experimental research approaches. One is required to be selective in how one defines and constructs social problems – only those that suggest cognitive-behavioural solutions, whose success can be measured by controlled experiments, are compatible with the chosen model of research. Macdonald rejects particular definitions of social problems because they do not easily lend themselves to favoured interventions and models of evaluation. These models depend on a perception of social problems that is individual and reductionist, and that concentrates on behavioural risk factors. Using the credibility of the medico-scientific paradigm it perceives effectiveness and quality only in positivist and empiricist ways. Their attempt to isolate variables and assess their relationship is too simplistic and too narrow to make available the diversity and scope necessary to understand the complexity of human experience.

These structural problems risk being minimized in the rush to formulate forms of service delivery that come to be regarded as the cure for social problems.

Experimental methods are not free from value judgements. The problems investigated, how they are investigated and by whom, and the interpretation and implementation of results are all subject to researchers, to funders and to policy makers who initiate research. In a political climate that purports to value 'empowerment' and user participation and choice, the dominance of experimental methods lies uneasily alongside government rhetoric of independence, social inclusion and an end to poverty (see Jordan, 2000). In experimental research the individuals studied have no part in the planning, execution or interpretation of the experiment, and their knowledge is dismissed as lay knowledge and therefore irrelevant, since it is expert knowledge that counts. They are regarded as acted upon rather than as actors, as to be 'known' rather than 'knowers', and although they may contribute to the research, this is solely as respondents to questions fashioned by the researchers. These conditions do not fulfil an ethical framework informed by social justice.

A further key question concerns the extent to which policy makers take account of the results of the research they commission. Some authors have suggested that the rational model of systematic experimentation, whereby policy makers wait for the results of evaluation before acting, is the exception rather than the rule (Oakley, 2000). At the same time, most research is equivocal and inconclusive, yet can be used to underpin policy initiatives. In the USA, for example, Head Start, an early intervention for disadvantaged children, was trumpeted as a success, even though the evaluation evidence for this was weak (Weiss, 1991). In the UK, the research suggests that incarcerating young people is ineffective in preventing reoffending. Yet recent government policies have resulted in increasing imprisonment for greater numbers of people aged under 18 (NACRO, 2001). In immigration and asylum policy, legislation has become increasingly draconian, even though the evidence for the government's main justifications for this is very weak indeed (Humphries, 2004b). Policy makers are often driven by prejudice, ideology and political expediency, and research, with its cautious and sometimes inconvenient conclusions, may be too awkward and slow for the perceived urgency of political and social action.

What is required here, as in judging all research, is an informed and healthy scepticism and a resistance to the current hegemonic status of ways of knowing that are experimental above other forms of knowledge. What is also required is less reliance on a single approach to social research. Combining the strengths of the experimental method with the strengths of other methods will go a long way towards avoiding its weaknesses while exploiting its power in the service of social justice.

main points

- Experiments involve the random allocation of participants to groups, the manipulation of variables and the measurement of effects

- Experimental designs are widely valued and used in social work research

- Questions have been raised about the appropriateness of experiments in research involving people

- Experiments cannot take account of structural dimensions of social problems

- Ethical concerns include:
  - issues of control by and dialogue with research participants
  - the exclusion of the wider social structural context
  - silence on organizational influences on the research

stop and think

- What advantages do experimental designs have over other methods in research in social work?
- What do you consider are the problems of 'cause and effect' methods for the study of human beings?
- What are some of the ethical questions that arise in experimental design, and how can they be addressed?
- In considering the appropriateness of experimental methods, when might you decide to use them. Think of a topic and write down a few questions on that topic which you think would be addressed by an experimental approach?

- Denscombe, M *The Good Research Guide for Small-Scale Social Research Projects*, 2nd edn (Maidenhead: Open University Press, 2003), Chapter 4
  A practical introductory text to social research. Chapter 4 explains the basics of experimental research in accessible language.
- Harvey, L and Macdonald, M *Doing Sociology: a practical introduction* (Basingstoke: Macmillan, 1993), Chapter 5
  A good introductory text. Chapter 5 takes the reader through the process of statistical analysis.
- Kirk, S A (ed.) *Social Work Research Methods: building knowledge for practice* (Washington, DC: National Association of Social Workers, 1999)
  Almost all the chapters by individual authors describe experimental methods to examine aspects of social work practice.
- Vanstone, M 'Behavioural and cognitive interventions', in I Shaw and J Lishman (eds) *Evaluation and Social Work Practice* (London: Sage, 1999, 219–34)
  A book chapter offering detailed description of experiments in crime reduction, and giving international examples.
- Sarantakos, S *Social Research* 3rd edn (Basingstoke: Palgrave Macmillan, 2005), Chapter 8.
  A general research text, clearly and usefully presented. Chapter 8 gives attention to the nature and types of experiments.

4 Participatory research

Introduction

Research approaches that emphasize participation (known both as 'participatory' and 'participative') have gained currency in recent decades, and converts range from small users' agencies to United Nations organizations. Governments in a number of countries now insist that participation of service users must be a central aim of research as well as the planning and delivery of services. At the same time however, as observed in Chapter 2, research ethics committees often operate on assumptions that do not recognize the democratic participation of service users, leading some authors (for example Truman, 2003) to question the appropriateness of criteria used by such committees in making judgements about participatory research.

In a sense, of course, all research is participatory, whether respondents are required only to provide information or whether they are centrally involved in design and implementation. The key difference between conventional and participatory strategies lies in the location of power in the research process. Cornwall and Jewkes (1995, p. 1669) identify four modes of participation:

- *Contractual* – people are contracted into the projects of researchers to take part in their enquiries or experiments;
- *Consultative* – people are asked for their opinions and consulted by researchers before interventions are made;
- *Collaborative* – researchers and local people work together on projects designed, initiated and managed by researchers;
- *Collegiate* – researchers and local people work together as colleagues with different skills to offer, in a process of mutual learning where local people have control over the process.

In 'shallow' participation, researchers control the whole process, while with increasingly 'deep' participation there is a movement towards relinquishing control and devolving ownership of the process to those whom it concerns. Thus participatory research (PR) aims towards a 'collegiate' research mode, with acknowledgement that at different stages of the process movement from one mode to another may take place at different stages. Both researched and researchers become engaged in a process of mutual learning and analysis. There are no distinctive methods associated with PR, and one of its characteristics is an innovative adaptation of conventional research methods. So although it has become mainly associated with qualitative methods, there are also examples of the use of quantitative methods. The basic principle is that methods, as with all aspects of any study, are controlled by those most affected.

PR is based on a theory of participation that holds that 'top-down' policies, planning and research are both inappropriate and ineffective, and that local perspectives, interests and priorities should inform any initiatives that require the co-operation and involvement of the people affected by them. The approach has both an ideological and a functional foundation. On the ideological level, the idea of participative approaches recognizes that poor and disadvantaged people are in a power relationship with decision-makers and researchers, that this is not to their advantage, and that controlling research, involvement in decision-making and implementation of policy initiatives are crucial towards their taking control of their lives and their environment. This aspect has had an appeal for social workers because it seems to fit comfortably with values of empowerment. The functional aspect is the recognition that policy initiatives can only be sustained if they have meaning for those affected by them, and maximizing participation results in better designed, more effective and valid outcomes. Thus the approach has become very attractive to policy makers as well as progressive researchers. The two elements described above are not necessarily incompatible but, as we shall see, there is a tension between them that is seldom considered in discussions about the issues raised in participatory research.

Origins of PR

Also known as 'new paradigm' research (Reason, 1994), and 'emancipatory research' (Barnes and Mercer, 1997), the PR approach accepts 'participation' as a universally acceptable 'good', and much of the early momentum came from 'developing' countries where the ideas underpinning PR were seized upon as part of the resistance to colonial or neo-colonial practices. It emerged in the 1970s and a leading practitioner in this field defined it as:

> a three pronged activity . . . a method of social investigation involving the full participation of the community . . . an educational process which is a means of taking action for development. (Hall, 1977, p. 1)

The key words in this definition are *participation, education* and *action*, and, as Martin (1994) says, PR is thus a process of social inquiry and learning for both researcher and researched, and has the explicit intention of collectively investigating reality in order to transform it. Martin says the features of PR are that (i) it originates within the community; (ii) it seeks to involve marginalized groups; and (iii) it recognizes the strengths and power such groups have and seeks to build on them. In spite of its ambition to be inclusive, PR was for a number of years dominated by male perspectives, and it was not until 1981 that Hall asked 'How can PR be human centred, not man-centred?' (Hall, 1981, p. 17). More recently a distinctively feminist approach to participatory research has emerged (Maguire, 1987, 1996; Martin, 1994, 1996).

One of the best-known theorists in PR is Paulo Freire, a Brazilian educationalist, whose ideas in *Pedagogy of the Oppressed* (Freire, 1972) have been adopted on a worldwide scale, and claimed to be empowering for poor people, women, disabled groups, the homeless and unemployed, and others who might be described as oppressed. Social movements such as the women's movement, the disability movement, the lesbian and gay movement and indigenous peoples' movements have seen the potential of PR and, as well as a feminist literature, there is now a thriving literature in fields such as disability (Barnes and Mercer, 1997), lesbian and gay studies (Truman 2000) and indigenous peoples' concerns (Tuhiwai Smith, 1999). In social work and social care policy there are a number of proponents of participatory research, notably Peter Beresford who runs the Centre for Citizen Participation at Brunel University in the UK, specifically to pursue participatory methods. It has found its way into the academy, bringing with it a critique of conventional research approaches, and has been adopted by governments towards 'citizen participation' in the identification of social needs and planning and delivery of services. In health policies in the UK, the Healthy Cities project, initiated by the government in the 1990s prescribed participatory research as a central strategy in engaging people in identifying their health needs (Rootman et al., 2006). Prominent advocates of PR in health and social care are de Koning and Martin (1996) and Dockery (2000).

Principles of PR

PR takes an explicitly political stance, focusing on empowering disenfranchised and marginalized groups to take action to transform their lives. As Cornwall and Jewkes (1995) say, 'Different actors, each with their own knowledge, techniques and experiences, work together in dialectical process, through which new forms of knowledge are produced' (p. 1668). In their view ideally the initial agents of change become redundant as the people most affected take over the process for themselves. These authors see it as more of an attitude of approach than a series of techniques. In PR research activities are expanded to encompass performance (Mienczakowski, 2000), art and story-telling (Wilkins, 2000), as well as the use of more conventional methods such as focus group discussions, structured questionnaires and depth interviewing.

When it emerged in the early 1970s, PR was regarded as an alternative social science method that challenged the premises of neutrality, objectivity and value-free research on which traditional scientific research had been based. As Tandon comments, 'the distance between the researcher and the researched, the dichotomy of the subject and object, the reliance on statistical and quantifiable techniques all were subjected to a comprehensive critique' (Tandon, 1996, p. 20). An even more fundamental challenge to scientific research was the question of knowledge and knowing. PR asserted that the knowledge of the scientist was not the only legitimate knowledge, that different kinds of knowledge were to be valued, and in particular the knowledge of 'the researched' was to be accepted on equal terms with expert knowledge. It was argued that such knowledge should be central to the conception, design and methodologies employed in researching human meanings. A key objective in PR is the attempt to achieve a situation where power is shared among researchers and participants, and the emphasis is on research *with* and *for* participants, rather than research *on* them. Below are basic principles accepted by most adherents of PR:

- a bottom-up approach with a focus on locally defined priorities, processes and perspectives
- striving for equalizing of power among researchers and researched
- the process is characterized by a genuine dialogue between researchers and researched
- control over definition of problems, methods, analysis and action is with those affected most by the study
- the emphasis is on processes rather than only on outcomes
- the role of the researcher is one of facilitator and catalyst rather than director

Hall's three activities that he regards as central to the approach – research, education and action (1993, p. xiv) – are focused on (i) engaging people as researchers themselves and legitimating the knowledge they have; (ii) developing in people a consciousness of the origins and nature of their oppression and exploitation; and (iii) mobilizing people into action in order to control and change their situation. The key components of *participation, education* and *action* make PR explicitly political, with the aim of bringing about a more just society through what Freire (1972) called conscientization. Park describes it as

> both cognitive and transformative; it produces knowledge that is linked simultaneously with and intimately to social action . . . people who desire knowledge to bring about a more free and less oppressive world engage in the investigation of reality in order to get a better understanding of the problems and their root causes. The real investigator in this case is not the traditional researcher who, as a technical expert, relates to the 'subjects' of research (questionnaire respondents, interviewees, participants in an experiment) only as objects of inquiry, the source of data. Rather it is the ordinary people with problems to solve who form a partnership with the researcher, for learning about the dimensions of oppression, the structural contradictions, and transformative potentials open to collective action. This is the 'participatory' part of participatory research. (Park, 1993, p. 3)

As is clear from this quote, one of the differences between PR and some other forms of research is that both the processes and outcomes of research are to be *useful* to oppressed social groups, to make a difference to their lives, to transform the circumstances that create and exacerbate their oppression. There is a clear objective that on both an individual and a social level, people involved are empowered to take action towards influencing policies and implementing social change measures. In this sense, PR has close similarities to some forms of action research, discussed in Chapter 5.

Cornwall and Jewkes (1995) describe a number of models of PR, particularly used in the field of health, including Participatory Rural Appraisal (PRA), Development Leadership Teams in Action (DELTA) and Theatre for Development. Within all these approaches methods are seen less as a means to an end than as offering ends in themselves by being concerned directly with relations of power. Ideally it should be 'the oppressed' who initiate the research, since they have knowledge about the problems they face, and PR assumes they are the origin of any moves towards change. In practice, it is researchers, and those who employ them, who take the initiative and who attempt to stimulate communities to take an interest in the research activity. It is argued that communities' powerlessness may prevent them from organizing themselves, and the researcher becomes a central person in acting as a focal point for action. This requires skills in developing trust, in interpersonal and political engagement and in drawing influential people into the process. It also involves developing an awareness of marginalized groups within communities, and ensuring that their perspective is heard. It requires facilitation ability in order to help the community to define the problems they want to investigate, and to make these manageable for research. It entails knowledge of a range of research options, and helping communities to make decisions about the appropriateness of different methods.

Examples of PR in social work and social care

PR draws on all available social science approaches (though it rejects certain techniques that dictate the separation of the subject from the 'object' of research). The examples below give a flavour of the range of methods that have been used to try to achieve the ideal of maximum participation. Most of these are qualitative, but there are examples of quantitative approaches worth examining too.

Day care on the move

Mark Baldwin (a British academic) was asked to evaluate a project at a day centre for adults with learning difficulties (Baldwin, 1997). The Centre management was concerned about its future direction, and purchased a package called Changeover to help them and users consider ways forward. Changeover claims to offer a structured basis for development that genuinely involves service users and which is grounded in O'Brien's five accomplishments (O'Brien and Lyle, 1987) as its value base. It consists of four modules called, 'Our service now', 'Options for change', 'Learning from others' and 'Looking to the future – action plan'. Changeover stipulates a core group as the main vehicle for managing the process of change, made up of a wide range of people – those who use the facility, carers and parents, local people and allies. The limitations of this model led to a decision to develop a process of what Baldwin calls 'participative action research' (PAR) (see Chapter 5). The core group remained, but a model was devised so that all staff, carers and users were to be involved, since they should be party to any decisions made, as change depended on these being owned and used by them. Participants were allocated to Changeover groups and made their way through the modules. Ideas were passed backwards and forwards, and the job of the core was to make sense of the ideas of the other groups, check these out with the groups and then move on to the next stage of the process. The Centre staff facilitated all this. As may already be obvious, this took up enormous amounts of time and was rather testing on the commitment of the facilitators, to say nothing of the group members. In the process a number of techniques was used – group discussion, brain-storming, SWOT analyses and so on, culminating in an identification of particular areas for change. In order to take these forward, participants chose a project group to develop their own area of interest (themes mentioned are 'advocacy', 'catering' and 'outreach'). Baldwin reports that the confidence of service users has increased in both frequency and quality over the period of the project, for which he cites evidence indicating greater involvement in presentations, and in offering options for change and development of the Centre. Baldwin emphasizes the importance of staff and carers' understanding of and commitment to the process, and identifies communication as a key component. The issue of anxiety about possible change needed to be accepted and time taken to deal with it to prevent the project being blocked by the worries of participants. Lifetime experiences of being disabled by assumptions that people with learning difficulties are not able to have opinions or make choices was a struggle for the project, and needed attention if participation was to be genuine. People who have high support needs and who are not well disposed to being part of communal 'group care' were difficult to include in Changeover.

At the same time Baldwin's evaluation suggested a number of successes. He describes the project as 'anti-disablist' in that it provided opportunities for people to learn about choices and how to make them. It also refused to accept difference as a reason for non-involvement. He comments that participation has been the key to a change of culture in that routine practices are viewed differently and old ways of understanding are more readily questioned.

One of the problems with Baldwin's description of PAR is that it is difficult to identify the two processes he described, that is the Changeover project itself and his own evaluation of it. He did not say in what ways his evaluation was participatory, but the intervention he described was designed on a model of inclusiveness that clearly is an example of PAR. One has a sense of his role as evaluator as external, with no evidence of any participative research design. Nevertheless, we can appreciate the ways in which those involved with the Centre attempted to set up an action research series of events towards inclusiveness of all participants.

User-controlled research

Some writers in this field have taken the debate beyond equalizing the relationship between researchers and participants They argue that as users have become more experienced in participation, there is a growing understanding of how they can themselves design and undertake research, with implications for the role of those employed to conduct research (see Barnes and Mercer, 1997; Beresford, 2000; Evans and Fisher, 1999). This demand comes with the growing power of social movements, their development of coherent theory building, and the requirement for user involvement in community and child care internationally. Beresford claims that one key quality distinguishes user knowledges from all others involved in social care and social policy provision: 'they alone are based on direct experience . . . from the receiving end' (Beresford, 2000, p. 493). Thus instead of service users' experiences being defined by research 'experts', where the thinking behind research questions is so far removed from the way users see their lives, research comes directly under user control. It is also the case that the starting point for many service users' view of research is as part of a structure of discrimination and oppression – an activity that is both intrusive and disempowering, serving the damaging purposes of a service system over which they can exert little influence or control. As a result of this there has been an increasing interest in user control of research. Some service user organizations in the field of disability, for example, have their own research units, or commission their own research. Beresford's work suggests that user knowledge and experiences should control all elements – the origination of research, who gains from the benefits of research, the accountability of research, who undertakes the research, research funding, research design and process, dissemination of research findings, action following from research (p. 495). The study by Beresford and Turner (1997) is an example of these principles in action.

Evans and Fisher (1999) give some examples of how user-controlled research might work. They define user-controlled research in the following terms:

> It must bring service-users greater power to define their needs and the outcomes that matter to them. Service users must select the issues for research and acquire control over the funds to conduct it. We think that service users should wherever possible become researchers, so that their influence pervades the research: this includes responsibility for data analysis and for dissemination. (p. 104)

These authors describe research carried out by Wiltshire and Swindon Users' Network, established in 1991 to promote collective advocacy among users of health and social services in Wiltshire. The network set out to evaluate the Wiltshire Independent Living Fund (WILF), a third-party cash payment scheme. The first essential step was gaining control of the research funding, provided through the local social services department. Because of the organization's credibility, built over years of working with allies in the department, this was achieved. A wide invitation to participate resulted in a core research advisory group of users, where key decisions about the use of funds were made. Users were paid a fee to attend meetings, thus providing the support needed to allow them to participate. At an early stage an academic ally became involved, whose contribution was carefully negotiated and subject to a formal contract so that control would remain with the network. Baseline data were accumulated from records (with careful attention to issues of confidentiality), in an attempt to gain a profile of applications for support across the county, with which applications to WILF could be compared. A decision was made also to gather information directly from WILF users about their experiences. An interview schedule was drawn up by the advisory group over a two-day workshop, during which all members had a chance to ensure that the questions they thought important could be included. Four people were trained as interviewers (three of them were WILF users), the training facilitated by the academic and by a network member with research experience. A sample of WILF users was 'independently' selected for interview, and these were taped and transcribed. Two people from the advisory group read all the interviews, and four others combed through the transcripts for particular themes. The group also took responsibility for co-ordinating the writing up of the report, and for dissemination. The draft report was the subject of a day's review by the advisory group, who then took on roles for a presentation to the forthcoming network AGM. Evans and Fisher make the point that in such research expertise must be conceptualized as belonging with service users as much as with professionals, and that professional skills lie as much in facilitating user-led and user-controlled research as in technical skills traditionally reserved to the 'researcher'.

This research was of course not devoid of problems, particularly in accomplishing tasks and moving on from the process of advisory group members recounting their experiences. There were also ethical tensions relating to confidentiality and in dealing with official data that had been gathered using conceptualizations of disability which the group found unacceptable. An important lesson from the experience is that the way these researchers chose to conduct research is not easily or quickly achieved. Close, joint collaboration with allies in statutory organizations was only achieved after several years developing relationships of trust between practitioners and service users. Control of the budget and the design of the research would not have been acceptable otherwise. The literature on PR consistently emphasizes the importance of building trust, but seldom acknowledges the long, slow process that may or may not result in mutual confidence.

In any case, most research is time-limited and under pressure to deliver quick results.

Gay men's health

I include the example of Truman's (1999, 2000) PR with a gay men's health group because it is one of the few available instances of the use of quantitative methods within a participatory framework. Truman starts from the position that statistical studies are a fact of life in modern societies, and indeed are powerful tools in the hands of powerful people. This being the case, there is an argument for changing the way social statistics are produced, so that the needs of marginalized groups, currently unrepresented or misrepresented in them, are made visible and given attention. Truman was involved in a large-scale (n = 1000) health survey of men who have sex with men. Significantly, the initiative came from a gay men's health group, Healthy Gay City (HGC), located in the north-west region of England, which operated both as a service provider around HIV/AIDS prevention and education and also as a user group. It was decided that a survey might provide data which could be used to influence purchasers and fundholders, since the organization was dependent on raising funds for its survival. Data were needed to show that health needs existed amongst the gay and bisexual population, and how those needs might be met through funded initiatives. HGC enlisted the help of a sympathetic academic (Truman) with expertise in organizing social surveys, who was also committed to a participatory mode of working. Instead of simply working to their brief – designing the survey, recruiting interviewers and analysing the findings and presenting them with a final report, she wanted to adopt an approach that would involve them centrally in the process, and would allow members of the group itself to develop research skills, and to share their knowledge and expertise.

The way this was done was to break the research down into small stages and to involve about six members of the HGC group at each stage, so that objectives of the stage could be discussed and strategies agreed. For example, at the sampling stage, the small group agreed on a community sampling approach that allowed the survey to reach depth and breadth of a population that is heterogeneous – not only those on the 'gay scene' who would fill in a questionnaire, but those who would not voluntarily fill in a questionnaire (by interviewing), those not on the 'scene' (through a snowballing technique), gay interest groups in, for example, student societies, churches, choirs. As a result the study was able to identify 1000 respondents by going beyond those who socialize on the gay scene to 'hidden' groups such as those who live in rural areas, gay men over the age of 50 as well as those under the age of 18 – ' this extensive coverage was achieved not by drawing on textbook ideas about sampling but on the expertise contained within the gay community' (Truman, 1999, p. 154). As a consequence, it is probable that a more sophisticated and representative sample was achieved than would otherwise have been the case. Because of this, the report presented to funding bodies carried a great deal of weight, since the survey had captured views about health needs across a widely disparate group of people. In this study, the main reason for using this quantitative approach was that HGC knew it would be influential with the audience they wanted to reach. They needed a 'respectable' piece of research that policy makers would accept as 'factual evidence'.

Other models of PR

There are variations on PR that are focused on the participation of people in areas where there is high illiteracy, and to reduce dependence in research on being able to read documentation associated with it. PRA is one example of this. PRA has been described as 'an approach and methods for learning about rural life and conditions from, with and by rural people' (Chambers, 1992, p. 1). As this description implies, it has been used mainly in 'developing' countries with rural economies, though its principles are applicable more generally. It grew out of disillusion with anti-poverty biases of conventional research and out of a concern about the limitations of questionnaire surveys. On the positive side, it has also been helped by recognition that rural people are themselves knowledgeable on many subjects that touch their lives and such knowledge needs to be tapped by methods that might be seen as unconventional but which, for practical purposes, require to be explored.

Applications of PRA continue to draw on qualitative methods such as focus group discussions, observation and interviewing, but more emphasis is placed on facilitating visualized analysis (Cornwall and Jewkes, 1995; see also Welbourn, 1992), giving opportunities for local people to explore and represent their perspectives in their own terms. They choose their own symbols from easily available materials, to represent aspects of their lives in a shared medium, which can then be amended, discussed and analysed. Participatory mapping is a central technique in PRA and can include seasonal calendars to illustrate complex interrelations among different factors over the year, such as those between, for example, the incidence of disease, patterns of rainfall, levels of migration and food availability. Timelines, time trends, flow diagrams and visualized biographies of problems offer a means to represent historical information visually. Activities carried out with different interest groups (e.g. women, men, the young, the old) highlight intra-communal differences, exposing assumptions of consensus within 'communities' (see Cornwall and Jewkes, 1995 for more detail). In this way social maps can be constructed, identifying local facilities, household attributes (for example ownership of farm animals or women's employment in domestic industries), social stratification, the distribution of vulnerable groups and the take-up of services. In health the mapping concept has been extended to participatory maps of the body, in an attempt to bridge profession-als' and local people's different understandings and languages in the areas of, for example, family planning, mental health and child care. In these ways researchers become learners, and begin to appre-ciate ways of communicating that otherwise they would not have imagined.

The DELTA approach and Theatre for Development referred to earlier also have unique features. DELTA offers process-oriented ways of identifying and responding to local concerns, and building confi-dence and trust through a long-term commitment. Facilitators conduct 'listening' surveys in communities and prepare 'codes', such as pictures or songs, which reflect local problems. Each 'code' is then discussed and analysed with focus groups or at an open meeting, within the context of human relations exercises that build self-esteem and motivation. Through this analysis, plans are made for action. Action provides further reflection, discussion and analysis.

Theatre for Development approaches involve adult educators and development workers building scenarios through listening surveys, and creating dramas as 'codes' as a focus for discussion with audi-ences in places where people gather together. Some projects have integrated members of the audience into the drama. Participants are invited to comment on, modify and take part in the sketches. Analysis takes place not only through discussion but also through the process of dramatization itself. People are invited to intervene in sce-narios from everyday life, breaking the narrative flow by posing ques-tions and challenges to the audience, and are encouraged to explore possible solutions. Spectators become actors and acting out becomes a rehearsal for action. Mienczakowski (2000) describes such a process in his work in the mental health field in Australia, and Ong et al. (1991) offer an example in an urban setting in the UK.

These are examples of how participatory methodologies offer ways in which learning approaches can be responsive to local priorities and committed to change. Such approaches are not confined to 'developing' countries, but can be used in needs assessment, service planning and development and a range of other settings anywhere.

Drawbacks of PR

This way of working presents a number of challenges. Some of these are to do with the actual process of making it happen, and others are to do with disciplinary conventions, academic credibility or funding priorities. Its detractors claim that PR is not objective because of its explicit political bias, that its claims for participation are not achievable and that it is vulnerable to incorporation by powerful groups. I shall discuss these objections under the headings of methodological, technical and political questions.

Methodological questions

Objectivity

From a methodological perspective one of the criticisms of PR (and of other research with an openly political objective) is the question of objectivity. How can PR be objective, since the whole enterprise is motivated by the political goal of changing the conditions of the poor and powerless? And does not the involvement of the beneficiary of research in the investigative process seriously compromise the results? PR, in common with other approaches that are not based on the scientific model, is often regarded as lacking rigour, reliability and neutrality. It is argued that truth must be pursued for its own sake and that the methods used must be technically sound. I have addressed some of these issues in Chapter 1 and here confine myself to a summary of the points. The accusation of lack of objectivity rests on an assumption that impartiality is both possible and desirable and that every effort should be made to separate research practice from politics. PR adherents reply that the definition, interpretation and solution of social problems and social need are all profoundly political questions that are, on the whole, in the hands of relatively powerful groups, and exclude perceptions and participation of marginalized and poor groups. What PR offers is an opportunity to hear the voices of these groups in an unmediated and direct way, thus increasing the validity of any findings.

Reliability and validity

A central principle in PR is the notion of dialogue, which cannot be achieved through a research process of simply responding to questions framed by a researcher, because these questions do not allow people to speak in a full voice. Oppressed people need to speak to each other as whole persons and as autonomous human beings. Part of this process entails ordinary people acquiring research skills, an activity traditionally reserved for technically trained personnel. This of course raises questions of reliability and validity. Reliability requires that the data-gathering instrument be standardized across all respondents. The questioner is instructed to administer the questions under uniform conditions, to keep social distance from the respondent and to avoid on-the-spot amplifications or clarifications of the questions. By contrast in PR the emphasis is on validity of data, and it is assumed this depends on the subjects fully empathizing with the purpose of the study, thoroughly understanding the intent of the questions, and wanting to give the needed information in the best way they know how. There is of course the question of whether this leads to collusion between researcher and researched, where the research subject gives the answers they think the researcher wants.

The nature of knowledge

A fundamental argument in debates amongst researchers adhering to different research paradigms is the question of who can be a knower, and what kinds of knowledge are legitimate? Gaventa (1993) tells a story of a friend who knew a particular geographical area well and had over the years come to be something of an expert on damage done by mining companies in the vicinity. One day he discovered a stream heavily polluted by silt from a mine higher up the mountain, so he brought a government inspector to see it with a view to prosecuting the mining company. The inspector consulted his maps of the area and then declared, 'I'm sorry, I cannot take action. According to my map, there is no stream there.' With a sentence that was underpinned by the authority of official knowledge, the problem was rendered a non-issue. Corporate exploitation had been protected by the state, buttressed by the power to define what constituted a 'problem'. Formal, 'scientific' knowledge dominated over informal knowledge and experience, even to the extent of becoming ludicrous. This illustrates the points made in Chapter 1 of this book, that there is more than one kind of knowledge, that knowledge is validated by the status of 'the knower', and that the power to name is more important than the knowledge itself. This is why it is important that those affected by research are supported to make their voices heard.

Technical questions

A number of questions arise regarding the complexities and difficulties of implementing PR. Because authentic and meaningful participation and control is so important in PR, there is a preoccupation in the literature as to the extent to which participation has been achieved in any particular study. Martin (1999) sets out a number of issues of concern here:

- *Sharing control with 'the community'.* Control over the research is rarely devolved completely on to 'the community', nor do 'communities' always want it. Research is the researcher's 'business', and others have busy lives and priorities that do not necessarily include involvement in research. They may be sceptical as to whether it is worth investing their time and energy in something without any guarantee of benefits from it. Cornwall and Jewkes (1995) comment that community participation often seems to carry more significance for outsiders than it does for the poor. In the event, some groups will be excluded because other more pressing needs demand their time and energy.
- *The level of confidence of participants.* Often people are not confident that their view matters, or indeed is wanted, or they feel they do not have research skills or appropriate knowledge. They may see the researcher as expert and therefore with skills others do not possess, and thus are discouraged from taking part. Enormous efforts may have to be made to involve them.
- *The motivation of people to become involved.* Once participation is secured, there is no guarantee that it will continue, or it may be intermittent and inconsistent. Commitment and interest waxes and wanes over time, and participants can experience task exhaustion. This is a big risk in PR, which is often a time-consuming business.
- *Fear and suspicion.* Many communities have been researched *ad nauseam* and have seen nothing for their efforts. Their experiences may lead them to believe that talk of control by 'the community' may be no more than rhetoric, or that any control they have may be limited and not over significant elements of the research. False hopes have been raised too many times before.
- *Including marginalized and less influential people.* Achieving sustained involvement from people who are oppressed by poverty, especially women who have to work hard for their families to survive, may be an unrealistic goal, especially where there are no resources to compensate people for their time and effort

Political questions

Political questions arise on a number of different levels, from issues of interpersonal power to government control. A basic assumption of PR has been its polarized view of 'the oppressed' and 'the oppressors'. In Marxist and Freirean approaches class has been the determining factor, with poor people occupying the role of the oppressed, and oppressors being people in powerful positions who exploit the labour of the poor. Freire's early work did not acknowledge gender for example, where a man who is oppressed by his boss can in turn oppress his wife. Feminists have developed the uses of PR to focus on women's oppression and as a means of attempting to empower women (see, for example, Maguire, 1987 and Martin, 1994, 1996).

Linked to the point above, the notion of 'community' is also problematic, because it tends to romanticize the concept as small, homogeneous and integrated or contained within a clear physical or geographical boundary, whereas all communities have competing needs, interests and values related to power relations around not only gender but also class, 'race', sexual identity, age, and so on. The representation of community needs as homogeneous has resulted in research with fictitious communities, because not all have had opportunities to speak. The search for consensus (as in the focus group, a popular method in PR) is misleading, since conflicting needs and interests are often not reconcilable.

There is also the tricky issue of who is to be excluded. Some community members such as formal leaders often represent those whose views have dominated over less powerful people and may for example hold patriarchal or nepotistic values or endorse practices that others regard as harmful and unjust. There will also be differences of wealth, gender, age, religion, ethnicity and power. If some are to be excluded from participating, one outcome might be that the processes and decisions resulting from the participatory dialogue are undermined and sabotaged, and damage done to community relations. Clearly participation should be achieved that will involve all, but not necessarily together and with a recognition of competing, contested interests. As Cornwall and Jewkes (1995) reflect:

> On the one hand, working through local power structures invites manipulation of the research according to the agendas of the powerful. On the other, working outside (and inevitable potentially against) these structures can weaken both the potential impact of the project at a wider level, as well as invite continued marginalization'. (p. 1673)

In addition to these problems in PR, Truman (2003) discusses a number of ethical dilemmas that arise in the actual process of doing PR (i.e. that are not only concerned with 'getting the methods right'). In her research evaluating a community gym for mental health services users, she was confronted with ethical dilemmas from the outset in discussions with the management committee before the work began, in the payment of expenses to participants, concerning informed consent and to do with involving people who were experiencing acute illness at the time of the research. These dilemmas are of course not peculiar to PR, but they suggest that awareness of the importance of addressing them at every stage is central to best practice.

Conclusion: PR and social justice

PR is explicitly concerned with the sharing of power and with equity and justice. However, as is clear, PR is not an easy option, is complex, time-consuming and holds a number of dangers and dilemmas for both communities and researchers. In some contexts it is totally inappropriate to involve local people in collecting sensitive information (e.g. on HIV). Some local knowledge can have potentially harmful and unintended consequences that cannot be foreseen. Some approaches to PR have been criticized for romanticizing the views of participants and ignoring the problems of privileging service users' perspectives regardless of what their views are. The dominance of the expert view is replaced by the dominance of the lay view, and all expertise discredited. The ideal of dialogue, where the knowledge of experts is brought into service in local communities' defining of needs, is lost in such a situation, and usually the importance of dialogue within organizations themselves is ignored. The need to take account of networks of power relations within communities, which are not homogeneous, and within the organizations where researchers are located, makes PR a rather complex process.

The volume edited by Cooke and Kotari (2001) raises a number of questions about what they call the 'tyranny' of participation and identifies three sets of 'tyrannies'. The first is 'tyranny of decision-making and control'. The question here is can participatory facilitators override existing legitimate decision-making processes? Democratic processes already functioning, may be bypassed by, for example, focus groups which are not necessarily representative, and are then used as the basis for important political decisions that affect whole communities. The second tyranny is 'tyranny of the group' – might group dynamics lead to participatory decisions that reinforce the interests of the already powerful, through a manipulation of group processes? The third concerns 'tyranny of method'. Have participatory methods driven out others, which have advantages that participation cannot provide?

The authors' answers to all of these questions is yes, these are very real dangers, since participatory approaches can be compatible with top-down planning systems, and have not necessarily heralded changes in prevailing institutional practices of development. Mosse (2001) points out that 'participation' is sufficiently ambiguous to allow many different readings and rationalities that can validate action from different points of view.

There is also a cautionary note to be drawn from the popularity of PR internationally. Government agencies use participation to reach expenditure targets through enrolling non-governmental organizations or community institutions in implementation. Participation can be used as a means to reduce operations and maintenance costs. Marketing agencies may see participation as a means to enhance an organization's profile. For some voluntary organizations participation may mean patronage and reputation-building.

> The idea of participation can become a self-validating theory of the relationship between successful outputs and people's involvement. As such it could be seen as a crucial tool for project management – not to shape the implementation of programmes . . . but to produce internal coherence and manage relationships 'upwards' with donors . . . [But it can] come to manage the internal contradiction between high-profile 'participation' on the one hand, and the 'strong control over programme delivery' and expanded patronage on the other. (Mosse, 2001, p. 30)

In other words, a link is established between the ideological 'good' of participation/participatory research, and efficient, economic implementation, thus legitimizing systems that are not necessarily in the interests of participants. 'Local knowledge' becomes compatible with bureaucratic planning. This points to the danger of naivety of assumptions about the authenticity of motivations and behaviour in participatory processes. Its quasi-religious associations and the language of empowerment can mask a concern for managerialist effectiveness external to a community, and can obscure and sustain broader inequalities and injustice. Any theory of PR needs to incorporate analysis of the meaning of the concept to different actors who will have different agendas.

A related question that may be raised about the 'empowering' aspects of PR is not how much people are empowered, but for what? This is a reference to the notion that regulation works through empowerment. The educative aspect of PR is not *inherently* emancipatory, but can act as a way of disciplining the self by shaping the way people understand themselves, and empowering them to behave in ways that are confining and restricting, tantamount to 'subjection' (Foucault, 1988).

There is clearly much more to PR than first captures the senses. One must therefore conclude that it is not necessarily and inevitably conducive to a commitment to social justice and, as with all other methods, requires close examination regarding the origins, motivations and agendas of those who promote it.

main points

- PR is also known as 'new paradigm' and 'emancipatory' research
- It is a 'bottom-up' approach that seeks to involve marginalized groups and to use their strengths
- It strives for equalizing of power between researched and researcher
- It is characterized by genuine dialogue
- Its critics say that PR is not objective and is too political, that participation is not achievable and that it can be hijacked by powerful groups

stop and think

- Why do you think participatory research is attractive to social work researchers? Write down as many reasons as you can think of.
- What do you understand to be the main values that inform PR?
- When might it be appropriate to use a PR approach?
- Can you think of any ethical dilemmas that might arise in PR?

taking it further

- Baxter, L, Thorne, L and Mitchell, A *Lay Involvement in Health Research* (Exeter: Washington Singer Press, 2001)
  A useful discussion of the move towards service user participation in studies in the health field.
- de Koning, K and Martin, M (eds) *Participatory Research in Health: issues and experiences* (London: Zed Books, 1996)
  A collection of international contributions, particularly from 'developing' countries describing a variety of models of PR.
- Truman, C and Raine, P 'Experience and meaning of user involvement – some explorations from a community mental health project' *Health and Social Care in the Community* 10 (3) 136–43
  A detailed and frank discussion of the process of doing PR in the evaluation of a community gym.

5 Action research

Introduction

Action research has been an attractive option for health and social care workers because the name conveys a sense of things happening immediately and therefore speaks to the practical and change-oriented nature of social work, rather than 'scientific' research as discussed in Chapter 3, which may often aim to gather knowledge without creating changes. Indeed 'pure' research may be explicit in its desire to 'disturb nothing' as an element of ethical research practice. An objective, detached view of the research problem in order to explain it is at the heart of the scientific method. 'Action research' appeals because it implies engagement with the social world and empowerment for relatively powerless people – the changes that take place in the course of the research are bound to be in the interests of 'the researched'. One of the founders of action research, Kurt Lewin (1948), set out explicitly to change the life chances of disadvantaged groups, and an underlying principle of the approach is not merely to understand the world, but to change it.

Grundy (1990) argues that the conditions necessary for action research are:

- the project takes as its subject matter a **social practice**, regarding it as a strategic action susceptible to improvement;
- the project proceeds through a **spiral of cycles** of planning, acting, observing and reflecting, with each of these activities being systematically and self-critically implemented and interrelated;
- the project **involves** those responsible for the practice in each of the moments of the activity, widening participation in the project gradually to include others affected by the practice and maintaining collaborative control of the process (p. 353, emphasis original).

Grundy makes the point that the idea of strategic action, which is deliberate, considered action undertaken to bring about change, distinguishes action involved in action research from other forms of action, which may be designed to assess the past or find out about the present. Such action, she says, often is not strategic, is backward-looking and does not bring about change and improvement.

Hart and Bond (1995) regard action research as particularly appropriate where problem-solving and improvement are on the agenda. They say this is especially so in health and social care professions, where the action research cycle of enquiry, intervention and evaluation mirrors the process carried out by professional staff in assessing the needs of vulnerable people, responding to them and reviewing progress. It also goes some way towards reconciling the 'theory-practice divide' in that these are inextricably intertwined. Some authors argue that inquiry is 'not just the mechanical observation of nature and others, but the intervention of political and moral illumination' (Harding, 1986, p. 241). As a result, action research becomes a process in which action and evaluation proceed simultaneously' (Reinharz, 1992, p. 180).

Origins of action research

Action research originated in the USA and came to prominence in the work of Kurt Lewin, a social psychologist who developed it among poor communities in the years after the Second World War. His approach was a form of research which could marry the experimental approach of social science with programmes of social action in response to major social problems after the end of the Second World War. He conceived a spiral of circles of activities which involved fact-finding, conceptualization, planning, execution, more fact-finding or evaluation, and so on. This was a radical departure from conventional research because 'participants' in the social world under investigation were to be involved in every stage of the action research cycle. Early experiments had shown the power of group decision in producing commitment and changes in attitudes and behaviour; action research was an attempt to incorporate group consciousness systematically into the research process (see Kemmis, 1990 for a fuller description of Lewin's work, and Chapter 3 for experimental methods). Since then it has been used in areas such as integrated housing, equality of opportunity for employment, the causes and cure of prejudice in children, the socialization of street gangs and the training of youth leaders (Kemmis and McTaggart, 1988). It has been applied in settings in the UK through the teachers-as-researchers movement and in Europe, Australia and internationally. The literature on action research is focused largely in the field of education, both in the training of teachers and in teacher-managed classroom projects:

> In its developed form, it offers all participants in the work of education a flexible approach to school improvement through critically informed action and reflection which is appropriate to the real, complex and often confusing circumstances and constraints of the modern school. (Kemmis and McTaggart, 1988, p. 7)

These ideas were circulating of course at a time before radical changes took place both in the organization of schools and in the content and prescription of the curriculum. However, even as late as 1998 it was still possible to identify action research for education change as 'a continuing, if subordinate aspect of the professional culture of secondary teachers' (Elliott, 1998, p. 12). There are now some descriptions of attempts at action research in social work and social care, and we shall consider examples later in the chapter.

'Action' research can be many things, may be carried out within a number of paradigms, and may range from experimental methods to participatory methods. It can be depicted as having two extremes, with a variety of points in between. At one end are what might be termed 'field experiments', modelled largely on controlled scientific experiments. According to Hart and Bond (1995) there has been a development from 'an Americanized form of rational social management to a more robustly democratic and empowering approach to change' (p. 12). In other words, action research can be a form of social engineering, where objectives are set in terms of changing human behaviour, action is initiated to influence the behaviour, its impact is evaluated, the next step is planned on a rational basis, action is modified, and so on within a framework of planning, acting, observing and reflecting. Those at whom the action is targeted do not necessarily consent to this process. Some modern writers warn that action research is being hijacked in the service of technical rationality, being suitable to adapt to controlling behaviour to produce predefined objectives or targets (Elliott, 2001), and indeed action research is compatible with some management theories and management styles.

At the other end of the spectrum there appears to be a concern only with immediate and local change, with little by way of preparation or evidence of change beyond personal testimony (the researcher's or that of random others). Between these two extremes a number of authors have attempted to set out principles for a disciplined framework of practice, and thus a variety of theoretical models has emerged.

Principles of action research

Most authors writing about this genre offer practical models rather than principles as such. Kemmis and McTaggart (1988), for example, set out the steps as they have developed these:

> In practice, the process begins with a *general idea* that some kind of improvement or change is desirable. In deciding just where to begin in making improvements, one decides on a *field of action* . . . where the battle (not the whole war) should be fought. It is a decision on where it is possible to have an impact. The general idea prompts a *'reconnaissance'* of the circumstances of the field, and fact-finding about them. Having decided on the field and made a preliminary reconnaissance, the action researcher decides on a *general plan* of action. Breaking the general plan down into achievable steps, the action researcher settles on the *first action step*. Before taking this first step the action researcher becomes more circumspect, and devises a way of *monitoring* the effects of the first action step. When it is possible to maintain fact-finding by monitoring the action, the first step is taken. As the step is implemented, new data start coming in and the effect of the action can be described and *evaluated*. The general plan is then revised in the light of the new information about the field of action and the second action step can be planned along with appropriate monitoring procedures. The second step is then implemented, monitored and evaluated; and the spiral of action, monitoring, evaluation and replanning continues. (p. 2, emphasis original)

Likewise, Cohen, Manion and Morrison (2000) propose an eight-stage model moving from identification of the problem, through preliminary discussions, reviewing the literature, redefinition of the initial statement of the problem, selection of research procedures, choice of evaluation procedures, implementation of the project, to interpretation of the data. This is very similar to processes of conducting research in any other model. The actual methods are not any different either.

Grundy (1990) distinguishes three modes of action research to demonstrate the paradigms and purposes of different models of action research. She names these 'technical', 'practical' and 'emancipatory' (p. 353):

■ A *technical* approach would be instigated by an 'expert' with technical skills, would have more efficient or effective practice as its objective and would be designed to 'produce', 'make' or 'create' something (e.g. a more efficient administrative system or an effective curriculum programme). The 'expert' would co-opt participants who would have little by way of input into the planning. Grundy says this type of action research does provide a stimulus for change, but there is a chance of manipulation where participants are regarded as instruments rather than agents of change. The absence of any obligation on the part of the researcher to initiate dialogue is contrary to the ethical standards we considered in Chapter 2.

■ Whereas 'technical' action research is judged on the extent to which an idea is implemented ('correct' action), *practical* action research has a moral dimension in that it is disposed towards action that is for the benefit of those affected ('good' action), though again they are only marginally involved in having a say as to what is to their benefit. It seeks to improve practice through the accumulated store of practice wisdom of those initiating the action. By reflecting on her/his knowledge, experience and intuition, the social worker will perceive what is in the best interests of her/his clients. S(he) then sets out to motivate them towards her/his objective by initiating the action research cycle. Grundy does point out however that the act of solitary self-reflection may result in self-deception, so the model requires the aid of one or more facilitator(s) to assist in the process of self-reflection.

■ 'Emancipatory' action research focuses on the institutional restrictions that impinge on practice where the individual or group is powerless to initiate change because of the strength of the 'system'. Action research will have to be more potent than either technical or practical approaches. Following Habermas's notion of 'critical theorems', Grundy argues that emancipatory strategic action follows from the disposition of critical intent. This refers to a frame of mind that is questioning of the motives and outcomes of current arrangements. It is fostered by the application of personal judgment to theory through reflection: 'the group needs access . . . to theory which has been subjected to the full rigour of scientific discourse, which can in turn be subjected to critical scrutiny by the group' (p. 359). It is envisaged that these group processes will give rise to enlightenment in the form of 'authentic insights'. This leads to a form of praxis, and action can be planned, followed by reflection, further enlightenment and further planning. There is an assumption that 'the group' will include representatives of organizations as well as service users, thus offering potential for genuine dialogue among them.

A number of authors regard the 'technical' mode as the most effective approach to action research. Payne and Payne (2004) describe one view of action research as a social experiment, in which interventions could be tested and successively modified on the basis of what is being achieved. They link this model closely with evaluation, which is undertaken to assess the worth or success of a programme, a policy or a project, and which also has an action orientation to introduce or support change. Evaluation studies focus on measurement of social inputs, outputs and processes, with observations made before and after intervention and the two compared. As is apparent in this description, evaluations can replicate classic scientific experimental methods.

A number of problems which have been identified with the experimental approach were discussed in Chapter 3. Briefly, these are first, in dealing with human beings the rules of the natural sciences may not apply. Variables cannot be controlled in ways which may be more possible in a laboratory setting, and it is therefore impossible to be sure that any changes can be attributed unambiguously to the intervention. Secondly, more often than not, no account is taken of the central issue of power relations in the process, with the assumption being made that the goals of the experiment are rational and unquestionable. An ethical research approach concerned with equality and social justice must ask questions about, for example, the legitimacy of management goals, about the elements of manipulation and engineering, and about the purposes of organizational problem-solving. It will also aim to involve participants in sharing power throughout the process.

Varieties of action research

It is important therefore to recognize that there are clearly distinguishable differences amongst models of action research, even though there may be shared aspects in definitions. Kemmis and McTaggart (1990) offer a general definition of action research as

> concerned equally with changing *individuals*, on the one hand, and on the other, the *culture* of the groups, institutions and societies to which they belong. The culture of a group can be defined in terms of the characteristic substance and forms of the language and discourses, activities and practices, and social relationships and organization which constitute the interactions of the group. (p. 16, emphasis original)

Different models of the approach emphasize different dimensions described in Kemmis and McTaggart's definition, but Winter's six key principles are commonly understood to characterize action research. These are:

- reflexive critique – the process of becoming aware of our own perceptual biases
- dialectical critique – a way of understanding the relationships between the elements that make up various phenomena in our context
- collaboration – everyone's view is taken as a contribution to understanding the situation
- risking disturbance – an understanding of our own taken-for-granted processes and willingness to submit them to critique
- creating plural structures – developing various accounts and critiques, rather than a single authoritative interpretation
- theory and practice internalized – theory and practice seen as two interdependent yet complementary phases of the change process

Cohen, Manion and Morrison (2000) comment that these and other definitions imply the consensual, co-operative nature of action research, that is that action research is a *group* activity and is not individualistic. They regard this definition as too restricting, giving examples of action research as individualistic, as in Grundy's 'technical' mode, for instance. Cohen et al. are concerned to point out especially the consensual model's associations with the 'practitioner-researcher' movement, and with the notion of the 'reflective practitioner'. They identify two main camps in action research – those in the tradition of Schön (1983) emphasizing an individualistic reflective practice, and those who are advocates of the 'critical action' model (broadly similar to Grundy's 'emancipatory' mode). The distinction is an important one, since it raises the question of whether either or both can be compatible with ideals of social justice. The former is criticized for being focused on an individualistic view of improving effectiveness, similar to Schön's (1987) idea of 'reflection-in-action', and for viewing the practitioner as relatively isolated and neglecting wider structures (Cohen, Manion and Morrison, 2000). As was discussed in Chapter 2, this severely restricts the possibilities for an appropriate ethical practice.

In contrast, critical action research is unashamedly political, and takes dimensions which involve political action. In Grundy's language, 'emancipatory action research' seeks to develop participants' understanding of illegitimate structural and interpersonal constraints that prevent the exercise of autonomy and freedom. For many action researchers research becomes a political tool for social change and reconstruction when it is used to promote the interests of disadvantaged groups. It has been used since the 1920s (Whyte 1991). The characteristics of this model of action research are the personal involvement of the researcher, the emancipatory aims of the research, the active involvement of the researched and its critical perspective, that is its opposition to certain established policies and practices. Sarantakos (2005, p. 334) sets out the basic principles of critical action research as:

- commitment to the cause of the study: research is not a task but a duty
- emancipatory nature: explaining social structures and pointing to the causes of problems
- active involvement of the respondents in the study, working together with the researcher
- opposition to established systems, policies and practices
- political nature of the study, its causes and consequences
- applied nature of the underlying research; it focuses on solving problems
- commitment to a critical paradigm, which drives the research and its political basis
- *empowerment* of participants to effect change in their own environment
- commitment to *change and reconstruction* of the social order
- *value-laden* procedures and operations (emphases original)

In other words, the researcher is not just an investigator but a collaborator and a facilitator.

For Cohen, Manion and Morrison (2000) the distinction between the individualistic and the critical camps lies in their interpretation of action research. For the former, action research is an improvement to professional practice at the local level, and for the latter it is part of a broader agenda of changing the profession and changing society.

The model put forward by Bradbury and Reason (2003) does not necessarily embrace either an individualistic or a critical paradigm, but takes a much more liberal stance. These writers see the core concern for action researchers as doing research *with*, rather than *on* people. For them action research is (i) grounded in lived experience; (ii) developed in partnership; (iii) addressing significant problems; (iv) working with, rather than simply studying, people; (v) developing new ways of seeing/theorizing the world; (vi) leaving infrastructure in its wake. They stress the importance of a new institutional emphasis on forging closer bonds between the fragmented spheres of knowledge generation and knowledge application. They envisage that for example in research alongside social work practitioners, the practitioners may become co-researchers themselves, in effect bypassing what they call 'the traditional, constructed separation between research and application' (p. 157). In their view, all action researchers must strive to align the interests and agendas of all involved in a project so as to be able to work in collaboration. Their *Handbook of Action Research* (Reason and Bradbury, 2001) defined action research as:

> a participatory, democratic process concerned with developing practical knowing in the pursuit of worthwhile human purposes, grounded in a participatory world-view. It seeks to reconnect action and reflection, theory and practice, in participation with others, in the pursuit of practical solutions to issues of pressing concern to people. More generally it grows out of a concern for the flourishing of individual persons and their communities. (p. 1)

This is a consensual model that assumes all interests are compatible, and does not consider the implications for action research where interests are conflicting (as does Sarantakos above, for example). In many action research approaches the emphasis is on co-operation, collaboration and participation. This is usually regarded as unproblematic, except in terms of the instrumental aspects (for example, the effort, time and costs involved in engaging people in the research).

PAR

A predominant model within the Reason and Bradbury assumptions is PAR (participatory action research; see also Chapter 4). The term PAR has been adopted by those who associate themselves with empowerment and democratic versions of action research. This model has two basic principles. It is concerned with:

- *changing* or *improving* a social situation
- *involving* those most affected. (Alston and Bowles, 1998, p. 164)

The second of these principles makes it clear that any change or improvement to a situation will be in negotiation with and using the definitions of those most affected. The aim is to avoid the top-down and manipulative elements associated with experimental methods, and together to engage in a cycle of activity that is committed to 'develop a plan of critically informed action to improve what is already happening; to act to implement the plan; to observe the effects of the action in the context in which it occurs; and to reflect on these effects as a basis for further planning, subsequent action and so on by means of a succession of cycles' (Kemmis and McTaggart, 1988, pp. 9–10). The process here is similar to that described for experimental methods, but the crucial ingredient is the researchers' engagement with others in a participatory movement towards agreed social changes. In this sense, PAR shares a similar philosophy with other kinds of 'participatory' research.

Curiously however, these same authors, along with Reason and Bradbury, are motivated by the belief that structural conditions must change if emancipatory aims are to be met. The struggle and therefore the conflict that is implied in this is not explicitly acknowledged.

'Empowerment' is a central concept in all these approaches, but its definition can range from a focus strictly on the professional sphere of operations, and on professional development, to that of 'taking control over one's life within a just, egalitarian, democratic society' (Cohen, Manion and Morrison, 2000, p. 233).

In summary, then, action research can be many things ranging from experimental to participatory, and can employ many different methods that may or may not involve participants in genuine dialogue. It may or may not take account of institutional and wider contexts and to varying degrees target these for change as part of its objectives.

Examples of action research in social work and social care

A number of texts have been produced which offer a step-by-step guide to conducting action research, notably *The Action Research Planner*, edited by Kemmis and McTaggart (1988), which, although written from a background in education, has much to offer those interested in action research in social work and other related professions. The same authors have drawn together a collection of the best-known articles on the topic in *The Action Research Reader* (Kemmis and McTaggart, 1990). In social work itself, some authors have identified action research as a way of overcoming the unhelpful division between research and practice – those who think and those who do (Weyts, Morpeth and Bullock, 2000). The demand for research-mindedness in social work practice has led to action research being seen as one way of achieving this, through studies that involve practitioners and service users and that can be useful to those who create the knowledge.

Recruiting foster carers

Metcalfe and Humphreys (2002) describe the process of conducting action research to study the impact of including foster carers in the recruitment of other foster carers. They set out their definition of action research, drawing on Hart and Bond (1995):

> Action research is an approach to research rather than a specific methodology. It involves the identification of a problem or situation which requires improvement, followed by a process of enquiry and a planned intervention for change and evaluation. [It] is further characterized by: research with groups rather than an individual project; having an educative value for those involved; and being founded on a research relationship in which those involved are part of the change process. (p. 437)

In the view of these authors, the process involves the continuous feedback of research results to all parties, and must take account of the differences in values and power of those involved in the research, recognizing that participants are concurrently solving a problem and generating new knowledge. The aims of the research they describe were to assess the value of information evenings with foster carers as a recruitment method; to analyse the impact of involving experienced foster carers on home visit contracts; to compare two recruitment campaigns, run in 1999 and 1998; and to explore motivating and deterring factors in those interested in fostering. These aims were said to be clear but flexible, and capable of being developed and adapted as the project progressed. A fundamental strategy in refining the aims for the research was a series of 'critical conversations', which they said were pivotal in establishing the collaborative, action-orientated nature of the project. They describe ten action research cycles aimed at getting colleagues on board, including consultation with a university supervisor, a series of dialogues with foster carers, team and team manager, setting up research workshops to establish colleagues and foster carers as stakeholders, information evenings, team discussion, evaluation of the process, interviews with prospective foster carers, debriefing meetings with experienced foster carers, diffusion of findings to the team and other stakeholders, team meetings to agree an action plan for influencing recruitment strategy – the action cycle of planning, acting, observing and reflecting described by Grundy (1990). The process took 12 months and methods included some quantitative comparison of data from the two campaigns, as well as qualitative interviewing and analysis of 14 interviews. The themes generated from the interviews provided evidence that assisted the team in planning future work, and led to the routine involvement of foster carers in information evenings and an increase in applications.

Metcalfe and Humphreys consider the 'critical conversations' to be an important basis for achieving the aims of action research. They also identify the use of 'insider information' (team priorities, knowledge and access) as advantaging the process, and they claim that the action research cycles of planning, action and evaluation mirrored practice already well established in the working dynamics of the team: 'while aspects of the research were over and above the everyday practices of the team (for example the semi-structured interviews) many other elements of the project were easily incorporated and therefore did not stand apart as an entirely new process imposed on colleagues' (p. 445). As a result the parallels between practice and action research were very close. The team were said to have experienced the research cycles as 'professionalizing and empowering' (p. 445) and a new language, which incorporated research into practice, began to develop in the team's conversations about their work.

Of course the drawbacks of the processes described are the amount of time involved, the significant increase in workload, the costs incurred and the pressure from the organization to produce results quickly and economically. Metcalfe and Humphreys have shown that if these constraints can be overcome or regarded sympathetically by employers, action research can be a method that leads to understanding and improvement of practice.

But taking this example, a number of points can be made. The work of Metcalfe and Humphreys is reminiscent of both Grundy's 'technical' and 'practical' action research, geared to improve efficiency and effectiveness, and with a concern for improving practice. But can it be said that the work of Metcalfe and Humphreys constitutes a move towards social justice? Are prospective foster parents disempowered or oppressed, *per se*? Is there evidence of an 'empowerment' model in their project? The initiative appears to be successful partly because the aims of the organization and the service users coincided, although their motives may have been different. It certainly met government and organizational objectives to involve users and carers in designing and delivering services and in finding a solution to the social problem of the numbers of children requiring loving homes. It actively involved team members, a crucial factor in its success. To answer the social justice question, we would need to know how successful the project was in changing practices within the organization. For example, did it lead to an involvement of disadvantaged groups – poor people, disabled people, people from minority ethnic groups, single people, lesbian and gay people – in the training, and to what extent did this contribute to a widening of the range of social groups recruited as foster carers? We would also need to consider the impact on organizational structures that may attract some groups more than others to foster. Moreover, we are not told (and in fairness, the research did not claim to go this far) whether subsequent placements included any increase in the numbers of 'hard to place' children finding a home. So although action research seems to have been achieved to some extent, there is no indication of whether the changes went beyond some increase in foster parent applications. This should be part of ongoing evaluation. The risk is that action research may become an end in itself. It needs to be part of an ongoing process that continues to track any impact it may have made.

Community care assessment

Baldwin used a version of action research – participative inquiry – in his involvement with teams of social workers in their use of discretion in community care assessment (Baldwin, 2001). Finding conventional qualitative interviewing unsatisfactory in that interviewees felt unable to 'own' the outcomes of the research, he chose co-operative inquiry as a more suitable approach, deliberately setting out to achieve dialogue and a sharing of power with participants. Two groups were formed, one of five hospital-based social workers and the other a disparate collection of social workers. They met separately, eight times over six months, convened and recorded by Baldwin. It was agreed that the aim of the meetings was to

> set up cycles of action and reflection to investigate the possibilities of practice development over time, within (their) restricted role as care managers, while at the same time exploring the use of discretionary social work practice . . . professional development was believed to be in serious jeopardy within the new role of care manager imposed by a management agenda ruled by resource constraint rather than service provision. How achievable was practice development, using cooperative inquiry as the motivating force? (p. 290)

In order to make this process manageable, the hospital group focused on a specific bureaucratic procedure to investigate differences in practice. The document chosen was a consent pro forma, to be signed by potential service users to allow the worker to contact third parties to seek information about the user. The authority saw consent as good practice since it reflected partnership. However it emerged that at times seeking consent was a threatening experience for some service users, and in these cases social workers did not ask for a signature. The focus for inquiry was therefore the use of social work discretion in the implementation of this procedure, and the research question concerned the extent to which agency policy was being undermined by their discretion.

The group devised a technique of investigation and recording that involved recording their reasons for not requesting a signature, every time they *should* have requested one. They were required to justify their actions through a process of what Baldwin called 'reflection-in-action' ('why am I practising like this right now?') and 'reflection-on-action' ('why did I ask *that* person to sign the form but not *this* person?'). This led to a discussion about the nature of intuition and reflection, and to the observation by the researcher that at some point the workers recognized that a particular individual met some undefined criteria that meant s(he) could 'cope' with being asked to sign the form. But how did s(he) know when the threshold had been crossed? As a result of the use of a system of recording, a much more reflective practice was developed, and Baldwin recorded that 'as a result, there was an increase in the number of forms signed without a consequent increase in service user or worker anxiety' (p. 291). He did not share how he was able to draw this conclusion. One of the important conclusions from this process was that group members were able to differentiate the use of knowledge that was informed by the participatory and empowering values that they espoused in theory from the more unaware or stereotypical practice that they recognized occurred if they were not engaged in reflection: 'practising with discretion but without reflection was recognized as ineffective or potentially oppressive' (p. 291).

Baldwin saw co-operative action inquiry as important in allowing the group members to establish new areas of understanding, some of them previously realized insights and others that were the result of revisiting and adapting formerly held knowledge. The research went further than simply increasing the proportion of consent forms signed, and, for example, there was reported to be a wider discussion on the supervision and support systems, and on how workloads might be freed up to allow more preventative work to be carried out. In terms of process, the research progressed through a number of cycles of action and reflection, with participants introducing issues that then became topics for the groups. Baldwin did raise the question as to whether such action research would change anything in organizations that were wedded fundamentally to scientific managerialism, but argued that it had potential to set up a dynamic and reflective environment which could force out unreflective discretion regarded as the norm in street-level bureaucracies. This entailed a sense amongst workers that they could, after all, participate in developing policy and practice within the organization. In this way the approach fulfilled Elliott's criteria that reflexivity must entail both self- and organizational-critique.

Baldwin's description of the process of action research can be characterized as within the Schön 'reflective practitioner' model, and Grundy's 'practical' model. It has a number of interesting features.

First, his description of carrying out conventional qualitative interviewing confirms that such an approach may be useful in collecting particular kinds of data, but it does not necessarily create changes in practice, nor do participants 'own' the data, even though they may be asked for their views of a draft report. The group process was more effective in identifying aims and concerns that had day-to-day relevance for the workers. Moreover, the group was encouraged to identify a specific practice (completing consent forms) that was within their control, where they could move to an understanding of the factors that influence their behaviour, and change that behaviour. Finally, engaging in the process may lead to a consideration of wider issues for debate and action.

What is somewhat worrying, however, is the implication that the organization objective to increase the numbers of consent forms signed is a positive move *per se*. We are not told any detail of, for example, why social workers were reluctant to ask some people to sign the forms, beyond the statement that service users sometimes felt anxiety about agreeing to this. Could it be that one of the issues social workers were aware of was the coercive nature of the request? In other words, if anyone had refused to sign, would that have led to a withdrawal of the service being requested? What ethical dilemmas does such a circumstance create for the worker? And what are the consequences of signing the form? To what uses is it put? Does it become a *carte blanche* for seeking information from and sharing information with any other organization as expedient? What about the issue of discretion at that level? Is a one-off signing of consent a permanent permission to the organization?

These questions are not to argue that seeking consent is not important, but because the research being described here does not set the procedure in the wider context it risks using co-operative action inquiry to legitimate bureaucratically rigid restrictions on human rights. However, having said that, one practical outcome of Baldwin's research did appear to be an impact on management systems in terms of supervision and a growing confidence in taking advantage of the opportunities for participation within the organization.

Drawbacks of action research

Above I have set out some of the drawbacks of action research as they arise from the two projects examined. A perusal of the literature revealed similar problems in other practical examples of action research, especially in the field of education where most of the work on the approach has been carried out (see, for example, Atweh, Kemmis and Weeks, 1998 which has 'Partnerships for social justice'

Table 5.1 Strengths and weaknesses of action research

Strengths	Weaknesses
It encourages public participation	It allows no replication
It encourages stakeholders to take active responsibility in the project	It may verify preconceived ideas of the researcher
It furthers emancipation	It is biased towards the interests of certain groups
It serves the public interest	It cannot assure representativeness, objectivity and generalizability
It is set to promote change	Low credibility due to the involvement of non-professionals in the project
It makes social and political processes transparent to the public	No control of the nature of the findings and quality of research design

Source: S Sarantakos, *Social Research*, 2005, 3rd edn. Reproduced with permission of Palgrave Macmillan.

as a subtitle to the book). However, most focused on practice issues rather than organization or institutional change, which perhaps reflects the difficulty in achieving such changes through critical action research. Yet the essence of critical action research is said to be its political nature in taking sides with those who are disadvantaged and in working towards social change. Although the emphasis may be more on qualitative than quantitative methods, the technical aspects are not very different from other types of research. It is the theoretical framework that is the key factor in distinguishing it from other approaches. Sarantakos (2005, p. 337) sets out both strengths and weaknesses, which I have replicated in Table 5.1.

It must be said that Sarantakos's list of weaknesses takes positivist assumptions as the norm for measuring quality, and they also imply that action research uses an exclusively qualitative methodology. The issues raised here by Sarantakos are those for which qualitative methodology is criticized generally. In terms of the strengths of the approach, one of its main values for social work is its applicability and its (potentially) emancipatory purpose. However, this also has come under scrutiny and the absence of convincing studies confirms its problematic nature. Cohen, Manion and Morrison (2000) argue that the jury is still out on the question of whether critical action research is socially transformative. Among the reasons they give are that:

- it is utopian and unrealizable;
- it is too controlling and prescriptive, and therefore moves towards conformity;

- it undermines the significance of the individual practitioner-researcher in favour of self-critical communities – 'why *must* action research consist of a *group* process?' (p. 233);
- it assumes that rational consensus is achievable, that rational debate will empower all participants (i.e. it understates the issue of power and renders the conditions of equality suspect);
- it overstates the desirability of consensus-oriented research, which neglects the complexity of power;
- power cannot be dispersed or rearranged simply by rationality;
- it is naive in its understanding of groups and celebrates groups over individuals, particularly the 'in-groups' rather than the 'out-groups';
- it privileges its own view of science (rejecting objectivity) and lacks modesty;
- it is elitist while purporting to serve egalitarianism.

Some of these criticisms are perhaps more legitimate than others, and some of them need not necessarily be the case, for example elitism and lacking in modesty. There are however problematic aspects of critical action research similar to those in participatory research (see Chapter 4). There is a heavy dependence on rational debate and the notion of persuasion through argument, and it is manifestly the case that argument does not change the views of those with an investment in power and with firmly rooted prejudices. Moreover, in much of the literature there is an unproblematic view of group processes and an ignoring of conflict and interest (including that of gender, class and 'race'). All of these dimensions require further acknowledgement and debate, and recognition of their having to be confronted. They do not necessarily constitute an argument for abandoning action research as a significant and rigorous tool in the process of democratizing research more generally, but they do suggest the need for wider collective effort in achieving its aims.

Conclusion: action research and social justice

One of the enduring features of action research is that it concerns practice –the real, actual, concrete, particular activities of people in local settings at specific historical moments. This, of course, makes it useful, though not necessarily just. Therefore, as we have seen, it has both emancipatory and social engineering potential. It might be argued that the versions which most lend themselves to goals of justice and equity have ingredients such as collaborative, collective and reflexive processes of action and reflection; the capacity to encourage people to reflect critically on their social relationships, their accustomed ways of interpreting themselves and their actions, and in turn how this shapes their identities and sense of agency; and ways of helping them contest and release themselves from the irrational constraints of social structures. This version of action research involves not so much solving problems as addressing the questions that make the problems intelligible as problems. It emphasizes a questioning of lived experience over an acquisition of instrumental knowledge.

main points

- Action research is change-oriented and focuses on the here and now
- It can operate within both realist and constructivist paradigms
- It proceeds through a spiral of cycles of planning, acting, observing and reflecting
- It is usually regarded as reflexive and collaborative
- It is criticized as utopian, as relying on rational consensus and as being naive about group processes

stop and think

- In what ways is the 'immediacy' of action research an advantage to social work?
- What do you think are the differences between 'reflection' in action research and 'reflexivity' as discussed in Chapter 1?
- What are the main features of an 'emancipatory' model of action research?

taking it further

- Kemmis S and McTaggart R *The Action Research Planner*, 3rd edn (Geelong, Victoria, Australia: Deakin University Press, 1988)
  A detailed guide for designing action research. It's a rather old text, but still relevant.
- Reason P and Bradbury, H *Handbook of Action Research* (London: Sage, 2001)
  An invaluable resource for action researchers from two of the foremost writers in this field.

6 Case study research

chapter

Introduction

As with a number of approaches considered in this book, case study research is not a method *per se*, but is an attempt to study a phenomenon in depth, using a whole range of approaches. It is associated with both realist and constructivist paradigms, the former believing that there are cases 'out there' that can be captured by empirical inquiry and the latter believing that cases are the constructs of researchers and/or research participants (see Chapter 1 and Platt, 1992a for an exploration of these beliefs). This chapter will deal mainly with case studies as they are commonly understood and used within a constructivist paradigm, using qualitative methods, since they are often the main form of inquiry in qualitative studies. The case study assumes that things may not be as they seem and privileges in-depth inquiry over coverage: understanding 'the case' rather than generalizing to a population at large (Stark and Torrance, 2005, p. 33)

A 'case' may be an individual, an organization, a group, an event or an issue. It might involve comparison of a number of cases. It might entail examination of the implementation of a particular policy from the point of view of a specific group affected by it, for example, such as multi-professional working in one or more mental health team(s), or of post-qualifying training in a particular educational institution (Gillman, 1996).

Social work students are often attracted to case study research because it seems easy and sounds familiar. It is however quite different from the use of case studies in teaching, where a single case can be used to draw lessons for practice and where essential features can be changed for the purpose of learning. Case study research attempts to approach a real-life phenomenon from the inside, using a range of methods. The study seeks to examine the phenomenon in depth in order to analyse thoroughly details that might be lost in any other type of research such as a larger survey. Although one of its limitations is that it is not possible to generalize from the case study, studying one example of a group of survivors of domestic violence, for instance, can often allow a researcher to identify a great deal of information that will reflect the experiences of the population of domestic violence survivors. In the words of one author, the case study 'defies the social science convention of seeking generalizations by looking instead for specificity, exceptions and completeness' (Reinharz, 1992, p. 174). Thus it is claimed that it can draw on specific cases to suggest more general implications.

Origins of case studies

There is a long history of the use of case studies, and Mayhew's nineteenth-century studies of the London poor used the method to powerful effect, because the experiences of poverty were conveyed in the words and the stories of the people most affected (Mayhew's research is discussed in Chapter 10 on social surveys). More recently, Platt (1992) traces the practice of using case studies back to the Chicago School of Sociology, which pioneered ethnographic research (see Chapter 9), and indeed to casework in American social work. The development of case studies seems to have been overtaken by enthusiasm for participant observation, which dominated qualitative research approaches for most of the 1950s, 1960s and 1970s. However participant observation is time-consuming and requires many months spent with groups being studied. Cheaper and quicker results were required, so a move was necessary from long-term to short-term studies. At the same time, during the 1970s there was dissatisfaction with experimental methods, regarded as revealing too little useful information. Case studies using interviewing techniques became widely used to gather data, and are currently to be found within a range of academic disciplines and research projects.

Quantitative researchers have used case studies in very limited ways and have regarded them as inferior to other approaches, especially experimental designs, and indeed writers such as Reid and Smith (1989), in their book on research in social work, assume no difference between case studies and single case experiments, describing the case study as 'the most elementary form of the single case design' (p. 104). Here case studies are considered as the exploratory stage of some other type of research strategy and are given very little import.

However Yin (1994) observes a shift from this hierarchical view of research methods where case studies were thought to be appropriate for an exploratory stage of an investigation, surveys were regarded as appropriate for the descriptive stage and experiments were seen as the only way of conducting explanatory or causal inquiries, towards a view where the case study method stands as a legitimate approach in its own right and can be both descriptive and explanatory. In his view the decision about method should be based on the kinds of questions to be answered (this point is taken up in Chapter 12). His book, now in its second edition, gives detailed guidance about implementation and is widely used in the social sciences.

Principles of case study research

As has already been emphasized, case study research is not a method of data collection, but is more a research model that employs a number of methods. In qualitative uses of case studies, the most common methods are interviews, documentary analysis and observation. Sarantakos (2005, p. 212) sets out the criteria that govern a case study approach:

- it is conducted in natural settings
- it pursues depth analysis
- it studies whole units not aspects of units
- it entails a single case or a few cases only
- it studies typical cases
- it perceives respondents as experts, not as sources of data
- it employs many and diverse methods
- it employs several sources of information

To this could be added not only that a case study pursues 'typical' cases, but the approach is also interested in untypical cases in order to learn about factors or dynamics that are not evident otherwise and that allow comparison with other cases.

The first criterion above about 'natural settings' suggests 'naturalistic', that is where people are going about their daily business, observed by the researcher, as in ethnographic studies (see Chapter 9), and, for example, David and Sutton (2004) associate case study research exclusively with ethnography, seeing the case study as a way of making participant observation manageable by selecting cases that will satisfy the research interests of the researcher in the setting. Stark and Torrance (2005) lean towards this view also. The case study approach is indeed compatible with ethnography, since it allows for depth and 'thick' description, but has been used with other approaches too. One of its attractions to students who may not have the time necessary for observation techniques, is that depth interviews and examination of documents are also available as a case study approach. Yin's definition of a case study puts it succinctly as investigating a contemporary phenomenon within its real-life context, especially when the boundaries between phenomenon and context are not clearly evident, and as relying on multiple sources of evidence (Yin, 1994).

So, the key elements are that the topic being studied is happening in the here and now, that it needs to be considered in its social context and that more than one method – triangulation of methods – is required to attempt to consider it in its totality. The here-and-now aspect needs some qualification. Case studies are most often of contemporary situations, but a case study may also be conducted of a past event (such as the English royal family's responses to the death of Princess Diana) or of a policy (such as the speeches in Parliament that led to the 1905 Aliens Act). Of course the purpose of such studies is likely to be to draw conclusions that are relevant to current events. The question here is what can be learned from the single case?

Often the notion of a 'case' is taken for granted and we do not stop to think what is a case? What are its boundaries? Where does the child, or the group or the agency or the policy, end and the environment begin? These are important questions for the researcher in designing any case study, and the answers to them will set the parameters of any research. Such parameters are necessarily artificial, since it could be argued that ultimately everything is connected to everything else. Stake (1998, pp. 88–89) offers a categorization of cases for study:

- intrinsic cases, selected and studied for their own sake, without the intention to generalize from the results (such as, for instance, the response of a particular school in a small town to the arrival of a substantial number of refugee children);
- instrumental cases, selected and studied to represent a set of similar settings, and with the possibility of generalizing from such cases (for example the study of a group supporting siblings of disabled children may offer information on the support needs of similar young people and may also contribute to theories of group dynamics);
- collective cases, selected from different settings to allow comparison (for example case studies of the practices of receptionists in several social work teams might be a focus for research interested in different intake systems and in ways 'need' is variously interpreted).

This categorization has a limited usefulness and needs some expansion. The idea of intrinsic case study makes sense at the level of researchers choosing a topic because they have a special interest in it, but they cannot avoid generalizations in that readers draw their own conclusions and apply them to other situations. It is therefore difficult to extract intrinsic from instrumental, except in terms of what might be the primary interest in the case. The notion of collective cases is clearer in that it is obvious that more than one instance of a phenomenon is involved, but at the same time comparison of different elements within any case study (whether of a single instance or multiple instances) is surely implied by the nature of the approach. Implicit in the notion of a 'case' is the idea that there are enough similar and separate elements in what is to be investigated to allow comparison. In a case study of a single event such as an individual's responses to a bomb explosion, there will be a range of intellectual, physical and emotional reactions at different times that can be compared and analysed. In a case study of a multi-professional team, one assumes that by interviewing members of the team one can uncover experiences of the formal and informal structures, and perceptions of roles in the team. Not only do we expect to be able to identify similarities and differences among individuals in that particular team, but we expect also to be able to connect the study to studies of other teams, assuming that many aspects are essentially the same and some are different.

There is a temptation for researchers to 'tidy up' cases and to see them as homogeneous units to make them manageable, as in experiments where variables are closely controlled. A 'case' for study may be a group of disability activists, but such a group cannot be abstracted from its context or the contexts of the lives of the people who belong to it. The meaning of membership of the group is tied up with structures, not only of government and organizational policies, not only of the meaning of the notion of 'disability' in any given society, not only of class, 'race', sexuality, age and gender, but with recognition of relationships, continuities, discontinuities, resources, in an attempt to understand the 'whole' – what Schostak (2002) calls 'a multilayered symbolic network that need not display any internal unity or consistency' (p. 23). It will be clear that the choice of a case study as a research project is not an easy option, and that identifying boundaries is a complex process.

The question of when to use a case study approach has been addressed by Yin (1994) who says

> case studies are the preferred strategy when 'how' or 'why' questions are being posed, when the investigator has little control over events and when the focus is on a contemporary phenomenon within some real-life context. (p. 1)

Examples of this might be: how do professional groups and the family of a West African child understand each other's cultures, and why does each respond to the other as they do? How do agencies pursue their different roles in multi-professional ways of working with an elderly man living alone in the community? How and why do service users participate in the activities of a university social work course?

Let us take the first example and unpack it a little further. Here the case study might entail the researcher collecting data from different members of the family and from the social worker, the health visitor, the teacher and any other workers involved. The question arises about the context and the extent to which it should be studied – the policies and management of the various workers' organizations, the beliefs and practices of the family's community, the legislation and statutory instruments governing education and care of children. All of these to some degree or other would be brought into the equation, and would constitute the boundaries of 'the case'. At the minimum the researcher would expect to learn about the family's and the various workers' beliefs regarding child care and child-rearing, the rationales for their behaviour, and points of consensus and conflict. The study may offer understanding of why certain decisions are made and their consequences, and the influence of environmental factors on the behaviour of all involved. It may lead to the development of basic theoretical concepts regarding, for example, the factors that contribute to good practice in cross-cultural child-care work; family functioning; interpersonal interactions; individual development; decision-making; organizational structures that facilitate or obstruct the interests of families and children.

In designing case studies, a number of questions have to be asked:

■ is it to be a single case or multiple cases?
■ if it's a single case, am I looking for a case that is typical of the phenomenon that interests me? Or one that is extreme or unique, or that might reveal something new?
■ if it's a multiple-case design, what criteria shall I use for making the choice – am I looking for similar or contrasting patterns?
■ how much of the context/wider environment do I need to include?

Some of these questions can be answered by selecting the topic and beginning a list of the basic questions to be answered by the case study. This can help to define the boundaries, set the priorities, identify the evidence to be collected and generally give some direction to the project.

Interviewing

I consider interviewing here because it has become one of the key methods of case studies. It is of course used in a whole range of research approaches, and is a familiar tool of all professional groups working in the fields of health and social care. There are different approaches to interviewing, and here I offer a brief comparison before concentrating on qualitative interviewing. Quantitative interviewing is taken up in Chapter 10 on social surveys. The kind of interviewing technique chosen for a research study depends on whether the researcher is working within a realist or a constructivist paradigm. In a realist paradigm, the researcher attempts to avoid interviewer bias by acting in a neutral way, by giving no indication of whether s/he agrees with the views being expressed and by controlling the questions by asking them in a sequential way. All of this is in the interests of getting at the 'truth' of what the interviewee really thinks. In a constructivist paradigm, interviewers try to make the interview more like real life, informal and conversational. They will use their personality to 'befriend' interviewees so that they open up and share their views in some depth. The research instruments that are used for these different approaches may be structured questionnaires, semi-structured interview schedules or unstructured interviewing. Structured questionnaires consist of a list of questions that are always asked in the same order, using the wording as set out in the questionnaire. Answers are recorded without comment. Semi-structured interview schedules act as a kind of *aide-mémoire* to prompt the interviewer about the areas to cover, but without stipulating in what order and allowing for flexibility in the wording. Unstructured interviews allow the interviewee to talk about those aspects of the topic s/he thinks important without too much control from the interviewer. The rationale for qualitative (semi-structured or unstructured) interviewing is a familiar one to social workers – only by developing a trusting, intimate relationship with the person being interviewed will the researcher be able to get to the truth of what s/he believes. The more it appears the two people have in common, the more willing the respondent will be to open up and share sensitive information and feelings. This argument has been taken to the point where some researchers insist, for instance, that only women should interview women and only black people should interview black people. However, Finch (1984) identifies the potential dangers in this and the risk of unethically eliciting information that interviewees would not normally share and may regret afterwards. This kind of interviewing requires much integrity on the part of the researcher, though there is a tendency in this debate to see the interviewee as passive, as manipulated by the interviewer and as without her/his own judgement as to the boundaries of her/his responses.

There have been a number of concerns expressed about qualitative interviewing. One is the question of the extent to which the data given are an outcome of the relationship (does a befriending encounter lead to respondents lying because they do not want to offend or because they want to please?). On the other hand it could be argued that people always respond in the context of the relationship, and that this is as true for the administration of structured questionnaires as it is for more informal interviewing (Gomm, 2004, p. 177). There is also the issue of accountability. Researchers in the qualitative mould are not able to make available the conduct of interviews that have taken place so that the process can be scrutinized by readers. Very few reports of studies tell us about the actual process of the interview, including those used in the case studies considered below. One way to address this is to tape record interviews and to make those tapes available for examination. Tape-recorded interviews have the advantage that they leave the interviewer free to concentrate on what is being said (though they do need to be switched on and they often break down!). Use of them requires the consent of the interviewees, who may not always be willing to give it.

Focus group interviews

Interviews may also be conducted in groups, and the focus group is a particular model of this. Again the degree of structure can vary from highly structured to relatively unstructured. Here the idea is to use the interaction between members of the group to stimulate discussion about a topic, in the anticipation that the discussion will be more wide-ranging and more detailed than in an individual interview. Members of the group usually have some characteristics in common (age, gender, experience – of being an overseas student at a university, for example) and the number in the group is small, between six and ten people. Focus groups can be used as the main research tool or they can be used at an early stage for generating relevant topics, which will help in designing other methods. They are also used to clarify results gained from other means. There are obvious ethical issues raised by focus groups, anonymity and confidentiality being fundamental ones that cannot be guaranteed by the researcher. At the same time, focus groups do give a large degree of control to the research participants in that they can set the terms of the discussion and can dictate what is important and what is not. There are also risks associated with group dynamics more generally – the silence of some members, the dominance of others, the scapegoating of some, and the use and misuse of power. Considerable groupwork skill is required to pursue this method. There is also the practical question of recording the discussion. Tape-recording is inappropriate because of the number of people involved, and involving another person to take notes (the recommended solution) is expensive and difficult to achieve.

Overall, qualitative interviewing requires careful preparation, especially in decisions about the nature of the areas to be discussed with interviewees and the importance of keeping the interaction relevant to the research topic. David and Sutton (2004) offer a helpful guide to designing semi-structured individual interviewing as well as focus-group interviewing.

Examples of case study research in social work and social care

The two most distinctive features of case study research are (i) the definition of a 'case' may range across individuals, groups, documents, organizations, even countries, as illustrated by Geoghegan and Powell (2006); and (ii) it uses a whole range of methods and research approaches within the general model of 'case study'. Most of the methods described in this book can be brought into play to meet the demands of case study research.

Lesbian and gay foster carers and adopters

Steve Hicks, for example, used Foucault's genealogical method (see Chapter 8) in his case study of lesbian and gay adopters and foster carers (Hicks, 2006). His aim was to demonstrate contemporary manifestations of family ties. He also wanted to understand the way the concepts of 'kinship' and 'ancestry' were used by this group, and what counts when we use the term 'relative'. In this way he hoped to contribute both to a description of the range of patterns of family life and to the development of theories of kinship beyond the dominant assumptions about blood ties and marriage. His goals were therefore both practical and theoretical. The case study consisted of interviews with 40 lesbian and gay carers and with 30 social workers within fostering and adoption agencies. The criteria for selection were that the carers were lesbian or gay couples who were fostering or adopting children and that the social workers had fostering and adoption as their area of specialism. The study was set in the wider context of debates about what constitutes 'the family' and about the ways in which ideas about this in social work have changed over time. Linked to this Hicks examined documentary evidence in the form of debates in the British House of Commons and the 2002 Adoption and Children Act that for the first time allowed lesbians and gay men to adopt jointly. In these ways his study is an example of triangulation of methods (Greene, Kreider and Mayer, 2005)).

In analysing and presenting his findings, Hicks organized this around themed opinions of those interviewed that he identified as emerging from the data. There was not of course a clear division across different groups (e.g. the carers on the one side and the social workers on the other), and indeed some people held varied and contradictory views. Examples of the themes chosen are:

- the primacy of heterosexual relationships (the 'best' way to meet children's needs is to have a mother and a father, what Hicks calls 'heteronormative views');
- stereotypes of gay and lesbian relationships are incorrect (i.e. quoting research to 'prove' that gay relationships are not short-lived, not damaging to children, and so on, what Hicks calls 'corrective reading' of the research);
- lesbian and gay parenting is no different from heterosexual parenting – the sexuality of the parents is private and irrelevant, what Hicks calls 'strategies of normalization';
- lesbian and gay parenting is both different and legitimate (i.e. it represents a purposeful rejection of heterosexual ways of family living – redefining and re-creating identities out of difficult histories, both of children and parents, what Hicks calls 'everyday life experiments').

Within these categories Hicks uses quotations from individuals to illustrate and elaborate on the opinions that were offered to him. Although there was no clear division between social workers and parents, he did identify a tendency on the part of social workers to adopt heteronormative positions: 'traumatizing children again because they haven't got a mother and father is reinforcing differ-ence'; 'lesbians and gay men can talk themselves dumb to the child about his or her needs and how to meet them, but they can't turn themselves into a father and a mother which I think is the child's basic needs' (p. 766). Hicks uses the discussion to explore how the idea of 'natural parenting' works to assert and maintain hierarchies of adult relationships, and how these discourses are challenged by the views and the practices of lesbian and gay parenting. He also notes how applicants were vulnerable to accusations from social workers of being 'too political' – 'this need to promote and promote and promote raised a big question for us about how resolved was he with his stuff?' (p. 771). What is important from a practice perspective is the reported instances where lesbian and gay applicants were subject to additional requirements in the assessment process (p. 767). As a result 'strategies of normalization' as described above were far more likely to constitute the approach taken by potential carers than, for example, any hint of 'everyday life experiments'.

Hicks's article addresses other aspects of kinship and parenting, but from a research methods perspective it demonstrates a number of things about a case study approach. First a focus on two groups of people who have common characteristics – self-identified lesbian and gay couples who are all foster carers or adopters, and social workers who are all working in teams specializing in fostering and adoption – allows both for depth in exploring their views and for comparisons between the groups and among individuals. They are not of course representative of all lesbian and gay carers and specialist social workers, but the themes emerging draw on themes in the wider society and are likely to be typical of the range of views held. Moreover, the literature in this field has reflected similar variation of views. What the study shows is that although there have been significant moves forward in respect of social work practice in this field, arguments against lesbian and gay foster care and adoption, or an insistence on male and female role models, are still very much present within practice. It is doubtful whether methods other than a case study such as this one could have made these complexities available. An interesting observation is that the goal of the research was not to 'make recommendations' as to how practice can be adjusted to prevent discrimination (a common feature of dissertations and other research), but to ask how social workers can drawn on the kinship practices of lesbian and gay carers to expand the boundaries of 'the family', and indeed 'what we might become rather than what we are' (Hicks, 2006, p. 773). Hicks's purpose in reporting his research was to develop theory about the notion of 'kinship' so that practice in social work and in the wider institutions might move towards a less discriminatory treatment of those who do not match the heterosexual norm.

Refugee children in the UK

Jill Rutter (2006) chose a different case study approach to that of Hicks. She was interested in the educational attainments of children from refugee communities and, as part of her project, she selected three communities for comparison. The three (Congolese, Somali and Southern Sudanese) have had different experiences both in their country of origin and since their arrival in the UK. The case studies were very specific in focusing on one element of that experience – the educational attainment of children aged 11–16. Here I shall examine Rutter's strategy in relation to one of the communities, the Southern Sudanese, mainly because it is the only one she describes as a 'success story'.

Rutter gathered detailed data on six children (she does not clearly set out their gender), gathered from a variety of sources. In order to make any sense of their experiences, she needed to set the research in context. This was done through documentary analysis, followed by interviews with the children and with teachers. The documents used were as follows:

- *2001 census.* This listed the number of people born in Sudan and resident in the UK at the time of the census.

- *Refugee Council statistics.* This showed the number of asylum applications to the UK during the peak years of application.
- *Historical and demographic descriptions.* These built a picture of Sudan, its range of ethnic groups, their location, languages, religions, and so on.
- *European and UK research.* This provided information on reasons for coming to Europe, movement between Europe and the UK, occupation, class, educational level and the location in the UK of refugee communities.
- *Local council needs analysis.* Rutter says there is very little written about Sudanese people in the UK, but was able to identify a study carried out by a local authority (Brighton and Hove) regarding the needs of Sudanese refugees in its area, which she drew on for her research. This did not include data on the educational achievement of children. All of this background was an important framework for the detailed data collection. This again is an example of triangulation of methods, a characteristic approach in case study research. This needs some explanation.

Triangulation

Triangulation fulfils a number of roles. It gives a more holistic picture of the phenomenon to be studied than the use of only one method, for example interviews. The aim here is for misrepresentation or distortion to be avoided, and for findings to achieve a measure of validity. Also within a constructivist paradigm it offers a range of perspectives on what the reality or the 'truth' of a situation is. There will never be a consensus about 'what happened' and it is important to attempt to draw a complex picture rather than a simplistic one that is one-dimensional. As well as methodological triangulation it is possible to have investigator triangulation (where more than one researcher looks at the same phenomenon); theory triangulation (data is approached from the point of view of different disciplines or theories, such as behaviourist, feminist and functionalist approaches); and data source triangulation, where the researcher views a phenomenon at different times and in different places, such as social workers in meetings, with clients, in the pub, to see if their behaviour or their views change (see Schostak, 2002 for a full discussion). Of the examples above, Rutter in particular has carried out a thorough methodological triangulation.

However, her report of the study does not tell us anything about where the children were living (e.g. whether they were amongst the larger Sudanese communities in inner London, Brighton, Manchester and Birmingham or whether they were in smaller communities). We are also not told how and why they were selected, but we are told that they had been in the UK for an average of 2.1 years, that two of them were unaccompanied, three were living with relatives, and all of them came from homes where English was spoken by one or more adults. They were all described as an elite group, with parents in senior posts in government of equivalent positions (though the adults in the homes where they lived in the UK were mostly in low-paid jobs).

Having presented relevant data from these varied documents, and funnelling in from the wider picture to the environment of the six children, her detailed research consisted of:

- *interviews with the children to collect life histories;*
- *analysis of the children's homework diaries* where they were available;
- *educational data from school records;*
- *interviews with teachers* who gave their views on individual children.

Rutter's conclusion is that Sudanese children were enjoying some educational success in the UK (although one might question whether such a conclusion was warranted, given the small numbers studied). She attributed this to the children's confidence in a distinctly southern Sudanese identity and their maintenance of cultural forms that valued education. Other factors related to the southern Sudanese being an elite group of migrants. They came from homes where fluent English was spoken and all of the children had entered school able to speak some English. High teacher expectations also contributed to the children's achievements, as did escaping the label of being traumatized and thus uneducable (Rutter, 2006, p. 204)

Rutter's study took the analysis to an even more focused level, in that she offered a couple of vignettes of particular children – describing their backgrounds, their experiences of persecution, their route to England, their interrupted education, a technique that is often very helpful in putting flesh on the bones of a study and bringing it alive for the reader.

The other two groups in Rutter's study (Congolese and Somali refugee communities) had fared less well than the Sudanese community in terms of the children's educational attainment, and data from the three studies were used to draw out lessons for practice and for policy changes in respect of the education of refugees. She also attempted to make a theoretical contribution and, in particular, challenged what she calls 'the hegemony of trauma' (p. 37), where it is assumed that all experiences of refugee children include a prior traumatic event, ignoring the experiences of trauma that result from their official treatment in the country of refuge.

Throughout, Rutter might have been more precise about her sources and more rigorous in reporting her methods, but the elements of her case study are clear from the point of view of research strategy. They demonstrate the various layers that need to be built up in order to make sense of what emerges at the micro level. If the individual detail is presented outside of a context it can often be quite meaningless.

Rutter's work also illustrates the Russian-doll complexity of case studies. In her work we can see a case study of a community, both in its country of origin and in that of its refuge; we can see a case study of a small number of children with the common characteristic that they share a broadly similar background and experience of flight; and we can see a case study of the histories and achievements of individual children. Put it all together and it becomes a rich, triangulated narrative that adds weight to the conclusions drawn from the study.

Drawbacks of case study research

Like all research methods, case study research is not free of problems, even though it remains a useful and popular method. There is no doubt that it has been treated with disdain by some researchers and has been regarded as the least desirable in the hierarchy of strategies. As with some other qualitative approaches, criticism has focused on a lack of rigour and carelessness in designing studies. This of course is not necessarily a result of the intrinsic weakness of case studies, but often of the way investigators approach them. The usual complaints about biased views and the possibilities for the researcher's beliefs to influence interpretation have been posited, but what is often forgotten is that bias can be a feature of other research strategies also.

Sarantakos (2005) sets out what he views as the weaknesses of case study research:

- results relate to the unit of analysis only and allow no inductive generalizations;
- findings entail personal impressions and biases and hence there is no assurance of objectivity, validity and reliability;
- research cannot be replicated;
- there is limited access to the field and to the personal and subjective information that constitutes the basis of case studies;
- the interviewer effect may cause distortions – even the presence of the researcher in the field can be destructive. (pp. 216–17)

It will be apparent to readers that these criticisms are based on positivist perceptions of reality and that they take quantitative rules as the norm against which all other approaches are judged. Nevertheless, concern persists that case studies do not lend themselves to generalization. After all, how can one draw general conclusions from a single case? Yin's (1994) answer to this draws comparisons with experiments:

> In fact, scientific facts are rarely based on single experiments; they are usually based on a multiple set of experiments which have replicated the same phenomenon under different conditions . . . Case studies are generalizable to theoretical propositions and not to populations or universes . . . the investigator's goal is to expand and generalize theories and not to enumerate frequencies. (p. 10)

Here Yin is claiming that case studies can contribute to analytic generalization rather than to statistical generalization. In other words, by building up evidence and by each case study adding to the pool of similar research, we can construct a picture of the ways in which different environments and circumstances are typically understood and responded to by different groups of people. As noted above, the criticism about absence of generalizability is only valid if we assume that the rules governing quantitative approaches provide the measuring rod for all research. If we understand qualitative approaches on their own terms – the importance of openness on the part of the researcher, the commitment to attempt faithfully to represent the views of research participants, and so on, then there is merit in Yin's defence of the case study.

There is also the issue of resources invested in case study research, not mentioned by Sarantakos. They take too long to complete, they produce long narratives that are inconclusive and they seldom offer practical results. The criticism that case study research takes too long to complete is less true now than it was some decades ago and, as we have seen, case studies do not inevitably mean participant observation, which is a time-consuming activity. The presentation of case study findings is challenging, and busy managers and policy makers are not interested in great detail. They are looking for ways forward. The practice of offering a short summary alongside the detailed report is one way forward. Another is to produce two reports, one containing detailed evidence, the other a shortened version. This too is time-consuming but is worth the effort if the study is to be read and taken seriously. Nevertheless there is no doubt that reports of quantitative approaches are often much more instant in their impact than case studies can ever be.

Conclusion: case study research and social justice

As we have seen, a 'case' may be defined as people, policies or other social phenomena, an analysis of which can lead to a critical understanding of social practices. One of the advantages of case studies for purposes of social justice is that, because of their nature as a tool for achieving depth and for focusing on specific units, whether representative or not, they are able to identify and describe in great detail the meaning of experiences of oppression to those affected by them. This kind of research has been popular in feminist and other studies that aim to 'give a voice' to those silenced as a result of power relations (see also Chapter 7). The examples of the work of Hicks and Rutter show how the views and achievements of disadvantaged groups can be a powerful indicator of the state of equal rights and opportunities, and can contribute to both policy and theory development. Although the purpose of case study is not to represent the world, its usefulness to policy makers and practitioners as Stake (1998, p. 104) points out, is in its 'extension of experience'. Vicarious experience (the imaginative sharing in the experiences of others) is an important basis for influencing actions and options, and should not be under-valued in research. At the same time, the case study researcher's intense interest in personal views and individual circumstances can raise ethical questions about exploitation, as discussed above. Although this is an issue in all research, the unique aspects of case study methods in attempting to delve deep, may lead to those studied risking exposure and embarrassment if they are not consulted and given access and power of veto over what is written about them.

main points

■ A case study is an investigation of a topic within its social context

■ In qualitative research, case studies are often the main form of inquiry

■ In quantitative research, case studies are usually subsidiary to other methods

■ Interviews (individual or group) are often the preferred method in case studies

■ Case studies triangulate methods, e.g. interviews, analysis of documents, observation

■ They are an attempt to achieve depth rather than scope

■ A 'case' may be an individual, a group, an organization, an issue, a country

■ It is not possible to generalize from case studies, in the sense understood in quantitative research

- What do you think are the advantages of case study research?
- When might you choose a case study method – think of examples of research questions?
- In your examples, where do questions of social justice figure?

taking it further

- Ragin, C C and Becker, H S (eds) *What is a Case? Exploring the Foundations of Social Inquiry* (New York: Cambridge University Press, 2005)
  A discussion of the different meanings of a 'case', and an exploration of taken-for-granted understandings.
- Stake, R E *The Art of Case Study Research* (Thousand Oaks, CA: Sage, 1995)
  A useful guide to the main elements and pitfalls of case study research.

chapter **7** # Critical social research

Introduction

Critical social research is, like the other approaches discussed in this book, a distinctive approach to studying social life, drawing on specific beliefs about the world and how it operates. The conventional notion of scientific research has been underpinned by an assumption that what is shared across disciplines is a similar scientific method and uniform standards that can be applied across the scientific community. This has been unsettled by critical research that regards the 'scientific method' based on positivist concepts as unsatisfactory because it deals only with what can be observed 'objectively' and does not locate social phenomena in their historical and political context. It asks awkward questions about the social interests served, masked or denied by research as well as other practices. Critical social research is grounded in critical theory, and this requires some explanation. As Nancy Fraser has said:

> A critical social theory frames its research program and its conceptual framework with an eye to the aims and activities of those oppositional social movements with which it has a partisan, though not uncritical identification. The questions it asks and the models it designs are informed by that identification and interest. (Fraser, 1989, p. 113)

Here Fraser openly aligns critical research with oppositional movements and debunks any notion of research as a neutral activity, though she is careful to emphasize the importance of rigour and honesty. Critical social research for many years had an exclusive interest in class and only comparatively recently has attempted to incorporate other social divisions into its analysis (see Harvey, 1990). So although critical approaches to social research are distinctive, they have influenced and are closely allied with other major social critiques such as Marxism, feminism, theories of anti-racism, some postmodernist approaches and disability, age-related and sexuality studies. In the discussion that follows here I employ the basic themes of critical theory to discuss the potential of a critical social research in the service of social justice, and I examine attempts, particularly within social work, to construct a methodology for critical research.

Origins of critical social research

Early theorists who have come to be associated with critical theory are C. Wright Mills, Marx, Weber, Durkheim, and in the early twentieth century the Frankfurt School, well known for its emphasis on the importance of studying society systematically as an historical totality rather than as a fragmented collection of mechanical functions. The Frankfurt School argued that such analysis 'should not take the form of an indifferent, value-free contemplation of social reality, but should be engaged consciously with the process of its transformation' (Morrow, 1994, p. 14). These themes continue within critical approaches to social research – a commitment to a particular way of understanding social problems and a desire to make changes that will benefit oppressed groups.

In the 1970s and 1980s Habermas took the themes of 'crisis' and 'contradiction' as a research agenda (Habermas, 1987), leading him to identify four basic areas of inquiry: forms of social integration, family socialization, mass media and mass culture, and potentials for protest. Habermas's themes are particularly relevant in countries across the modern world, given the preoccupation with the integration of minority ethnic and cultural groups in the context of global terrorism, changing family forms, concerns over youth cultures and crime, and the influence of the world wide web and other mass information and communication vehicles. The focus on crisis and contradiction can take account of phenomena such as environmental and anti-nuclear movements, and other single-issue and counter-culture movements linked to minorities (sexual, racial, gender-based, disability). It can cover religious fundamentalist movements and cults and self-help movements. In this respect Habermas is careful to 'differentiate emancipatory potentials from potentials for resistance and withdrawal' (1987, p. 393). In other words, 'resistance' should not be interpreted necessarily as having progressive potential, but can have conservative and even fascist intentions. This is where critical approaches claim to offer a value base that allows researchers to discriminate between processes that further human resistance to oppression and those that serve to reinforce it.

Principles of critical social research

This approach to research has politicized social research in unprecedented ways. Although many approaches to social research could claim to be 'critical', research influenced by critical theory is intrinsically critical and constitutes a very specific approach (see Humphries, 2005). The main presuppositions are:

- social structures are oppressive, maintained through political and economic power, and supported by a range of legitimizing strategies
- these legitimations should be made visible for examination and to identify the oppressive and exploitative practices they underpin
- by focusing on specific topics, taken-for-granted understandings are examined for their relationship to wider social and historical structures
- it seeks ways to combat oppressive structures
- the critical social researcher is reflexive and flexible enough to engage with these power dynamics

In other words, critical social research is interested in domination and in the social arrangements that perpetuate power relations to create forms of alienation and inhibit the realization of human imagination and possibilities. Feminists and others have added to these beliefs in identifying the particular ways in which women, black people, disabled people, gays and lesbians, the young and the old all experience distinctive forms of domination. Central to all these critical approaches is a concern with praxis – the idea that knowledge does not end with finding out about how reality is constructed but is about changing it. A fundamental assertion of critical approaches is that every form of social order entails some forms of domination, and that a critical–emancipatory interest informs struggles to change these relations of domination–subordination. Research is one of a number of strategies that contribute to this struggle. Its distinctive contribution is a grasp of the complexity of domination (some of these were discussed in Chapter 2) as well as the methodological problems involved in studying it.

Critical social research cannot be easily located within either a realist or a constructivist paradigm, as discussed in Chapter 1. It is anti-positivist in the sense that it acknowledges the problem of interpreting meanings in social life. At the same time it does not deny the existence of objective facts, and indeed insists on examining the institutional structures that constrain and control relatively powerless people. It insists equally that 'social facts' are interpreted by human beings, and that we 'create society at the same time as we are created by it' (Giddens, 1982, p. 13). It points to the possibility of change in human behaviour in response to knowledge about that behaviour, and to the potential of human beings to change structures and therefore the future. An analysis of the complex ways in which domination is produced, reproduced and resisted, constitutes the methodological challenge of critical research.

At the same time, it is argued that this strong political commitment should not result in the facts being ignored or distorted: 'to be sure, critical research has a strong ideological content, but this is held in check by the commitment to analyze social reality' (Morrow, 1994, p. 26). A critical research methodology asserts that questions about justice, freedom and equality should be explicitly addressed as part and parcel of its approach. Harvey (1990) describes it as a 'critical-dialectical perspective' (p. 1). It is 'critical' because it draws attention to the relations of power that shape social reality. It is 'dialectical' because it attempts to analyse subjective and objective realities as intertwined and mutually implicating one another. A feature of the approach is a constant back-and-forward movement between the topic studied and the political and historical context in which human behaviour takes place. For example, a study of the experiences of users of mental health services will be not only descriptive but explanatory in that users' experiences will be set within a framework of historical and contemporary images of mental health and illness, the ways in which institutions and services have developed in response to these, and current priorities and resources. In contrast to a purely interpretive notion of social life, or one concerned only with social causation, both of these dimensions are central to the very essence of critical research.

There are no distinctive methods that characterize this approach (though some methods are more compatible with it than others), and critical researchers are pragmatic and pluralist in their choices. However, it does require a critical pluralism that directs attention not only to the ways in which research problems are constructed, or the ways in which such construction shapes the choice of methods, but also to the political contexts informing such choices. This brings us back to the central point, that critical research is informed by an explicit research programme that sets an agenda linking its theory with its methods. Its methods stretch across a wide range of research tools such as observations, both participant and non-participant; formal interviews with random samples; semi-structured, unstructured and in-depth interviewing; key informants' testimonies; analysis of personal and institutional documents; mass media analysis; archive searching; examination of official statistics; and reviews of published literature. Furthermore critical social research also uses a wide variety of analytic techniques: ethnographic interpretation, historical reconstruction, action research, multivariate analysis, structuralist deconstruction and semiological analysis (Harvey, 1990, p. 196). Where they differ from other strategies is in their strong explanatory (as opposed to interpretive) focus, and their attention to the interplay between structures and individual meanings. Although concerned with contemporary phenomena, the connection with historical processes is an ever-present influence.

Thus, for example, a critical ethnographic study of black children in the British education system would certainly have an interest in interactions between the children and their teachers, the value placed on education by parents, the meanings of school for the children themselves, and so on. However it would analyse these in the context of a history of class, gender and 'race' oppression and exploitation, and current prevailing ideologies about youth culture, class, gender and 'race'. It would look for ways in which these pervade relationships among the actors in the study, along with resistances, alternative ideologies and strategies of resistance. The goal is to produce an analysis in its totality, with history, ideology, structure and praxis as its key elements. A focus on questions of power, ideology and historical genesis defines the character of all critical methodologies.

There have been attempts to bring together critical perspectives with some aspects of postmodernism. Peter Leonard, one of the *enfants terribles* of Marxist social work in the 1970s, attempted to bring together Marxism and feminism with elements of postmodern deconstruction in order to reconstruct an emancipatory project of welfare by building on 'what is worthwhile in the radical traditions of feminism, of socialism and of anti-colonial and anti-racist struggles' (Leonard, 1997, p. 163). Fawcett et al., (2000), Fook (2002) and Pease and Fook (1999) have all offered more recent examples of what a social justice model of research based on a critical postmodern feminism might look like.

Reflexivity is a central feature of critical social research (discussed generally in Chapter 1). In whatever sphere scientific knowledge is elaborated, it must continually return to its point of origin. All data requires interpretation, and researchers' interpretive skills only become possible through our experiences and prejudices and, as Morrow (1994, p. 238) points out, denying or suppressing them can only distort the communication process and our ability to interpret others. A critical perspective acknowledges that knowledge is always and inevitably interested, and that all research approaches inherently carry a sense of what should be the case. Research discussions about child abuse, crime, care of elderly people, and so on, are saturated with implicit and explicit value judgements that are often taken for granted and unexamined. The argument suggests that any discussion of research needs not only to take account of history and context, but should be reflexive in that the researcher makes available the characteristics and beliefs that intertwine with theoretical discourses. In the examples I offer below, I include studies based on socialist, feminist, anti-racist and disability studies – topics that are not mutually exclusive, as will be seen.

Examples of critical social research in social work and social care

Critical approaches in social work have included topics such as violence (Kelly, 1988, Mullender and Hague, 2005), ethics (D'Cruz and Jones, 2004), black women's experiences (Bernard, 2001), mental health (Ferguson and Barclay, 2002), children (Jones, 2002), disability (Fawcett, 2000) and more general social work topics (Dominelli, 1999, 2002). Here I offer a selection of examples.

The mental health needs of asylum seekers

In 2002, Iain Ferguson and Aileen Barclay published their study into the mental health needs of asylum seekers in Glasgow. They conducted seven focus groups containing between four and six participants, and nine individual interviews, seeking to answer the following questions:

- What are the major factors which asylum seekers in Glasgow identify as impacting on their mental health and well-being?
- In what ways do these pressures affect their social and emotional functioning?
- What are the main ways in which they cope with these pressures (personal/informal supports/formal supports)?
- How helpful are these strategies/supports?
- What new services, or changes to existing services, would asylum seekers like to see in place to help them cope with the pressures which they experience? (Ferguson and Barclay, 2002, p. 13)

The methods used were conventional qualitative methods to conduct a needs assessment, although the researchers were careful to employ a model of research that was 'user-led' rather than 'service-led'. That is, at every stage they involved asylum seekers – as key informants in drawing up the research questions; by starting from asylum seekers' perspectives on mental health issues rather than using a diagnostic approach; and at the final stages of the process, by presenting the findings to respondents for discussion and/or amendment in a group setting prior to publication of the report (see also Chapter 4 on participatory methods), avoided very structured data collection instruments such as questionnaires, on the grounds that they carry the perspectives, experiences, assumptions and knowledge of the designers of such instruments, which are likely to be very different from those of the respondents. Focus groups and semi-structured interviewing were chosen as more conducive to identifying the health needs and expectations of the asylum-seeker population in a culturally sensitive way. The researchers saw the needs being assessed as in the context of the trauma experienced in the past and in the present, rather than employing an 'illness' model devoid of wider structures. The study did not attempt to collect epidemiological information or to measure levels of disability, but treated episodes of mental disorder as a result of 'stress, enduring vulnerability and coping difficulties' (Onyett, 1992, xi, quoted on p. 12 of the study report). This avoided any pathologizing of the asylum seekers themselves, and foregrounded structural determinants as factors affecting mental health.

The research explored not only negative but also positive experiences of living in Glasgow and of services, in an attempt to offer an holistic view of asylum seekers' lives in Scotland.

There are a number of features of the research approach that justify its description of 'critical'. First, the authors set their study in a wider context by:

- identifying the significance of the 1999 Immigration and Asylum Act which introduced compulsory dispersal of asylum seekers across Britain, regardless of individual wishes or connections with communities, and initiated a voucher scheme whereby income support was no longer in cash but in vouchers that could be spent only in designated shops (this latter scheme became chaotic to administer and was disbanded two years later);
- pointing out that hostility against asylum seekers was fuelled by both the tabloid press and by politicians of both main parties, resulting in 'asylum seekers' becoming a term of abuse. As a result some communities, especially those affected by poverty and unemployment, often also those where asylum seekers were concentrated, responded in an abusive and racist manner. The agencies and services proved unable to respond appropriately to the needs of asylum seekers

The researchers clearly set their study in this context, and described their respondents' lives against this background, setting up a dialogue between personal experiences and social and political conditions. In particular, ongoing mental health problems were linked with stress resulting from the voucher system, dispersal, the slow rate of decision-making about their asylum status, racist harassment and the local council's policy of housing asylum seekers in some of the most deprived areas of Glasgow. There were other linked concerns of course, such as social isolation, health problems, fears about personal safety, waiting times for medical treatment and lack of interpreting services, that contributed to uncertainty and instability. The important point is the interaction among structural, institutional and cultural factors in which politicians, the media, agency workers and local communities are all implicated (albeit not with uniform responses), and their impact on the mental health of people fleeing persecution elsewhere. This analysis led the report authors to call for changes in legislation such as an end to vouchers and dispersal, shifts in policy to avoid concentrating asylum seekers in deprived urban areas, a campaign of public information to counter misinformation and hostile reporting, and an imaginative programme of education in schools, which would counteract some of the racist stereotypes in circulation. In this way the research was able to contextualize individual and private worries within a much bigger scenario that went some way towards explaining why mental health problems persist and even worsen after people have fled from immediate dangers in their country of origin. The report is not without specific and immediately recommendations that will improve the support offered to this vulnerable group, but it recognized that these need to be accompanied by a shift in the ways asylum is regarded at all levels of society.

This research report does seem to have brought to the fore the perspectives of the people interviewed and it is punctuated throughout with the voices of the asylum seekers themselves, through frequent direct quotes from them, and it pays tribute to the resilience and courage of the respondents in making a new life for themselves. Nevertheless the authors show how services can be disempowering – 'their situation in Britain is characterized by an almost complete lack of power over every aspect of their lives, a lack of power that seeps away at their sense of self-worth and corrodes their mental and emotional well-being' (p. 62).

One limitation of the report in terms of an ambition to be 'critical research' is that the historical analysis might have been extended to draw not only on recent legislation and policy regarding immigration and asylum but also on a much longer history, dating from the beginning of the twentieth century. This would have demonstrated the connection between the use of stereotypes of peoples not regarded as 'belonging', the country's perceived economic needs and the resultant selective control of who is allowed to enter and who is excluded, regardless of any human rights obligations towards asylum seekers. The use of racist stereotypes to justify repressive policies might have been shown as part of this history, thus sketching the continuities and changes over time. However, no doubt the researchers were constrained by the remit given to them by the funders, the Glasgow Association for Mental Health, whose interest is with the immediate and practical needs of service users. In any case, a critical approach to social research will be inevitably controversial and may as a result risk being dismissed and discarded, an outcome the researchers would want to avoid. The question remains, however, whether such an analysis would have resulted in different recommendations, and whether indeed it is relevant to research that is geared to the practical end of improving services in the 'here and now'. Critical researchers would counter this by arguing that such changes, while important, are no more than 'tinkering at the edges', leaving the root issues of power, powerlessness and vested interests untouched. The immediacy of practice should not be an excuse for neglecting the need for radical transformation of social reality.

Health inequalities

The volume edited by Graham (2000) shows how both qualitative and quantitative approaches to research can be used within a critical social research framework to highlight inequalities in health and to offer a critique of government policy. The book's value position is set out at the outset:

> This book turns the spotlight on the link between social inequality and individual health. It does so by focusing on socio-economic inequality: on the fact that how well and how long one lives is powerfully shaped by one's place in the hierarchies built around occupation, education and income. (p. 3)

The editor places the analysis in an historical framework by showing that an association between socio-economic position and health dates back to ancient China, Greece and Egypt, and that today, in older industrial societies, greater prosperity and better health for the population as a whole has not brought about a narrowing of inequalities in income and mortality. She points out that most research in this field gathers data from individuals, their lives, habits and lifestyles, an approach that obscures the multi-layered structures of disadvantage that contribute to socio-economic inequality. Graham, by using and analysing statistics collected for a variety of purposes by the Office for National Statistics and other official sources, shows that geographical location, class, ethnicity and gender, as well as lifestyle, contribute to levels of health and ill-health and to morbidity and age at death. Life expectancy has continued to rise for men and women in all socio-economic groups, but is greater for those in higher socio-economic groups. Similarly the decline in death rate has been greater in the higher classes. There is a concentration of premature death in areas of high deprivation. Other statistics link health status differentials to employment and unemployment (men's and women's), housing and household structure. An important conclusion from the analysis, based on a number of studies, is that income inequality is an important determinant of health in richer societies:

> A series of studies has found that population health is related less to how wealthy a society is and more to how equally or unequally this wealth is distributed. Life expectancy is higher in more equal societies. (Graham, 2000, p. 12)

Graham gives the example of USA and Greece. The USA has a gross domestic product per capita which is over twice as high of that of Greece, yet life expectancy is higher in Greece than in the USA. In countries such as Finland, Sweden and Denmark with redistributive economic and social policies, poverty has not increased inexorably with the rise in unemployment.

This is an example of how a critical research approach may be taken to conduct secondary analysis of statistics collected for other purposes, and to make national and international comparisons, being mindful, of course, of the limitations of and the flaws in statistical sets.

Graham and her colleagues go further than setting out the statistics. In the tradition of a critical approach, their analyses are explanatory in offering ways in which the association between socio-economic status and health can be understood. They are careful to point to multiple chains of risk, 'running from the broader social structure through living and working conditions to health-related habits such as cigarette smoking and exercise' (p. 14). However, in identifying factors at the individual level, Graham points out that although lifestyle influences have been a major focus of national strategies to improve health, they make a relatively small contribution to health inequalities. Further, it is pointed out that perceiving oneself to be worse off relative to others may carry a health penalty in terms of increased stress and risk-taking behaviour. Attention is also drawn to the ways in which people act against, as well as within, their class circumstances. Such explanations avoid blaming the poor for their own ill-health, and attribute to them struggles that may change their circumstances.

In this example the research described in Graham (2000) goes further than the Ferguson and Barclay study could go, in identifying the historical links among industrialization and its wane, the national distribution of health status in rural and urban areas and the politics of contemporary European health policy. This discussion takes the debate beyond individualistic and victim-blaming explanations towards the ways in which increasing poverty and income inequality serve to undermine the effectiveness of policy initiatives.

Service user participation – survivors of domestic abuse

Hague, Mullender and Aris (2003) and Mullender and Hague (2005) reported their research examining the extent to which women survivors of domestic violence are regarded as a service user group in their own right. They approach the research from a feminist perspective and against a long history of men's violence against women in the domestic sphere, explained as both economic inequality and a disdain towards women generally. They reject negative assumptions of a passive 'victim' status and labels such as 'learned helplessness' and place value on the women's knowledge and experiences. The researchers were concerned that in spite of government policy on service user participation, abused women have rarely been involved in service and policy development to any extent, and black and minority ethnic women have been even more excluded than white women. They aimed to find out whether women have a voice in specialist domestic services. The research consisted of two stages, using both quantitative and qualitative methods:

Stage 1
- a questionnaire-based mapping of all inter-agency forums (around 200), refuge-based services (around 350) and other domestic violence projects;
- analysis of relevant documents;
- semi-structured questionnaire to key professionals in domestic violence projects nationally;
- non-participant observation at selected forums, support groups, workshops and meetings;
- four focus groups with female domestic violence survivors of diverse ethnicity.

Stage 2
This stage focused on user participation by abused women in three main study areas, two further policy profile sites and four detailed case study locations, including those where good practice was believed to exist. Study sites were selected to give geographical and demographic spread, varying presence of multi-racial populations, a rural/urban and Wales/England split and varying presence of refuge projects and of active consultation procedures in place. Eighty five declared domestic violence survivors were interviewed, supplemented

by interviews with groups of women, giving a total of 112 women interviewed. In addition 82 semi-structured interviews were carried out with officers of statutory, voluntary and community organizations and multi-agency forums, as well as interviews with key personnel in national agencies. A variety of relevant meetings were attended and further analysis of policy and guidance documents was conducted. The methodology is described in more detail in Mullender and Hague (2005).

The quantitative findings confirmed that few of the women were involved in domestic violence inter-agency forums and few of the forums and projects had any clear idea about how best to involve survivors. Consequently most of the abused women felt that service providers had overlooked their views. The qualitative findings helped to shed light on the reasons for this, highlighting of course the usual practical obstacles (e.g. transport, poor health, caring responsibilities). However it was at the level of attitudes that the most entrenched blocks to full user participation took place. There was a difference between 'consultation' and 'having real power' in relation to policy and practice-related decisions, and agencies tended to overstate their success in achieving participation of users. Moreover tokenistic gestures included a variety of delaying tactics, diverting users into alternative agendas, legitimating professional decisions by having users present and inviting individuals rather than talking to representative groups. An important finding was that psychological weaknesses may be exaggerated or attributed to survivors in a blanket way, so that professionals regard survivors as vulnerable 'while they are still in the experience' (Mullender and Hague, 2005, p. 1333), and therefore not ready to join in decision-making forums. This is a justification that could potentially exclude all women survivors (and all service users). An interesting finding was the extent to which survivors of domestic violence do take part in almost all multi-agency and other forums, but are not necessarily able to reveal themselves as such. These are mainly in professional roles or are activists in a wide range of settings. These participants preferred not to be 'out' and thus risk being stigmatized by colleagues, given how hard it is for professionals to accept as equals those service users who have been labelled as unable to cope or to make their own decisions.

The research also identified examples of good practice in the form of new participation methods – information exchange, one-off meetings between women and policy makers, survivors' forums and advisory groups and the use of political and community theatre, art and poetry to raise the voices of abused women.

Overall the study was a large-scale attempt to understand the obstacles to empowerment of women survivors through real participation in decision-making in services that affect them directly. It attempted to be representative in its geographic and demographic spread and in its involvement of women with a range of ethnic identities. That they are not seen as a 'user group' in their own right is a reflection of their continued marginalization in social spheres of influence.

The research is 'critical' in that the feminist authors explain women's lack of participation in the public sphere in terms of wider patriarchal and economic power related not only to their example but also to a more general absence of women from public decision-making. The research has significance too for the involvement of other service users and the extent to which they are able or are allowed to influence policies that affect them. Organizational systems such as top-down managerial practices, tactics such as professional tokenism and institutional cultures resulted in silencing survivors' voices, both those of women representing user groups and those of employees in the organizations. Mullender and Hague limit their conclusions to the problems of user participation as a policy and the resultant flawed, incomplete and dangerous practices that could result. They do, however, raise the question as to why, when women have their own body of theory and their own user-run services and in the light of the Women's Movement for recognition, domestic violence survivors are still marginalized in user consultation and the provision of advocacy.

Black mothers and child sexual abuse

Claudia Bernard's study of representations of black mothers in child sexual discourses seeks to challenge some professionals' views of mothers as 'collusive' and 'to blame' in sexual abuse cases. She was also concerned about the 'casual reliance on . . . assumptions of culture-centred suppositions to explain child sexual abuse in black and minority families' (Bernard, 2001, p. 3). She set out to understand the women's lived experiences and to assess critically the interplay among structural, cultural and emotional factors in their responses to the discovery of sexual abuse of their children. Primarily, the research sought to examine the way 'race' and gender coalesce to influence black mothers' help-seeking and protective strategies. She conducted in-depth, semi-structured interviews with a sample of 30 self-selected mothers who described themselves as black British of African–Caribbean origin (Chapter 3 of Bernard's book is worth reading from a methodological perspective). The analysis is dialogical among themes such as gendered power relations within black families, divided loyalties and ambivalence about the treatment of black men and black communities in the criminal justice system, the distorted beliefs of professionals about cultural practices and their intense and often racialized scrutiny of mothering ability in the aftermath of sexual abuse, often to the exclusion of fathers. As a result Barnard was able to show the complex matrix of influences on such mothers' motivations and coping processes, and to recognize the relationships of power at personal and institutional levels: 'importantly, the contradictory elements of mothers' experiences need to be unravelled for making sense of the conditions for women that lead to having conflicting loyalties that impact their parenting ability' (p. 97). Not only was Barnard able to offer a number of recommendations to help practitioners understand and deal with this complexity in grounded situations, but she also insisted that practitioners should not accept uncritically an interpretation of risk that pays little attention to the broader social and political context in which black mothers' parenting is constructed. This context includes an understanding of unequal social structures related to 'race' and gender, and the ways these impact on both professional practices and black mothers' responses to abuse of their children.

Other examples of critical research are available. For example Fawcett (2000) has a feminist postmodern take on disability, using a 'deconstructive textual analysis' on her study consisting of interviews of 25 women and men (p. 70). Her analysis focuses on the detail of their discourses about disability, and consists of paying attention to styles used, emotional tones and intensities, omissions, variations, contradictions, paradoxes and interpretive shifts found in the text of the interviews. She uses the analysis to contribute to the refinement of a social model of disability 'within a more nuanced world-view drawing from feminist and postmodern accounts' (p. 74). She draws out some implications for disability rights movements.

Drawbacks of critical social research

A major area in which critical social research comes under criticism is in its partisanship, its identification with the poor and oppressed and its claim that it has a right to make moral judgements and to seek to uncover unequal social arrangements and change them. The question arises as to whether 'difference' in treatment inevitably means inequality of treatment. Moreover, researchers who treasure value-neutrality in the conduct of research argue that one's judgement is affected by any commitment to one side or another. Critical researchers counter this with the argument that no research can ever be value-neutral, and it is more ethical to declare one's values and political position than pretend to offer a 'view from nowhere'. This is a debate that is relevant to any research approach that takes sides with particular groups, and one which will run and run and thus contribute to ensuring that researchers' own political and moral predilections do not get in the way of evidence.

Another potential drawback of critical research is its preoccupation with the 'grand narratives' – the emphasis on historical and structural forces of power – that can sometimes obscure the experiences of individuals or groups being studied. This was a criticism of radical social work practice in the 1970s and 1980s, that its strong critique of social structures was not matched by strategies to improve the lives of the people it claimed to serve. There are however some examples available of the ways people have used research findings to challenge their social situation and make positive changes to their communities (see, for example, Harvey 1990), so it could be argued that this problem is not inevitable.

Critical research produces findings that are at minimum 'uncomfortable' and may be highly condemning of current social arrangements. Its insistence on a focus on the need for structural change makes it unpopular with officials and politicians who may feel unable or are unwilling to contemplate radical shifts in institutions. As a result there is a real risk that such research may be dismissed as unrealistic and 'biased'.

Conclusion: critical social research and social justice

A central feature of critical research is that it is not an end in itself, concerned with the construction of knowledge for its own sake, or with confirmation or falsification of particular hypotheses. It is predicated on producing knowledge for action by dominated social groups, for application by those seeking transformation of collective and individual identities and on changing social structures. There is no doubt that gender, 'race' and class are understudied axes of difference in all forms of inquiry, and this has constituted one of the main weaknesses of social research. Critical approaches have the capacity not only to address these and other social divisions but also to bring to bear understandings that aim to promote a just society.

However, such an approach may be more achievable in some settings than in others: for example, universities have lost a great deal of their autonomy in a political climate which demands studies that offer concrete answers to social problems, and where research is dictated increasingly by government departments. Opportunities for critical research directed towards informing social praxis may be more difficult to find. At the same time the near universal recognition that 'value-free' research is a myth offers opportunities to connect values and research in ways that are transparent and justifiable, whatever the setting. Of course one should not allow personal values to distort or bias the conduct or interpretation of research, but critical researchers argue that the best way to maintain vigilance against these problems is reflexivity and open self-consciousness about beliefs and values. Critical approaches to social research claim to produce knowledge for social change because a creative linking of the public and the private is at the heart of its urge towards praxis.

main points

- Critical research is concerned with dominant social interests
- It is aligned with oppositional social movements and is engaged in the project of social transformation
- It insists on an examination of the historical context of any topic studied
- Its methods are plural and wide-ranging
- It is criticized for being too partisan and lacking objectivity

stop and think

- What do you think are the distinctive features of critical social research?
- Do you think it is a suitable approach in social work research? If yes, think of a topic and make a list of questions a critical study might ask.
- How might critical research answer the charge of its being too partisan?

taking it further

- Harvey, L and MacDonald, M *Doing Sociology: a practical introduction* (Basingstoke: Macmillan, 1993), especially Chapter 1
  An introductory guide to social research and the philosophies that inform it. Chapter 1 shows how particular topics might be approached from different theoretical positions, including critical perspectives.
- Humphries, B 'From margin to centre: shifting the emphasis of social work research', in R Adams, L Dominelli and M Payne (eds) *Social Work Futures* (Basingstoke: Palgrave Macmillan, 2005)
  Sets out some principles of critical research that might contribute to social transformation.

8 Discourse analysis

Introduction

As with other research methods, discourse analysis consists of a number of approaches to research, with different assumptions and emphasizing different theoretical positionings. Some versions of it have been used very effectively in critical research approaches, as we shall see later in the chapter. Taylor (2001) describes the approach broadly as 'the close study of language in use' (p. 5). Weatherell, Taylor and Yates (2001a) describe it as 'the study of talk and texts . . . a set of methods and theories for investigating language in use and language in social contexts . . . it offers routes into the study of meanings' (p. i). It has developed over the past twenty years or so, reflecting changing views and conceptualizations of communication, culture and language, especially the question of whether language conveys a reality or *representations* of reality. In this respect discourse analytic research rejects a view of language as only a way of transmitting meaning from one person to another, as a transparent, neutral, information-carrying vehicle. Rather discourse analysis sees language as constitutive – as actually creating, negotiating and changing meaning. It is not a static system but is located in ongoing interaction involving competing attempts to fix meaning and pin it down once and for all. The study of discourse, therefore, confronts debates about what constitutes reality and 'truth', what are social problems and solutions and what is 'real', and about the very nature of meaning.

Origins of discourse analysis

The approach to critical social research discussed in Chapter 7 was a dominant mode of analysing society during the 1970s and 1980s. However, postmodernist perspectives on which discourse research is built are critical of the attempt to build grand theories that purport to explain all social relationships, and they argue that we can only understand the world in partial, specific and localized ways. They see the world as fluid, changing and complex, and power is not possessed by particular groups, Instead it operates in all social encounters and is exercised and resisted in all situations, what Foucault calls 'bio-power' (Foucault, 1980). The way to examine these processes is through the study of discourses – those configurations of language that produce certain outcomes. These configurations can be found in talk between individuals, in policy documents, in legislation, in speeches, and so on. The important thing is not whether what is said is right or wrong, but how it defines the way an issue is to be understood. There are, of course, many kinds of discourse research, emanating from different disciplines, and, as we shall see, Foucault's model has been criticized by other theorists.

Principles of discourse analysis

Weatherell, Taylor and Yates (2001a) set out emerging research traditions in the study of discourse: conversational analysis, sociolinguistics, discursive psychology, critical discourse analysis, and Foucauldian analysis. These can be used to analyse people's talk in everyday conversation or in formal interviews, but they can also be used in work with texts such as historical documents, social policy pronouncements, e-mail communications and talk among people at different levels of institutions. The two volumes produced by Weatherell, Taylor and Yates (2001a and 2001b) trace both the theoretical and methodological development of this kind of research. Broadly, the principles that are associated with discourse research are:

- meanings are historically produced in a particular culture at a particular time, so should be examined in that context
- it is not whether discourses are true or false that matters, but their effects
- experts and institutions routinely have the power to define the debate and to produce views of people and problems within discourses
- at the same time language provides ways of resisting such definitions
- the important focus is on the ways different discourses are mobilized in different arenas to produce different outcomes

Taylor (2001, pp. 7–9) distinguishes four foci of discourse analytic research. Briefly these are:

(i) A focus primarily on the language itself – patterns, structures, functions, vocabulary, 'regularities within an imperfect and unstable system' (p. 8).

(ii) A focus on interaction and the use of language. People engaged in a conversation are not seen as free agents, but their talk is shaped and constrained by what has gone before.

(iii) A focus on patterns in language in use – the set or family of terms that are related to particular topics or activities, and the ways meanings are created or eroded as part of ongoing social change. It describes this as the employment of 'interpretive repertoires' and is interested in social and cultural contexts rather than particular interactions.

(iv) A focus on identifying patterns of language and related practices, and to show how these constitute aspects of society and the people within it. It involves the study of the social and historical origins of discourses (genealogies). Language is used as a resource for studying something else, such as power and resistance, contests and struggles.

Although it is unwise to associate particular approaches too closely with specific disciplines, Taylor's first model is used largely within sociolinguistics, focusing as it does on the minutiae and technicalities of language use. Here I shall concentrate in more detail on the other three models.

Conversation analysis

The second model, broadly capturing the scope of conversation analysis (CA), can be used not only to investigate conversational interactions, but also to examine talk in workplace settings (institutional interaction). Its interest is in utterances as objects which speakers use to get things done in the course of their interactions with others. Wooffitt (2001, p. 51) cites an example, used by Harvey Sacks to develop the model, of a caller to a Suicide Prevention Centre neglecting to give his name when prompted by the centre agent. The utterance 'I can't hear you' was analysed to reveal how it was being used to achieve a specific task, that of declining to identify himself. The assumption is that lengthy utterances, phrases, clauses or even single words are used methodically in everyday interaction to achieve particular ends.

In CA the researcher is not interested in how power is mobilized in interaction, but is more concerned with the participants' own interpretations of what is happening, which can be observed from an analysis of the sequence of turns at talking. CA claims to offer insights into institutional talk, for example in court rooms, doctors' surgeries, calls to emergency services and TV news interviews. Heritage (1997) argues that institutional talk is distinctive in that its organization is different from recurrent practices found in everyday conversation.

Participants in institutions are normally concerned with specific tasks that are the business of the institution. Moreover talk is constrained by factors such as hierarchies within institutions that govern the behaviour of people in different locations in the hierarchy.

Wooffitt (2001) identifies a number of areas in which CA has proved useful. Speech therapists have found that CA's focus on the detail of interaction can be a valuable resource in understanding the ways in which speech disorders impact upon everyday conversational activity. Speech-based computer systems have drawn from CA research findings. Social workers could find CA a useful analytic tool, since ordinary language is one of the main sites in which our social identities are negotiated. It could be employed in understanding how parents socialize their children or in examining institutional norms. And there are some examples of the broader relevance of CA in the ways in which members of social categories interact. Kitzinger and Frith (2001), for instance, examined the process through which young women negotiate sexual encounters with men, especially in declining to have sex with them. They conclude that 'saying no' is not easy, and education programmes that advocate 'just say no' are, these authors claim, deeply problematic because they fail to recognize the complex processes at work. The work of these researchers has implications not only for education programmes but also for the ways in which workers deal with claims by men that they have misunderstood the signals.

However a more general limitation of CA is that although it is strong on description, it has little concern with explanation, 'with how discursive practices are socially shaped, or their social effects' (Fairclough, 1995, p. 23), and with relations of power in interactions. It does not help us to appreciate how social problems are constructed and ideas about them reinforced, sustained and challenged. We must look elsewhere for that.

Critical discourse analysis

Whereas CA aims to clarify what an interaction is for participants through the rigorous study of the evidence, critical discourse analysts argue that their work should be judged by its ethical and political effects. Their aim is towards socio-political goals such as combating inequality and exposing power relations. Van Dijk puts it this way:

 Critical discourse analysts take an explicit socio-political stance: they spell out their view, perspective, principles and aims, both within their discipline and within society at large . . . their work is admittedly and ultimately political . . . Their

> perspective [is] that of those who suffer most from dominance and inequality. Their critical targets are the power elites that enact, sustain, legitimate, condone or ignore social inequality and injustice. That is, one of the criteria for their work is solidarity with those who need it most. (Van Dijk, 1993, p. 252)

Here we can see echoes of critical research in the aim to uncover power relations and in the identification of the research with dominated groups. Indeed Fairclough (2001) adds:

> CDA is not just concerned with analysis. It is critical, first in the sense that it seeks to discern connections between language and other elements in social life which are often opaque. These include: how language figures within relations of social power and domination; how language works ideologically; the negotiation of personal and social identities . . . Second, it is critical in the sense that it is committed to progressive social change; it has an emancipatory 'knowledge interest'. (p. 230)

At the heart of critical discourse analysis (CDA) is a concern with understanding the nature of social power and dominance, how these are reproduced through discourse, and the nature of resistance to such dominance. CDA is interested in personal power only where it is enacted as an individual realization of group power, where it can be used to illustrate the power of one group over another. In other words, power and dominance are usually organized and institutionalized, often supported and legitimated by legislation and ideologically sustained by formal and informal writings, such as textbooks and the media.

Genealogical analysis

The other model of discourse analytic research comes much more directly from the work of Michel Foucault (1972, 1980), known as genealogical analysis. The key element of this theory is that discourse produces the objects of knowledge, and that nothing which is meaningful exists outside discourse. This has been understood by some as suggesting 'nothing exists outside discourse' (and is therefore a denial of the real effects of class, gender and 'race' relations for example). Foucault does not deny that things have a real material existence in the world, but he argues that it is discourses that give events meaning. The issue is not about what exists, but about where meaning comes from (Hall, 2001). It is a constructionist theory of meaning and representation in that it is discourse – not the things in themselves – which produces knowledge. Subjects such as 'childhood', 'madness', 'asylum' only exist meaningfully within the discourses about them. Moreover these discourses are historically specific. The forms of knowledge that were produced about, say, childhood differ radically from period to period, with no necessary continuity between them. Discourses are also culturally specific, produced, regulated by the disciplinary techniques of particular societies and times. Foucault's approach depends on the relation among discourse/knowledge/power and how this operates within institutional apparatus and technologies to regulate particular 'bodies'. Discourses about mental illness, for example, operate within psychiatric structures using technologies developed by psychiatrists to produce and control 'the mentally ill'.

Foucault's ideas about power reject the totalizing assumptions of traditional revolutionary theory and its hierarchical, centralized, top-down model of power. As we saw above, this is problematic for CDA researchers. However, Foucault does not deny that such monolithic power exists, but argues that the model does not capture those forms of power that make repressive forms of power possible, namely the myriad power relations that circulate at the micro level of society. Thus his model allows for power which emanates from the state, class and the law, but does not reduce it to this level, rather it makes way for the possibility of a network of power relations outside these centralized locations.

In social work, Fook (2002 – see Chapter 6 of her book) suggests that radical and structural beliefs (what we discussed in Chapter 7 as 'critical social research') have resulted in too rigid categories of class, 'race' and gender with little room for variation, for multiple identities or for individual change. As a result, social work service users may have stigmatized identities imposed on them, taking on 'disempowered, marginalised "victim" identity, because of being assigned to social categories based on fixed social structures' (p. 72). Fook argues that much social work research is based on this view of clients.

Social workers are not immune from the influence of these conceptions of self and identity, and these may become a taken-for-granted subtext in interviewing and assessment. Because they are not recognized by social workers as oppressive to and disempowering of interviewees, strategies employed by service users and others for resisting such imposed identities are misunderstood. For example, clients asking for help may become angry and aggressive if they find themselves being viewed for assessment purposes as helpless and unable to cope. One can see how an analysis of the interaction from a discourse perspective could be a useful means to make this process visible and to help social workers understand the responses of service users.

Examples of discourse analysis in social work and social care

One of the advantages of discourse analysis is its usefulness in documentary analysis, and its capacity to offer a framework for a systematic unpacking of discourses within social policy. Below are some examples.

New Labour policy

The first example is of CDA. It does not come directly from social work practice, but is important because it is a way of analysing social policy and therefore an important tool for social workers. Norman Fairclough (2000) carried out a CDA on the 'Third Way' policies of New Labour. He explained his reason for doing this: 'my view [is] that it is profoundly dangerous for my fellow human beings in this new (global economy) form of capitalism to develop unchecked, both because it dramatically increases inequality (and therefore injustice and suffering) and because it threatens to make life on earth ecologically unsustainable' (p. 15). Here Fairclough shows what he thinks of New Labour policies, explains that he will be using CDA politically and ethically, as described in the quote above, and declares his motives as seeking knowledge for the purpose of human emancipation. He sees government as a 'social practice'. He starts from the position that New Labour's Third Way – a reconciliation of liberal 'enterprise' with social justice – is impossible in reality and must therefore be achieved rhetorically through speeches or in public statements. He sets out to describe how that is done and to expose the ideological underpinnings in New Labour pronouncements. Language therefore is crucial in the effort to persuade the public that its policies are legitimate. Fairclough examines a range of New Labour documents using a framework of analysis that provides a coherent way of distinguishing the rhetoric from the reality by giving examples of what is said and what happens in practice, and showing the relationship between them. His analysis attempts to expose the gaps among, for example, New Labour's discourse of 'partnership' against how it actually governs, the discourse of welfare or pensions regulations against the experiences of claimants, and Blair's relaxed and inclusive style against evidence of control-freakery.

Fairclough does not claim that a critical examination of discourses is all there is to social life, but does argue that semiosis (i.e. all forms of meaning-making – visual images and body language as well as verbal language) is an irreducible part of material social processes. His aim is to see how language is articulated *together with other elements* – economic, political, cultural, and so on, and to show the connection between social change and relations of social power and domination. He does not see discourse as 'all there is' but insists on the importance of analysing language alongside these other aspects of social life. He is also concerned to include an analysis of resistances to dominant discourses, insisting that 'the way things are done does not exhaust the possibilities for the way things could be' (p. 160).

Below is a description of Fairclough's technique of CDA. His analytic framework consists of five stages:

1. *Focus upon a social problem that has a semiotic element.* Beginning with a social problem rather than the more conventional 'research question' accords with the critical intent of this approach – the production of knowledge that can lead to emancipatory change.
2. *Identify obstacles to the social problem being tackled.* This is done through analysis of the network of practices it is located within; the relationship of semiosis to other elements within the particular practice concerned; the discourse itself.
3. *Consider whether the social order (network of practices) 'needs' the problem* (whether those who benefit most from the way social life is now organised have an interest in the problem *not* being resolved).
4. *Identify possible ways past the obstacles.*
5. *Reflect critically on the analysis* (including the analyst's own social positioning). (adapted from Fairclough, 2001, p. 236)

Welfare reform

Fairclough applied this framework to a worked example focusing on an extract from the government's Green Paper on Welfare Reform, published in March 1998, which is worth reading in full for an understanding of the detail of his approach. The model is such that it can be adapted for application to a range of discourse genres.

Fairclough is critical of Foucault's sense of power as circulating and ubiquitous rather than as possessed by and attached to a particular class or group, in that he views it as having helped divert attention away from relations of domination. Fairclough does not subscribe to a view that the analysis should not be reduced to a deterministic notion of class. In claiming that a discursive event works ideologically, one is not claiming in the first instance that it is false, or claiming a privileged position from which judgements of truth and falsity can be made. The claim is that it contributes to the construction of relations of power. Nevertheless, CDA adherents cannot avoid questions of truth; indeed they have a responsibility (as do we all) to make judgements in debates about the great issues of the day. Fairclough concludes, 'Retreating into a helpless relativism when faced with issues such as war crimes in ex-Yugoslavia, which require judgements of truth and falsity, is in my view a serious ethical failure, whatever theoretical voices may be used to rationalize it' (Fairclough, 1995, p, 19). In other words, we cannot take a position that all views are of equal worth, or that no judgements should be made about 'right' and 'wrong'. Fairclough's method of discourse analysis involves researchers taking a stand that supports an ethical position of opposing oppression.

Autobiography from prison

Steve Morgan (2000) based his analysis of criminal autobiography primarily on the scheme set out by Fairclough when he carried out a textual analysis of extracts from an autobiography. His description of the study gives a detailed account of his methodology. He reproduces an account of a critical incident when the author appears in court as a young man, is found guilty and is condemned to prison. In the extract Morgan identified three dominant modes of discourse on crime and criminality, condemnation, resistance and celebration which are reflected in the account. He analyses the extract meticulously to identify crisis and contradiction, and leads readers to its central message: 'the legally and morally innocent child is sacrificed to the demands of quick and efficient court procedure by the setting aside of "tiresome duty"' (Morgan, 2000, p. 125). By a painstakingly detailed unpacking of the account, Morgan helps us to understand the perspective of the person labelled 'criminal'. He shows how it contributes to discourses of juvenile delinquency and its control by the challenges it contains to official and court discourses that 'make' delinquents through processes of diagnosis, explanation and classification for the purpose of forms of disposal. Morgan says, 'the important recognition . . . is that society's rejection of the delinquent may create a space for him to develop a personal and political analysis of identity which can confront and challenge the official accounts' (p. 128). Morgan insists on the right of excluded voices to be heard and he defends the discursive analytic method as validation of an examination of autobiographical documents, and as important objects of analysis in their own right. His treatment of the text links with wider structures of class and gender, and with contradictions in institutional practices which construct criminals in particular ways in order to justify forms of punishment. In these ways Morgan very clearly meets the ethical criteria discussed in Chapter 2 of this book in that he recognized the importance of dialogue with institutional practices and included this in his analysis.

The adherents to CDA, then, pay attention to how class relations function within the social system, intersecting with gender, ethnicity, and so on. The goal is to reveal how ideology functions tactically in the service of relations of institutional domination, and how resistance to domination is expressed. From awareness and critique arise possibilities of empowerment and change.

An agency case study

Viviene Cree used a Foucauldian genealogical analysis on a study of a voluntary social work organization to help make sense of the 'confusing, multi-layered, contradictory nature of social work policy and practice today' (Cree, 1995, p. 1). This is an example both of discourse analysis and of a case study of a single organization as discussed in Chapter 6. Cree argued that social work is best understood as a discursive formation – a collection of competing and contradictory discourses that come together at a particular moment in time to frame the social work task – and that there is no 'essential' social work task. To demonstrate this she used a single-case-study approach to trace the development of an agency over 80 years, which reflected the key debates in social work. In her case she not only used a Foucaudian genealogical framework but also threaded this with a feminist analysis to explore the place of women in social work. She says, 'Foucault's analysis of history, discourse and power provided the conceptual means for achieving my feminist objectives' (p. 6). She interviewed social workers, managers and management committee members past and present, corresponded with others and read documents produced by the agency at different points in its history, from its Victorian origins to the 1990s. She also analysed social policies and legislation relating to social work over a similar time frame. As a result, her research provides insights into what certain discourses have had to say about social work, its purpose and its goals, its subjects and its objects, its parameters and its aspirations, and its ambiguities and paradoxes that centre on women workers, clients and managers. She demonstrated how discourses within the agency both reflected and influenced shifts in social work policies and practices and, as such, offer an accessible and fascinating insight into the history of social work seen through the mirror of a social work agency.

Plummer's version of symbolic interactionism has much to offer towards progressive social change.

Categorizing crime

In contrast, Cicourel's (1976) work on juvenile crime offers an example of uses of *ethnomethodology*. His question concerned how 'crimes' and 'criminals' come to be seen and described, particularly how identifications and categorizations are done and how they contribute to the construction of the social order. (Readers might be interested to compare his approach to this, to the discourse analytic approach of Morgan, described in Chapter 8.) He started from the observation that in the course of our daily lives all of us make use of categories to describe the world around us. In terms of crime, we regularly use categorizations such as 'delinquents', 'criminals', 'working class', 'middle class', and so on, and in doing so we make the assumption that all of these are detectable and describable. We then go on to use them as a resource in discourses about 'crime'. Cicourel was interested in the journey of a criminal act and its perpetrator from the point it is reported to the police to its being recorded in official records as a 'crime'. He collected data by patrolling with the police in their cars, reading their reports, listening to their conversations about 'cases' and generally 'hanging around' in whatever situations he was permitted into. He observed that the police assemble a range of (tacit, not explicit) background expectations and norms, based on the repertoire of categorizations – they are able to 'read' the social environment, to distinguish between 'normal' and 'abnormal', to know what kinds of offences to expect and who is likely to be an offender. They patrolled areas where black people live more than other areas; they were more likely to stop young black men for questioning; they regarded certain young men as the most likely to have committed particular sorts of crimes. The study showed that police and probation officers used perspectives that produced written accounts that omitted ambiguity and standardized the reports of 'what happened' to bring them within their own practice domain of interest. In other words they tidied things up to show no uncertainty and to conclude that already specified action should be taken by them. These written records then formed the basis for further action with regard to the offender. They continually simplify, abstract, interpret and reinterpret the original event or action so that it is seen to 'fit' the logic of the law which requires standardized recipes for explaining the relationship between legal rules and behaviour (Cicourel, 1976, pp. 27–28). The importance of Cicourel's work is that it reveals the unreflected-upon and taken-for-granted assumptions that professionals carry

Discourses of unmarried motherhood

Jean Carabine (2001) examined historical social policy documents to trace a genealogical analysis of the way unmarried motherhood is spoken of and with what effects, and shows how

> discourses are . . . fluid and often opportunistic, at one and the same time drawing upon existing discourses about an issue whilst utilizing, interacting with, and being mediated by, other dominant discourses (about for example, family, femininity, morality, gender, race, ethnicity, sexuality, disability and class, etc.) to produce potent and new ways of conceptualizing the topic. (p. 269)

Carabine identified at least eight different discourses interacting to produce the notion of 'lone motherhood', including 'counter-discourses' challenging the representation constructed. One effect of the dominant discourses is that they produce the object of which they speak, leading to the idea that (in this case) lone mothers are a drain on the state, allowing government to make access to benefits and to housing more difficult or conditional. Carabine traced the ways in which lone motherhood has been spoken of at different times – as immoral and undeserving, as mentally deficient, as having some psychological lack, as exploiting men and welfare – illustrating that discourses are not continuous and unchanging over time, but are historically variable. For example, a current official view of single mothers is that they should work in order to merit state help and thus we have the government's New Deal for Lone Parents policy. Different constructions convey specific messages at any given time, and have certain effects and outcomes. This 'tracing' of the history of a topic, through the examination of discourses about it, is central to Foucault's genealogical method.

Foucault was not concerned with exposing ideology in the Marxist sense of revealing the 'truth' behind it. His project was to reveal something about the nature of power/knowledge in modern societies – the strategies, relations and practices of power in which different knowledges are embedded and connected. Below is a summary of Carabine's guide to doing Foucauldian genealogical discourse analysis:

1. *Select your topic.* Identify possible sources of data, including material suggesting counter-discourses and resistances.
2. *Know your data.* Read and reread it. Familiarity aids analysis and interpretation.
3. *Identify themes*, categories and objects of the discourse.
4. Look for evidence of *interrelationship* among discourses.

5. Identify the *discursive strategies* and *techniques* that are employed.
6. Look for *absences* and *silences*.
7. Look for *resistances* and *counter-discourses*.
8. Identify the *effects* of the discourse.
9. *Context 1* – outline the background to the issue.
10. *Context 2* – contextualize the material in the power/knowledge networks of the period.
11. Be aware of the *limitations* of the research, your data and sources.
    (adapted from Carabine, 2001, p. 281)

Drawbacks of discourse analysis

The emphasis on language has been a focus of criticism, both from those who oppose discourse analysis and internally between, for example, Foucauldian adherents and adherents to CDA. Foucault's approach is dismissed as relativist in that there is no assumption of a universal 'truth' or 'what really happened' which will be revealed by the method. At the same time, it is more than just a study of language, since it takes account of the social context and the social relations within which power and knowledge occur and are distributed. Moreover the genealogical method attempts not only to expose the processes within which discourses are produced but also to describe the ways discourses are practised, operationalized and supported institutionally:

> Truth isn't outside power . . . truth is a thing of this world; it is produced only by virtue of multiple forms of constraint. And it induces regular effects of power. Each society has its regime of truth, its 'general politics' of truth; that is, the types of discourse which it accepts and makes function as true, the mechanisms and instances which enable one to distinguish true and false statements, the means by which each is sanctioned . . . the status of those who are charged with saying what counts as true. (Foucault, 1980, p. 131)

Knowledge linked to power has the status of truth and, applied in the real world, has constraining, regulating and disciplining effects. Thus the material realities are not ignored by Foucault, a position that would be unacceptable in any conceptual framework grounded in social justice.

However, in contrast, Fairclough's approach to CDA very explicitly sets out to address the material realities as well as the discourses that constitute and support them, and in this sense leaves no room for ambiguity about the importance of recognizing material inequalities and leaving no doubt that discourses are not 'all there is'.

Conclusion: discourse analysis and social justice

It will be clear from this discussion that discourse analytic researchers contest scientist models of research that seek objective explanations of an independently existing reality. Instead they aim to understand and interpret a world of meaningful social practices from the inside, finding themselves 'within a world of constructed meanings and practices, and seek to make this world intelligible' (Howarth, 2000, p. 127). They do this by exploring how and why social agents identify with and transform particular systems of meaning. They seek to locate these in larger historical and social contexts and thus to expand their significance and provide a basis for critique. These critiques are judged by the extent to which they provide new, meaningful and plausible insights into current social practices and the social and political phenomena investigated. As we have seen, some forms of discourse analysis are indifferent to political realities and constitute no challenge to an unjust status quo. For the purposes of this book, a Foucauldian approach has a helpful historical dimension which assists in making sense of current practices, but risks distortion by researchers who may ignore material realities, so important to any push towards social justice. Critical discourse analysis is also potentially conducive to an aim of social justice, since it sets out to unmask ideologically permeated and often obscured structures of power, political control and dominance, as well as strategies of discriminatory inclusion and exclusion in language use (Wodak et al., 1999). If the model on offer can ally itself with those who suffer political and social injustice, and can uncover the rhetorical strategies that impose certain political beliefs, values and goals to the exclusion of others, then it has a contribution to make to a better world. It requires to travel beyond an analysis of such discourses, to make transparent the relationship between discursive action and political and institutional structures. It is not a linguistic and semantic study of discourses *per se* that is sought, but an exploration of their specific social significance and function. Social life is more than discourse, and the popularity of discourse analysis carries risks that it becomes impossible to recognize the relationship with social processes. In particular, an examination of discourses for purposes of social justice does not perceive discourses as static but rather as dynamic, vulnerable and ambivalent. Discourse analytic research holds out the possibility that discourses and social realities are capable of change and alternatives are always available.

■ Discourse analysis sees language as creating, changing and negotiating meaning, and not as a fixed and transparent way of transforming knowledge from one person to another

■ Its objective is to make clear the relationship between discursive action and political and institutional structures

■ Language also provides a way of resisting dominant discourses

■ Discourse analysis asserts that meanings are historically produced in a particular culture at a particular time and need to be examined in that context

■ Discourse analysis is criticized for suggesting that language is 'all there is'

stop and think

■ What are the features of discourse analysis that might make it a useful approach for social work research?
■ What are the main differences between critical discourse analysis and genealogical discourse analysis?
■ What uses of discourse analysis might make it unsuitable in meeting the ethical standards suggested in Chapter 2?

taking it further

■ Antaki, C, Billig, M, and Edwards, D 'Discourse analysis means doing analysis: a critique of six analytic shortcomings' *Discourse Analysis Online, 2*
■ Potter, J 'Discourse analysis and constructionist approaches: theoretical background', in J T E Richardson (ed.) *Handbook of Qualitative Research Methods for Psychology and the Social Sciences* (Leicester: BPS Books, 1996)

9 Ethnographic research

Introduction

Ethnography is concerned with writing about and describing cultures. Ethnographic approaches to research take the view that an appropriate way to understand the social world is to take an insider's view in an attempt to understand other people's world-view, and to study the meanings that people attribute to events and actions. The way to do this is in naturalistic settings, in being close to people going about their daily business. In this sense it is located within a constructivist paradigm. A key method is participant observation, where the researcher attempts to saturate herself/himself in the culture and the world of those researched, either overtly or covertly, and to record the realities of those involved in this world. This is in direct opposition to the rules of the physical sciences, where the researcher must control the environment in order to study relationships among variables, and where s/he remains distant with a view to maintaining objectivity. Instead ethnography acknowledges that all research has an impact on its subjects and the ways in which they construct their reality, and can never have a 'fly on the wall' perspective. For this reason the notion of reflexivity (as discussed in Chapter 1) is central to ethnographic research.

Origins of ethnographic research

Ethnography as a form of inquiry is now over a century old, but has changed over time and has a number of different forms. It emerged out of a rejection of scientific research as inappropriate for the study of human beings (see the discussion of paradigms in Chapter 1), and as denying social complexity and human agency in favour of over-simplistic predictions based on cause-and-effect models. Philosophers such as Weber (1969) were concerned to find a basis for conceptions of knowledge that did not rely exclusively on sensory experience, as was the case with realism/positivism. Weber argued that social action occurs when a social actor assigns a meaning to his or her conduct and/or environment and, through this meaning, relates it to the action of others. Actions are the result not of stimulus-and-response mechanisms, but through an *interpretive* process. It is the aim of the researcher to understand this interpretive process and discover 'the motives, the reasons and the goals which lead people to act in the ways they do' (Benson and Hughes, 1983, p. 42).

The heyday of ethnography was in the 1950s, 1960s and 1970s when it was fashionable for (usually young, male) researchers to carry out participant observation with people on the margins, for example drugs users (Becker, 1963), street gangs (Whyte, 1981; Parker, 1974) and men who have sex with men in public places (Humphreys, 1970). Other studies examined the behaviour of professional workers towards their clientele, such as Sudnow's study of the process of dying in hospital, examining class and 'race' discriminations by staff in dealing with death (Sudnow, 1967) and the behaviour of police towards young black men (Cicourel, 1967), doctors towards patients (Davis and Horobin, 1977) and social workers towards their clients and others (Davies and Kelly, 1976; Humphries, 1983; Smith, 1980). The approach associated with these beliefs stresses the detailed investigation of these interactions and usually consists in the researcher gaining access to the processes of people's daily living, and participating in these over a prolonged period, observing what happens, listening to what transpires, asking questions, reading documents and triangulating data (see Chapter 6) by any means available to throw light on the issues in which s/he is interested. Reporting of ethnographic studies is characterized by detailed and 'thick' description, extensive direct quotations from participants, and reflexive accounts of the reactions and reflections of the researcher herself/himself. Normally the researcher is known as such by the participants, and the assumption is that over time those being observed will relax and behave normally in her or his presence. Observation can take the form of covert involvement by, for example, the researcher pretending to 'belong' to the group being studied, or by her/his *actually* belonging – as a police officer, or social worker, etc. – and so having direct access to the field of study, but without disclosing that s/he is carrying out research. This deals with some of the problems of 'researcher effect', but the ethical issues raised by this behaviour have long been debated in the literature (Atkinson et al., 2001; Fine and Weis, 1998; Hammersley and Atkinson, 1995). On the whole, covert research is regarded as unacceptable (although, as discussed in Chapter 2, most codes of ethics have a 'get out' clause that allows for covert research in some circumstances).

Ethnographic studies are usually of 'subcultures' within one's own society, and the researcher attempts to be as involved in their processes and as insignificant as possible. That ethnography may take place within one's own society is not to say that the researcher can take anything for granted. One of the skills is to see phenomena anew, to render familiar events strange so that they can be made available as an object that can be studied and interpreted. This entails a description of complexity and contradiction, achieved through a triangulation of methods that bring together different perspectives on the topic of interest, with a view to producing a deep and detailed analysis of the environment.

In recent years these realist descriptions of social life have been challenged by postmodernist critics, and new versions of ethnography have been produced (e.g. Denzin, 1997; Clarke, 2004). Clarke, for example, points to the loss of certainties with the postmodern turn, and the emphasis on 'partialities, positionalities, complications, tenuousness, instabilities, irregularities, contradictions, heterogeneities, situatedness and fragmentation – complexities' (p. xxiv). She sees traditional ethnographic approaches as inadequate to capture such complexity, and calls for methods that elucidate contradictions, ambivalences and irrelevances; that take account of marginalized perspectives; and that go beyond 'the knowing subject' to address salient discourses within the situation of inquiry. Her book proposes a version of situational analysis as a means to achieve this.

Principles of ethnographic research

As with all research traditions, there is diversification and disagreement as to the nature and conduct of ethnography, and its genealogy includes phenomenology, existential sociology, symbolic interactionism and interpretive sociologies. All of these approaches share two basic assumptions:

> human beings are not merely acted upon by social facts or social forces, but are constantly shaping and creating their own social worlds in interaction with others; and special methods are required for the study and understanding of these uniquely human processes. (Benson and Hughes, 1983)

These principles are associated with the 'subjectivist' tradition of social inquiry (that is, reality is described from the point of view of the subject of the research and the meaning they attribute to events and speech), in contrast to the 'objectivist', 'realist' or 'positivist' tradition (that is, an independent external reality exists and is made known to the researcher by its action on her/his senses). Chapter 1 has a fuller discussion of the basis of these paradigms. However, as we shall see, both of these notions are problematic in practice.

Below I describe some of the assumptions in the major traditions of ethnographic research:

- the research focus is on the nature of social interaction, that is the dynamic social activities taking place among persons (the *social construction of reality*)
- human action is not only caused by social interaction; it also results from interaction *within* the individual (the *subjective construction of reality*)
- the concern is with the *present*, not past influences
- the human being is unpredictable and active in her/his world, and our action involves conscious choices
- what is real for us in our environment always depends on our own active intervention and on our interpretation of knowledge presented to us

The means to study these processes is inferred from what we *do* rather than from what we say. Human uniqueness relates to the ability to reason and to communicate symbolically with ourselves and with others. The emphasis is on the changing and dynamic nature of the social universe. The individual is not a consistent, static personality, but is always in a state of 'becoming', always undergoing change in interaction with the environment. From the research point of view it is important to observe people in different contexts, since behaviour, opinions and beliefs change and may even be contradictory, according to the context. Thus, for example, when a bystander sees a young person smash a ball through a window, his understanding will vary according to whether it is his window or his child, or what his relationship is with the owner of the window or with the child.

A version of ethnography, *symbolic interactionism* (Blumer, 1969), attempts to view the human being as a self-directing actor who exercises freedom and is creative, impulsive, spontaneous, and who realizes the possibility of refusing to conform and saying 'no' to expectations. Symbols such as words are a source of human freedom, to be used to construct new ideas and strategies. Limitations to human freedom are acknowledged, such as environment, and coercion and manipulation are recognized within the framework. The perspective assumes that human beings are rational problem-solvers and that society is a process of individuals in interaction – co-operating, role-taking, communicating in largely consensual ways. It credits humans not as being creative sometimes but as being creative in *all* situations. It credits all people with the capacity to make freely taken decisions, and its methodology attempts to locate an individual freedom that methods associated with realism cannot find. Crowds, groups, organizations, communities are all societies made up of individuals in interaction, who communicate with symbols and come to share a reality through this process. The researcher attempts to understand the symbols, and to describe how individuals decide on action – how they take account of others' views, how they interpret actions and how they act back and forth. The symbolism contained in a country's national flag, for instance, will lead to different interpretations of its meaning and of the beliefs of those who display it, and such interpretations will lead to particular actions on the part of those confronted with it. It is not necessary for participants to be together in one geographical location; for example, one might study professional groups interacting through the pages of a journal, learning about their shared language, the range of their beliefs, the ways they interact, the things they take for granted, and so on.

The approach acknowledges that society makes us through interaction with others, but with what society provides – symbols, self, mind, role-taking ability – we turn around and make society. We access this by observing and describing the ways in which individuals figure out situations, consider the actions of others, exercise control over their own behaviour, conform to and challenge rules. We can understand what is going on only if we understand what the actors themselves believe about their world – their vocabulary, their ways of looking at things and their sense of what is important. This approach could be a useful means to make sense of case conferences, for example, in the effort to take account of the social worlds of different professional groups and of parents of children under discussion. The methods implied here involve observing and interviewing people in real settings, personal accounts and life histories, and 'non-reactive' techniques such as, for example, written materials, non-verbal communication and audiovisual tapes.

A criticism of traditional versions of ethnography is that they do not take account of, for example, psychological predispositions or social structures, and are therefore conservative in their orientation. At the same time there are examples of those that make connections between individual actions and wider social patterns, and it can be argued that myriad small studies of social life can add up to a more sensitive and politically engaged understanding of the world than many of the multi-million surveys that lose out on understanding in the requirement for standardization of data.

Alfred Schutz (1969) offered insights into what he called the 'natural attitude', where human beings take the world for granted, not questioning its reality. As social actors in the everyday world, we routinely, without difficulty, without hesitation, attribute motives, beliefs, attitudes to others as ways of making sense of the world. How this is done, and in what ways, through talk and conduct, should be the subject of research. Garfinkel (1967) took up these ideas in his *ethnomethodology* approach and proposed to study the procedures people use in routine and mundane situations in the process of 'going about knowing the world' (Benson and Hughes, 1983, p. 56). Here the assumptions are:

- the meaning of everyday talk is dependent on the context in which the talk occurs: 'that is to understand an utterance, members must also know something about the particular circumstances in which the utterance was made, who the speaker was, the previous course of the talk, the relationship between the user and auditor, what is said subsequently, and so on' (Benson and Hughes, 1983, p. 101).
- actions are expressions of patterns enabling us to see what the actions are in terms of the meaning of the context – the 'documentary method of interpretation'

These dimensions offer ways of studying people in their social context. Ethnographic methods have been used in a broad range of settings, from the analysis of conversations, offering insights into the importance of the way people talk and the importance of studying it as a phenomenon in its own right, to group and crowd behaviour, the factors that influence it and the meanings of it to those involved.

Examples of ethnography in social work and social care

I have selected a range of ethnographic approaches to illustrate its variety.

Telling stories

The work of Ken Plummer (1991, 1992) is relevant to social work. His book, *Telling Sexual Stories* (1995) takes a narrative approach to the process of listening to people telling stories of sexuality and sexual experience. Instead of viewing these stories as reflecting actual facts of individuals' lives, he sees them as topics to be investigated in their own right, exploring how they come to be told, the role they play in contemporary lives and their political significance, with a view to contributing to a wider goal – the development of a sociology of stories. Plummer's version of *symbolic interactionism* views the social world as a 'vast flow of ever-changing symbolic interactions in which we are set adrift in a never-ending stream of practical activities' (1995, p. 20). Through symbols and languages, as human beings we are able to reflect upon ourselves and others, and we cannot but help acting in, on and through the world. And all the time we are telling stories about our pasts, our presents and our futures. Stories can be seen as a constant flow of joint actions, and individuals may adopt roles such as storytellers, coaxers or coercers of others to tell stories and consumers or audiences of stories. Plummer's method consists of encouraging people to talk about their lives (in his case specifically a variety of different kinds of sexual stories) in relatively unstructured ways. He is interested in a range of dimensions associated with telling sexual stories. For the purposes of this chapter a particular issue he raises concerns the social role that stories play in the lives of people and societies: 'how might stories work to perform conservative functions maintaining dominant orders, and how might they be used to resist or transform lives and cultures?' (p. 25). The case study by Hicks, discussed in Chapter 6 also describes 'conservative' and 'resistance' narratives. Plummer's analysis is set in a postmodern (or what he calls 'late modernist') framework, and he emphasizes changes over time, such as participant versions of stories that reflect 'expert' perspectives; stories of difference, multiplicity and a plural universe, replacing stories of the 'essence' and of 'truth'; and stories of deconstruction (questioning, unpacking beliefs) replacing categorically clear stories. One of Plummer's central themes is that the telling of stories depends on interpretive communities that will create and hear the stories:

> Without lesbian and gay stories, the lesbian and gay movement may not have flourished. Without the stories told by abuse survivors, the whole rape movement would probably have floundered. And recovery tales identified in their narratives a whole scenario of hitherto undetected concerns that have entered a public arena of discourse.
>
> And these stories work their way into changing lives, communities and cultures. Through and through, sexual story telling is a political process. (Plummer, 1995, p. 145)

In other words, telling stories of 'coming out', by lesbians and gay men, women's stories of rape and other stories of oppression not only helps the recovery of the individual through processes of sexual 'suffering, surviving and surpassing' (p. 50), it also interacts with a listening and receptive community whose dynamic interaction with the wider society potentially provides routes out of stigma and towards changing institutional practices. For example, the accumulation and making visible story after story of lesbian and gay sexuality not only gives confidence to this minority community but also brings pressure to bear on the wider society to take account of their presence and their perspectives. This may result (and has resulted) in changes in legislation, and in a shift of institutional practices and individual attitudes. At these different and interdependent levels,

about everyday life (and there are applications for child abuse, mental health, adoption, and so on) and the possible consequences for those systematically recognized as a 'type' and categorized accordingly. One lesson of this is that abstract, statistically correlated information on age, sex, ethnicity, number of offences, social class, and so on do not provide the researcher with the 'facts' or with material for understanding how delinquency (or any other social problem) is produced. The research focus has to get close to the negotiated character of phenomena labelled as delinquent, and how records produced as a result come to be understood. This approach has wider implications for how social workers create records and reports, the tacit, common-sense knowledge they use about what is a 'social problem' and the consequences for those who are labelled as a result.

Assessing 'need'

In social work Gilbert Smith conducted an ethnographic study of the notion of 'social need' as used by social workers in their everyday tasks (Smith, 1980). His participant observation study examined the way social workers employ 'need' as a *resource* rather than as a concrete reality. That is, their view of what constitutes 'need' is flexible and can change in different contexts. He pointed out that policy documents of the time were calling for more 'accurate' definitions of need that would make intervention more precise and focused. Through participant observation in social work area offices, he was interested in how the notion of 'need' was used. It was important for him not to try to record everything he observed, but to set boundaries around his area of interest. One of the early problems for ethnographic researchers is in deciding what to observe and what is irrelevant to the area of interest. Smith's research found social workers using several clearly separate ideologies of need, that varied depending on the context, to explain the nature of the problem to hand. He also identified different and competing ideologies in policy documents. His major contribution to research in the implementation of social policy demonstrated the importance of studying both the incoherence and ambiguity of policy initiatives and also the way professionals subjectively construe policy measures and strive to implement them in their practice. Without an ethnographic approach that brought the researcher close to actual practice, this complexity may not have been observed, and the meaning of the notion of 'need' may have been treated as commonsense and taken for granted. Hardiker (1977) found a similar situation pertaining in the probation service. The question to be asked of this kind of research is 'so what?' What difference does it make to know that policy documents are not internally consistent and that professionals are left to interpret and operationalize them in their daily work? Neither Hardiker nor Smith has examined the political implications of this for work with people in trouble. They might have addressed the ways in which individual professional discretion in defining 'need' leaves the way open for the operation of prejudices, for institutional bias and for definitions to be favoured that fit organizational resources. This issue is as alive now as when Smith and Hardiker conducted their research.

Drawbacks of ethnographic research

There have been a number of criticisms of ethnography. Traditional ethnographic approaches follow a particular set of social scientific rules. First it is important to note that they assume a posture of realism; that is, they have a commitment faithfully to reproduce reality. The goal is to create a factual narrative about the social world, so that what is recorded represents faithfully the intentions of the people studied, and how they perceive their own actions and those of others. In other words, the priority is to remain true to the phenomena under study, rather than to ensure that correct methods are followed. The social world is infused by social meanings:

> that is, by intentions, motives, beliefs, rules and values . . . As participant observers we can learn the culture or subculture of the people we are studying. We can come to interpret the world in the same way as they do, and thereby learn to understand their behaviour in a different way to that in which natural scientists set about understanding the behaviour of physical phenomena. (Hammersley and Atkinson, 1995, pp. 7–8)

There is a contradiction within this version of ethnography. Although the assumption is that the social world is constructed and interpreted by social actors, and the positivist notion of a 'reality out there' is rejected, in order to study the world of participants, the ethnographer must believe that it *is* possible to capture and describe that world to readers. In other words, the rules of realism are invoked to legitimate the telling of the narrative. Indeed some methodologists have attempted to produce rigorous, scientific systematized procedures for capturing that reality. *Grounded theory* is an example of this. Developed by Glaser and Strauss (1967), the purpose of the approach is to generate theory from data, rather than to collect data with a predefined theoretical formulation already in mind. Participants' responses and interpretation of events are filtered through the eyes of the researcher who then constructs a theoretical formulation (see

Corbin and Holt, 2005). The process involves concept identification, where the researcher codes the early data into initial concepts. S/he uses these to formulate more questions designed to clarify and elucidate these concepts. A process of alternating data collection and analysis takes place, concepts are modified and eventually a saturation point is reached when the data seem repetitive and no further concepts are emerging. An example of the methods is Holt's study of talent development in elite adolescent soccer players (Corbin and Holt, 2005). This involved observing interactions among the players and their coaches, and interviews with both players and coaches. After every field trip (period in the site of the research) he coded his data, drew out themes, went back to the field to test these by exploring them with his interviewees, revised them, went back to the field to test them, and so on, until he could not identify any more themes. He then analysed the data to theorize his results. It is a lengthy, expensive and time-consuming process, but it is defended as a method because it provides the stepping stones to develop and update a body of knowledge. There is a tendency in grounded theory to assume that theory emerges from the data in an unproblematic way to reveal a singular reality (Glaser, 1992), but recent versions acknowledge the possibility for multiple interpretations of any set of data (Denzin and Lincoln, 1994; Strauss and Corbin, 1998; Patton, 2002).

A further criticism of some forms of ethnographic research is a failure to deal with the implications of the assertion that researchers are part of the social world they study. Often researchers neglect to take account of their role in the construction of reality. The question arises as to whether researchers are capable of realistic reporting, that is of accurately representing the reality of the world of their subjects, when their *own* meanings, knowledge, common sense and activities are implicated in the data (see Hammersley, 1995). As Trinh (1989) says, things are not found, they are made. And the ethnographer 'makes them up' (p. 141). Some ethnographers would argue that objectivity is not attainable because our perceptions are inevitably selective and shaped by the understandings we bring to any situation. It is therefore more fruitful to explore these meanings reflexively rather than try to investigate reality as if it were separate (Taylor, 2002). In this case the researcher is placed squarely in the frame and her identity, beliefs and affiliations examined as part of the overall study. In this way, an honest account of her involvement shows not only the impact she has on the meanings and constructions emerging from the research but also the ways in which her own behaviour and beliefs are influenced by the experience.

Ethnographic research has also neglected the wider social context, an important point from a social justice point of view. Some studies have been concerned with cultures (so-called 'subcultures') on a small scale such as gangs, professional groups, religious organizations, the members of which are in contact with each other on a face-to-face level. Their interest in power, in the transmission of culture, in the mutual construction of reality takes place at a micro level, and identifying bigger patterns or making generalizations is not possible. True, the approaches are underpinned by an attempt to produce a narrative from the participants' point of view and to offer an account of their world, and this has led to other methods of research where participants' perspectives and influence have increased. However, in ethnography 'meaning' is always subject to the interpretation and analysis of the researcher, raising the question as to whether this is a method that truly reflects what was intended by the research subject (although, in fairness, this is a question inherent in all forms of research).

Ethnographies have also offered valuable insights into the 'careers' of drugs users, religious converts and others, and have informed methods of intervention. The downside of this is that they have also opened up private activities to public gaze, and this gaze has focused almost entirely on groups regarded as 'deviant'. Researchers went into the field and brought back tales of the natives, framed in relatively simple and unselfconscious ways that purported to be direct copies of an assumed reality. The ethical question persists – is ethnography no more than another surveillance strategy motivated largely by social control? If the ethnographer 'makes things' and 'makes things up', what does this imply for the power ethnographers have over their subjects?

Crises in ethnography

A number of crises have taken place in ethnography. The new global cultural economy is shaped by new technologies and shifting systems that flow across national boundaries. A litigation and compensation climate leads to subjects challenging how they have been written about, and researchers cannot presume to present uncontested and objective accounts of other people's experiences. Denzin's (1997) postmodern critique suggests a triple crisis of representation, legitimation and praxis (p. 3), confronting qualitative and particularly ethnographic researchers.

Representation

A fundamental problem with the early versions of ethnography which focused on 'deviant subcultures', concerned the politics of representation (how people are described by the researcher to the wider world), where life stories could be misread as negative stereotypes or hostile portraits of the poor and marginalized, regardless of the intentions of the author. This did not seem to be a concern of some researchers though there are exceptions. Bourgois (1995, 2002) sets out his ethical dilemma, explaining that he struggled with the potential misuse of his descriptions of the conditions of Puerto Rican crack dealers in New York, but

> at the same time, countering traditional moralistic biases and middle-class hostility toward the poor should not come at the cost of sanitizing the suffering and destruction that exists in inner-city streets. Out of a 'righteous or a 'politically sensitive' fear of giving the poor a bad image, I refuse to ignore or minimize the social misery I witnessed, because that would make me complicitous with oppression. (Bourgois, 2002, p. 15)

Bourgois explains that in writing about this community he tried to build an alternative, critical understanding of the inner city by organizing his central arguments and by presenting the lives and conversations of the crack dealers in a manner that emphasizes the interface between structural oppression and individual action. His intention was to attempt to restore agency, autonomy and the centrality of gender and the domestic sphere to a political economic understanding of the experience of persistent poverty and social marginalization in the urban USA. However, the issues of how research subjects are both represented and read remains problematic.

This is particularly important, given that the writing of ethnography has assumed that the world of those studied can be captured through the careful transcription of triangulated field materials – interviews, notes, observations, document analysis, diaries, and so on (see also Chapter 6). The author is able to reflect this world and to make available the experiences of subjects of the research. In other words, the literal translation of talk and actions is equal to lived experiences and its representation. Denzin asks a number of questions about this, arguing that language and speech do not mirror experience but rather that they create experience, and the meanings of statements are therefore always deferred, always in motion and cannot be 'captured', 'there can never be a final, accurate representation of what was meant or said, only different textual representations of different experiences' (Denzin, 1997, p. 5). This reflects the debates within discourse analytic research (Chapter 8) and raises questions about the authority claimed by researchers faithfully to recount the stories presented to them.

Legitimation

The crisis of legitimation concerns the traditional criteria used to evaluate and interpret ethnographic research. The authority of any text is established by references to a reality that exists outside the text, and is governed by the rule that the description truly reflects what happened and the meaning that was intended by what was said. It is trust in a text's claim to validity that gives it credibility and confirms its legitimacy. Some critics read claims to validity, triangulation, trustworthiness, truth, plausibility, etc., both as attempts to ground the work in the conception of 'the world out there' and as a bid for power over readers in setting the rules for persuading them of the author's particular version of reality. Validity is the researcher's mask of authority that allows a particular version of truth to work its way to the reader (Lather, 1993). Research reports operate in a world of competing discourses, and the researcher's point of view is only one of a number of truths, all of which claim legitimacy. This dimension of the power of the researcher to persuade his audience that his version of events is the valid one can sometimes be glossed over.

Praxis

The crises of representation and legitimation inevitably lead to a crisis in praxis and the question, 'is it possible to effect change in the world, if society is only and always a text?' This question is pertinent to our quest to evaluate research approaches that are compatible with an ethic of social justice. Praxis, as described in Chapter 7, is the notion that knowledge leads to action and that these have a reflexive relationship with each other. If there is no objective reality, only multiple accounts – any of which is as legitimate as any other, action becomes impossible, because all accounts are 'true' from someone's point of view. This is the conservative and reactionary heart of some forms of postmodernism that challenge any universal notions of 'human rights', 'justice' 'equality' or 'empowerment'. It is argued that these concepts must be framed and understood in situated and local accounts where, it seems, anything goes. This position is unacceptable within any framework of social justice, and although ethnographic accounts reflect multiple realities, they have to be interpreted and analysed. This cannot be done without value judgements being made.

Conclusion: ethnography and social justice

This leads to the conclusion that ethnographic research is always political, whether it ignores the bigger picture or draws attention to it in its presentation of multiple views of reality. Much ethnographic work fails to locate the day-to-day experiences of participants in a wider context, or to note how history, culture and political–economic structures constrain the lives of individuals. Studies are often reductionist in ignoring class exploitation, racial discrimination, sexist oppression and the subtleties of cultural meanings that should be addressed if understanding is to be enhanced. The political consequences of this omission can be dire for those researched. Bourgois (2002) describes a number of studies in the USA on poor families. On one of them he comments:

> Lewis collected thousands of pages of life history accounts from one extended Puerto Rican family in which most of the women were involved in prostitution. The 'culture of poverty' theory that he developed out of this . . . focused almost exclusively on the pathology of the intergeneration transmission of destructive values and behaviours among individuals within families. (p. 17)

Bourgois reports that Lewis's book became a bestseller in the United States, where it resonated with Protestant work ethic notions of rugged individualism and personal responsibility, and was instrumental in confirming the deep-seated contempt for the 'unworthy' poor that permeates US ideology. This notion of the 'culture of poverty', the 'undeserving' and the 'underclass' is not absent from UK research and the social policies that flow from it (Fairclough, 2000). Part of the problem is that a central method of ethnographic research – participant observation – gives the research access to the minute detail of individual actions, and encourages a documentation of this detail alongside a blinkered approach to history and power. The structures and institutions that form the context of these actions are largely ignored and therefore remain unanalysed.

Bourgois does not minimize the problem of attempting to keep the context in view while being embroiled in what can sometimes be the painful and chaotic events of the lives of the poor. He often experienced a confusing anger with the victims, the victimizers and with the wealthy industrialized society that generates such an unnecessarily large toll of human suffering. He found himself often 'blaming the victim'. Furthermore, he argues that a political economy analysis and a focus on structures can obscure the fact that humans are active agents of their own history (a criticism also levelled at some versions of critical research) rather than passive victims: 'ethnographic method allows the "pawns" of larger structural forces to emerge as real human beings who shape their own futures' (p. 18). He suggests that one way to view this is to regard the street culture he witnessed as resistance to social marginalization, albeit a destructive and negative resistance. He does not offer a resolution of this structural-versus-agency debate, but nevertheless is convinced that the depth of overwhelming pain and terror of the experience of poverty and racism needs to be talked about openly, regardless of the discomfort this brings.

One answer to the question of praxis is a political one, offered by Lather (1986, 1991). If a research account is stripped of its external claims to authority and the desire to produce a valid and authoritative text is renounced, it can be observed that *values and politics* govern social science, not an objective theory of knowledge. Lather calls for 'openly ideological' research that takes its lead not from the rules of science but from political movements inspired by the struggles of oppressed peoples. A good ethnographic text is one that exposes how 'race', class and gender work their ways into the concrete lives of interacting individuals, what Lather calls 'catalytic validity . . . the degree to which a given research project empowers and emancipates a research community' (1986, p. 67). This challenges profoundly the privileging of scientific knowledge. It contrasts with the realist regime which sees an underlying reality behind group façades and which turns ethnography into stable systems of meaning. Denzin describes it as a model of truth that is

> narrative, deeply ethical, open ended and conflictual,
> performance and audience based, and always personal,
> biographical, political, structural and historical . . . a new way
> of writing – reflexive, transgressive and simultaneously
> feminine and masculine. (1997, p. 266)

The suggestion of openly ideological research has aroused vigorous and acrimonious debate (see Humphries, 1997, 1998; Cealey Harrison and Hood-Williams, 1998; Hammersley, 1997). Yet what is opened up is the tiny moral tales – invisible in much ethnography – and how they link to the bigger story of oppression, exploitation and resistance. The fact is that everything that a researcher writes has an impact on those written about, as Bourgois has demonstrated. Sometimes she is accused of writing the wrong story or of not acting in the best interest of those studied. We do need to remember that writing is inscription, an 'evocative act of creation and representation' (Denzin, 1997, p. 26), and what we write is always open to challenge. At the same time, it could be argued that traditional forms of ethnography are morally indefensible in that they are voyeuristic and ultimately without a sense of purpose. If we are concerned not only to interpret the world but also to change it, ethnography just has to be more than this.

- Ethnography is an attempt by researchers to saturate themselves in the culture and world of those studied
- Data is collected in natural settings rather than in laboratory-like conditions
- It emphasizes subjectivity – the effort to capture the point of view of the research subject
- Ethnography has been questioned in terms of
  - its capacity for 'accurate' representation
  - its legitimacy as a method that can be validated externally
  - its contribution to a state of praxis

stop and think

- As a social work researcher, what kinds of questions do you think might be suitable for investigation using ethnographic methods? Make a list around a topic of interest to you.
- What might be some of the dilemmas in ethnography, in the context of the ethical criteria offered in Chapter 1?
- What do you understand by the crises of representation, legitimacy and praxis discussed in this chapter?

taking it further

- Hammersley, M and Atkinson, P *Ethnography: principles in practice*, 2nd edn (London: Routledge, 1995)
  One of the best-known texts on ethnography, accessible to those who are new to the approach.
- Taylor, S (ed.) *Ethnographic Research: a reader* (London: Sage, 2002)
  A collection of detailed examples of ethnographic research. Stephanie Taylor's introduction is very informative and a useful discussion of the basic assumptions.

10 Social surveys

Introduction

Surveys as an approach to social research is one of the most common (usually quantitative) methods found in the social work literature. Broadly it is based on realist principles and represents an attempt to capture certain features of social life in ways that allow general observations to be made, although surveys do not provide depth of understanding of phenomena. Kirk (1999, p. 191) offers some features of surveys:

- they can be of people, groups, organizations, communities or other units of interest such as journal articles;
- they can be used to explore topics, to describe complex relationships among characteristics and (sometimes) to identify causal relationships;
- they allow economic study of large populations by using relatively small samples;
- they provide a platform for generalization of findings to broader populations;
- they 'scan' a carefully selected group rather than intervene in the manner of an experiment;
- they use a range of methods of data collection – e.g. personal interviews, either structured or unstructured, telephone interviews, mailed questionnaires, agency records, other existing documents;
- they gather information at one point in time (though this may be repeated as in longitudinal studies).

And, as Reinharz (1992, p. 83) comments, surveys produce

> statistics [that] are powerful in part because they are concise. Their brevity makes them easily communicated to reporters and lawmakers who seek information. Statistics have legal force and are important in lawsuits concerning . . . injustices. Statistics are also powerful because they are easy to remember and comprehend. Survey results can be presented in pictorial

> form to people who are illiterate or to those who have little understanding of numbers. The fact that survey research is typically associated with government institutions and is costly may also enhance its prestige in the eyes of the public and of researchers, since nowadays, value often reflects cost.

In this quote we have sufficient justification for taking the social survey seriously as a major research approach.

Origins of social surveys

The original association of surveys was with the activities of the state making inventories of its possessions. However, in the mid-nineteenth century their use was fuelled by a motive of social reform and an improvement in the living conditions of the working class, and it became a central part of a new 'science of the poor' (Oakley, 2000, p. 132). Florence Nightingale was well aware of the importance of social background in interpreting health data. She collected survey data to demonstrate that childbirth deaths were higher in institutions than at home (Oakley, 2000, p. 117). However, the way such data was used raises concern. Mort's (1987) survey of the collection of data from the nineteenth and early twentieth century revealed an accumulation of 'facts' about the working class that were overlaid with moral codes leading to two central themes that represented the dangerousness of the urban poor: a link between poverty and immorality and disease, and the belief that disease spread from the dissolute to the sober and industrious. He demonstrated how objective 'facts' are overladen by moral discourses which have the purpose of controlling the sexual behaviour of certain groups.

There is no doubt that surveys have been used as a means for social control and to create social distance between middle class investigators and the socially marginalized objects of their censorial gaze – the unemployed, manual workers, prostitutes, the insane. But the survey method, in certain hands, has offered a means of exposing injustice and exploitation. Although the emphasis in the first instance was on *statistical* surveys without much detail of conditions of life, priority was shifted to the *experiences* of those surveyed, and the pioneer work of Henry Mayhew and Charles Booth in the late nineteenth century was significantly qualitative in nature. In Mayhew's words, history was being told 'from the lips of the people themselves' (1851, p. iii). In other words, the use of detailed case studies as a method in the survey, offered a vivid picture of the experiences of the human beings behind the percentages, told in their own unvarnished language (see also Chapter 6 on case study research). Nevertheless a weakness of these studies was their non-random sample, and the researchers' *assumptions* that the conditions they described pertained across the whole population of interest. Depth was insufficient without quantity. In Rowntree's (1941) surveys in York half a century later, the introduction of random sampling placed the social survey method on to a different plane, where the stories could be told on a grand scale and generalizations made with greater authority.

A major modern contribution to the building of evidence on inequality results from the surveys carried out by Peter Townsend and his colleagues over many years. His study of the links between poverty, ill-health and poor services produced the influential if controversial Black Report (Townsend and Davidson, 1988), followed quickly by another publication showing how people with ill-health were clustered in particular deprived communities (Townsend, Phillimore and Beattie, 1988).

As will be clear, survey research is a very powerful tool in persuading people of the legitimacy of particular constructions of social conditions.

Principles of social survey research

Survey research has a number of specific rules that guide its practice:
- the personal values and views of the researcher must be kept out of the research process in order to minimize personal bias and prejudice – known as objectivity
- quality in surveys depends on precise, consistent, accurate comparison in measuring concepts
- studies should be conducted in such a fashion that they can be repeated by other researchers, known as 'replication'
- research instruments or tools should measure what they are supposed to measure – known as 'validity'
- research instruments should produce consistent results regardless of the characteristics of the researcher or the context – known as 'reliability'
- sampling should be employed to ensure that findings are consistent with what appears in the target population – known as 'representativeness' (see the discussion below on statistical representativeness)
- representativeness leads to the capacity of the research to claim that its findings can be generalized to the whole population (group of interest) – known as 'generalizability' (see Sarantakos, 2005, Chapter 4 for a more detailed discussion of these principles)

Social surveys can be quantitative (questionnaires) or qualitative (interviews) or a mixture of both. However, the rules governing the approach set out above are those that apply to quantitative research more generally.

Variables

The concept of variables is central to survey research. A variable is something that can vary such as male or female, working class or middle class for example. The cause-effect relationship is such that if one variable changes, then other variables will change too. Surveys are designed around research questions concerned with identifiable variables of interest, such as gender, marital status, age, education, behaviour, attitudes, social conditions, health and so on, and the relationships among these. Each variable must relate to one concept only and has to be described in a way that makes it accessible to measurement, and research tools must be developed that are suitable for measurement. This is a complex process: the concept of 'poverty', for example, has to be translated into variables that are measurable, such as income, education, diet, housing, location, and so on, and data collected about these. Dimensions of poverty might go beyond the material to include recreation, type of work, integration into the community, and so on. A common design in survey research is cross-sectional, which involves the collection of quantitative data on at least two variables at one point in time and from a number of cases. These are used to look for patterns of association or relationships either in the group as a whole or in subgroups sharing characteristics, such as females' and males' attitudes to 'the family' for example (Lewin, 2005).

Sampling

A key technique in surveys is *sampling*. Where it is impossible or difficult to collect information about every member of the group or population of interest, a representative sample is taken – one in which the same range of attributes can be found in similar proportions. It is then possible to generalize the findings to the whole group. There are different approaches to sampling:
- *Simple random sampling* is one in which each population member has an equal chance of selection from the complete list, by 'pulling names from a hat' or assigning numbers and generating random numbers.
- *Systematic sampling* uses a sampling frame (a complete list of the population of interest, for example the census, or a school population of pupils, or all social services teams in a country), and a selection is carried out at regular intervals from the list.
- *Stratified sampling* orders the sampling frame according to one or more characteristics (for example people in different age ranges) and then selecting the same percentage of people or items from

each subgroup in order to ensure proportionate representation. This method is an attempt to ensure statistical representativeness that the selection represents the frequency with which particular groups appear in the population of interest. If 80 per cent of children in foster care in a borough were girls, then 80 per cent of the sample would be girls. If 14 per cent of the girls were aged 14–15 then a similar percentage of the girls would be in that age range.

- *Cluster sampling* can be used when the population of interest is large and widely dispersed, and involves an initial selection of subgroups such as geographical areas, or schools or hospitals, followed by a random selection.
- *Opportunity* or *convenience sampling* has easy access as the main criterion, such as selecting everyone who enters an agency looking for help.
- *Purposive sampling* involves cases which are handpicked for a specific reason, such as having received a caution from the police.
- *Snowball sampling* uses initial contacts to access other similar individuals – street workers introduce the researcher to other street workers, for instance. (see Lewin 2005 for further discussion of sampling)

There is little agreement on what is an appropriate sample size, and yet this is regarded as a crucial factor in the process. The larger the sample size the smaller the error will be in estimating the characteristics of the group, but the more expensive the survey and the analysis becomes, the less likely it is that students will be able to achieve it. Fowler (2002) suggests that major subgroups should contain at least a hundred cases and minor subgroups contain between twenty and fifty. Lewin (2005) says that in studies which aim to examine relationships between particular characteristics (e.g. smoking and health) there should be at least thirty participants. Harvey and Macdonald (1993, p. 121) identify their own list of sampling techniques, separate them into 'random' and 'non-random' and offer a quick guide to the advantages and disadvantages of each (as shown in Table 10.1).

Random samples are more representative than non-random, but finding a complete sampling frame or the resources needed does pose questions. Perhaps the best that one can do, especially in small-scale studies, is to attempt a sample that is as representative as possible, and to be aware of and be open about its limitations.

Questionnaires

Questionnaires help to structure the data collected in ways that make findings accessible to descriptive or statistical analysis. These

Table 10.1 Sampling techniques

Type	Advantages	Disadvantages
Random		
Simple	Gives a true random sample	Needs complete sampling frame Selection is time-consuming
Systematic	Quick to select sample	Needs complete sampling frame Widely dispersed sample
Cluster	Concentrated sample	May not be truly random Cluster only needs frame
Multi-stage	Random selection of concentrated sample Complete sampling frame for selected areas only	May not be truly random Frame needed at each stage
Stratified	Variables match population	Needs knowledge of strata
Area	Useful when no sampling frame	Not truly random
Non-random		
Convenience	No selection procedure	Not representative
Volunteer	Avoids selection problems	Not representative
Snowball	Useful to build sample	Not representative
Quota	Representative, no need for frame	Representative quotas need construction. Not random

Source: L Harvey and M MacDonald, *Doing Sociology: A practical introduction*, 1993.
Reproduced by permission of Palgrave Macmillan.

questionnaires can be self-completed or administered by an interviewer. They may be completed anonymously or the respondents may be identified. Questions are usually highly structured and the majority are closed (i.e. they require a short answer such as yes/no or a number or a time frequency, for example) because they are quick for respondents to answer and easy to analyse. They should be simple, clear and unambiguous, should not be 'leading' and should be asked one at a time (as opposed to 'either/or' type questions). Measurements such as the Likert attitude scales are sometimes used in surveys, asking respondents to place themselves on a scale of responses according to the extent to which they agree or disagree with a statement made. All these techniques make analysis of questionnaires more straightforward than if questions are left open (for example 'please give your opinion of . . .'). Surveys sometimes use means of communication other than words, such as for example the pictures used by Pitcairn (1994) when surveying people with learning disabilities, or face scales, which ask respondents to choose depicted emotions that indicate their response. Most texts recommend rehearsing (piloting) questionnaires on a small scale to identify questions that need clarification or are unsuitable or are positioned inappropriately. There are several good introductory guides available on questionnaire design, including David and Sutton (2004), Gomm (2004) and Somekh and Lewin (2005).

Exploring data using statistics

Most people are familiar with graphical representation and tables presented in easy-to-understand ways that are offered as analytical tools. Graphs and charts can often highlight patterns to vivid and dramatic effect. Statistical analysis of small-scale studies can be done by hand, but there is also a wide range of statistical tests that can be applied to survey data with the assistance of computers, and social scientists use (amongst others) a program known as SPSS (Statistical Package for the Social Sciences), of which there are several versions. Sarantakos (2005, Chapter 14) sets out the steps of quantitative analysis:

- Data preparation. Checking, editing and coding
- Data entry. Entering the data on a computer
- Graphic presentation. For example, presenting the findings in the form of graphs or tables
- Data processing and analysis. Conducting statistical analysis
- Interpretation of the findings. Explaining the meaning of data individually
- Conclusions. Proposing direct answers to the research question

The use of tools such as SPSS does not require researchers to understand the mathematical principles underpinning statistical tests, although in evaluating such research this can be a valuable tool. Authors such as Schutt (1996, Appendix 3) offers a step-by-step guide to understanding and using statistical packages. Harvey and Macdonald (1993, Appendix 2) as well as a number of other authors, give guidance for coding, and offer simple advice about the construction of frequency tables for each variable. Computer analysis can give data about the relationships between variables and the statistical significance of survey results. Statistically testing the results of surveys asks the question:

> are the differences between groups in the survey of such a size that they might be attributed to the chancy business of selecting samples . . . rather than reflecting real differences between groups in the population? (Gomm, 2004, p. 90)

Conventionally, statisticians regard any results which might occur by chance more often than five times in a hundred (the so-called *five per cent level*) as statistically non-significant, meaning that whatever

Table 10.2 Frequency distribution of gender and job status

Gender	Managerial	Team leader	Basic grade
Female (28)	3	5	20
Male (12)	7	3	2
Total (40)	10	8	22

caused the results to be as they are, it is safest to regard them as a result of chance. It is important to recognize that explanations of statistical tests raise complex questions. Identifying statistical significance does not tell us much about causal relationships – whether results are accidental or whether they are the result of fundamental dissimilarities, or researcher or sample bias or of the attitudes to the survey of those studied.

Many undergraduate students are likely to be using descriptive statistics, indicating the frequency of all categories, such as, for example, 'only 10 per cent of the young men said they used drugs more than twice a week'. Of course, the use of percentages assumes substantial sample numbers – if in the example above the sample is, say, 20 people, it is more meaningful to give the number of young men (2) as at this level percentages risk distorting the picture being drawn. The frequency distribution of two such variables (e.g. gender and job status) can be cross-tabulated into a bar chart or two-dimensional table, as shown in Table 10.2.

The table shows that of 40 members of staff in an organization, 70 per cent are female and 30 per cent male. However only 7.5 per cent of managers are women as compared with 17.5 per cent of men. This begs the question as to the relationship between the variables gender and job status. Does one 'cause' the other? If so, in what ways and what are the consequences? Similar issues in interpretation arise as in the use of statistical significance tests.

Examples of surveys in social work and social care

There are a number of examples of the use of surveys in social work, sometimes used in conjunction with qualitative approaches. Social work researchers in the USA, generally more oriented to clinical approaches than social workers in the UK, and more espoused to quantitative methods, offer some examples of surveys in Kirk's (1999) edited volume (which, although it advertises itself as a generic research text is almost entirely devoted to methods concerned with measurement of change).

Social supports in retirement

Potts, for example, surveyed senior citizens living in a retirement community consisting of 8,500 people, with a view to providing information that would allow social workers to offer appropriate services (Potts, 1999). Her sample (400, reduced to 99 in the final sample) underwent a number of measurements for quantity and quality of social supports, depression and physical health, in an attempt to examine the links between social support and health in older adults. Answers to a questionnaire were scored and analysed statistically along a number of indices. The main conclusion was the importance of distinguishing among different types of friends, classified by Potts as 'close', 'casual', 'club' and 'helpers' (p. 207). The study recommended that assessment should take account of the importance of friends living outside the community, the individual's capacity for intimacy, environmental barriers to self-disclosure and the possibility of support groups. These observations are in themselves useful, if fairly mundane, but a number of observations can be made, both theoretical and methodological. Because the study did not take account of the significance and social uses of discourses on ageing, the emphasis is almost entirely on a passive dependence on 'visitors'. There is no consideration of their unequal economic and social status, of how this is resisted, of the politics of age-segregated living as a model of housing, of whether older people feel in control of their lives, of their own activities of offering friendship to others, or of whether factors such as involvement in equality movements or other activism make a difference to their sense of well-being. The model of ageing that has informed the study is the dominant one of undifferentiated dependence, incapable of opening up other possibilities. This does the research subjects a disservice.

In terms of methodology, the study identifies a number of limitations. Because the sample was from one geographic location, the findings may not be generalizable (and no mention is made of the relative affluence of this group in respect of other groups). The sample finally achieved is tiny (the author of the chapter claims 46.2 per cent, but in fact it is under 25 per cent of the original random sample). Also, the design was cross-sectional, so that causal relationships could not be made (e.g. depression may impact on social supports rather than the opposite). The chosen quality scales were unreliable regarding proximity of support, and there was no consideration of the influence on well-being of ordinary everyday concrete tasks such as practical assistance or personal care. The possible significance of ethnic and cultural diversity or of experiences of racism were not considered, and gender was limited to a comment about the greater number of women than men in the study. Sexuality, mobility and disability were also absent. The result of all this is a use of the survey method that is both ideologically and practically restricted to a 'welfare' model of social care, designed to make clients 'comfortable'. It takes no account of their own view of their social needs (their responses were tabulated and measured within structured external frameworks) and ignores the structural and institutional context in which they live.

Carers of people living with AIDS

In contrast to the study described above, another US survey of Latina AIDS caregivers, although it did not address structural and institutional factors, showed sensitivity to culture, gender and socio-economic status as factors affecting reaching and maintaining a sample, survey procedures and issues in measurement (Land and Hudson, 1999). The study was designed to examine stress factors and coping mechanisms, the role of informal and formal services, especially their cultural sensitivity, and how socio-demographic background variables related to respondent stress. Methods centred on structured questionnaires and standardized instruments to measure variables, as well as in-depth interviews and open-ended questions. The discussion considered a range of methodological concerns in cross-cultural research, such as the difficulties entailed in obtaining a sample – a lack of trust among Latino populations generally, the stigma of AIDS, immigration status, the sensitive topic of sexual behaviour and the fear of exposure to neighbours and family members. The authors of the study also confronted the problem of cultural bias on the part of the designers of the research, and the appropriateness of many standardized scales of measurement. For example, those that tap culturally based behaviour, such as dimensions of coping or role definitions, are not designed for use with minority ethnic populations or cross-cultural research, and content tapping spirituality is lacking from most instruments. The researchers were particularly critical of the widespread use of the Likert-type scale, and the 'noted inability of varying cultural groups to reliably respond to its format' (p. 469). All of these factors can seriously distort findings, and since instruments play a prominent role in the diagnosis of dysfunction and the construction of knowledge about populations, attention to their appropriateness or otherwise is required.

In the UK, a number of social surveys have contributed to a deepening of understanding in a number of areas. Kelly and Regan's work on sexual abuse, for example, has exposed the range and the

consistencies of male abuse of children, taking the issue beyond individualistic and psychology-based explanations (Kelly, Regan and
Burton, 1995).

Child protection and ethnicity

Williams and Soydan (2005) report on a cross-national survey of
social workers' responses to issues of ethnicity in child protection
work. The respondents were social workers in the child and adolescent care and protection services in urban areas in Sweden, Denmark,
Germany and the UK, just over seven hundred in total. Responses
were obtained partly through mailed questionnaires and partly
through independent completion of the questionnaire at given
venues. The authors acknowledged the problems of cross-cultural
surveys, particularly the difficulties in standardizing questionnaires
across different legislation, administrative structures and practices.
They also recognized that linguistic subtleties and cultural understandings can result in different interpretations of material, including
the notion of 'ethnicity'. From a methodological perspective, the
survey incorporated a vignette into the questionnaire, and requested
responses to questions about the vignette. Half of those surveyed
received a vignette where the name of the child was common within
the particular country; the others received a vignette (a brief résumé
of a case study) where the child's name was recognizably Muslim.
The analysis of the quantitative data found that there were some differences in responses across national boundaries, but the most strik-
ing overall feature of the responses to the messages of the vignette
was that respondents in the study reacted in similar ways irrespective
of the background of the family. The report authors assert therefore
that the social workers were operating with a 'colour-blind' approach
in the procedures they followed.

This research concluded that the social workers' orientation was
towards reliance on professionalism and towards individualistic and
behavioural explanations over social structural considerations: 'this
leads them towards cultural/individual deficit models over a consideration of wider issues such as poverty, inequality, housing conditions, support networks, the effects of displacement and torture or
racism within their explanatory frame' (p. 915). Given the level of
discretion that individual social workers still have, it is useful to elicit
views as to what individuals would like to think they would do, to
expose the assumptions that operate at a face-to-face level and to
reveal the neglect of training on 'race' and ethnicity in social work.
There is a risk however that by offering a vignette and asking individual social workers to respond to it, the focus is diverted from policy

injunctions, bureaucratic procedures, managerial directives and the other institutional trappings that have been set up to deal with child abuse. The authors of the study do ask the question, 'Does an over-reliance on cultural explanations distract from significant structural factors such as poverty, unemployment, marginalization and exclusion?' (p. 917). They might themselves have included a section in the questionnaire about the influence of structural factors and about whether acknowledgement of these would have made any difference to recommendations for dealing with the case study.

Mothers and physical abuse

Vic Tuck's research on mothers who physically abuse or neglect their children argued explicitly for more emphasis on the socio-economic context in which parenting is performed, and the possible consequences of this for children (Tuck, 1995, 2000). As a practitioner, he was concerned about the presence of complex interconnections between poverty and abuse, and he undertook a survey of mothers in a neighbourhood characterized by social disadvantage and high rates of child protection referrals to the local social services department. The sample was representative of (reported) families where the mother was identified as the perpetrator of abuse. The research model was a conventional survey with a 'cause and effect' orientation – that is, the researcher set out to explore the role of material deprivation in 'causing' child abuse. As a result of the study, Tuck developed a multi-layered, multi-dimensional model to examine links among practical resources available to the women, their social relationships and neighbourhood support networks. The model was careful not to minimize the importance of the personal characteristics and backgrounds of mothers, but it was argued that harm to children is powerfully linked to 'deficits' in material resources available to families and complex interacting psychological stress factors.

Tuck's study had drawbacks. It did not consider the racial, religious and cultural backgrounds of the participants, nor did it specifically examine disability as a significant factor. However, his conclusions have important messages for how social work might respond, the key one being the importance of intervention strategies which have as their major focus the needs of 'vulnerable' populations of children and families rather than attempting exclusively to identify individual families where harm to children might be occurring. This is a progressive argument for movement beyond the confines of 'individual risk assessment' and its pathologizing potential, towards community-wide approaches that have a sharper child-welfare focus, based on comprehensive and co-ordinated family welfare services rather than knee-jerk responses to crises. This would mean building on community strengths and resources and working with the definitions of need and the aspirations they find there. Tuck insists that a refocusing of provision to recognize the daily realities of life for the families when social work is meant to assist may open up fresh prospects for welfare.

Decision-making in social work

A recently reported survey examined the extent to which disabled children participate in decision-making in social services departments (SSDs) in England (Franklin and Sloper, 2006). The researchers contacted all 150 SSDs asking if participation of children was taking place or had taken place in the previous 12 months. Questionnaires were sent to the 102 who responded saying that they had involved disabled children. In designing the questionnaire, one of the methodological problems the researchers had to tackle was the meaning of the concept 'participation' and how it might be operationalized. They describe a number of typologies of participation that have been used by other authors and in the end categorized the questions around the following themes: the nature of participation; the characteristics of children involved; characteristics of the participation activity; methods of involvement; support for children, young people and staff; and outcomes and lessons learnt. The article the researchers wrote does not reflect critically on this categorization, but one wonders whether further stages of refinement would have been appropriate. However, they were able to report that of the 71 authorities that responded (incidentally just under 50 per cent of all English authorities and around 70 per cent of those who said they did involve children), 57 reported the involvement of children in at least one of the categories identified. The most likely areas of involvement were in decisions about the children's own care, and the least likely were within child protection conferences or their own health plans.

The survey was an attempt to achieve a 100 per cent sample, which would have made the study completely representative. The non-response of 48 SSDs cannot necessarily be interpreted as their not involving disabled children. At the same time, it would have been relevant and interesting for some information to be elicited from the 27 authorities who confirmed that they did not involve children in decision-making.

The presentation of statistics which the authors offer is descriptive on topics such as the kinds of initiatives in which children participated, the ages and disability labels of the children, the range of partner agencies involved and the resulting changes in services.

There are a number of limitations of the survey, some of which are acknowledged by the authors, and most of which are also limitations of surveys generally. What the survey produced can only be seen as a snapshot of a moment in time, and cannot produce depth and meaning of the activities to the actors involved. The definition of 'participation' is unclear, raising questions about the reliability of the research instruments. Moreover, the information provided is from SSDs only, who, it might be argued, have an interest in projecting a positive picture of the involvement of disabled children, given government policies to encourage this engagement. This raises questions about validity. The authors say they intend to follow up with interviews with the children to gain their perspectives, an important development for the study. In the survey stage the children are treated as an homogeneous group, with no indication of the part played by gender, culture, ethnicity or a variety of disabling barriers – dimensions that are crucial to understanding how experience is shaped by these factors. However, initial information was collected by the survey method, providing pointers for designing the next phase of the study which will use a qualitative approach to examine children's views of participation, the supports and resources made available for this to take place, and the extent to which they think they have made a difference to services and gained some control over their lives.

Drawbacks of social surveys

Some of the drawbacks of survey research are similar to those of other quantitative approaches such as experimental ways of knowing as discussed in Chapter 3. There are huge problems in seeking to identify cause and effect where human beings are concerned, because they are reflective and self-conscious creatures, and therefore able to change the way they behave. The emphasis on objectivity tends to lose sight of the theory- and value-laden character of all research, and the interpretation and meaning of findings is determined to a large extent by these aspects. The power and ubiquity of survey methods is such that the statistics produced are often accepted uncritically. Yet many factors affect respondents' answers, and answers hinge on the exact form a question takes. Typically there is no opportunity for clarification and discussion of answers. A basic objection to quantitative measurement is that it treats facts as unproblematically given in the world. These result from categories that are the outcome of implicit theories about social life and social relationships – aspects that are obscured by claims to scientific rigour. This is not to say that survey research should be rejected wholesale. It is the claim to neutrality and objectivity that is at issue. Concepts used in measurement do not arise 'out of the blue', but are the consequences of what questions are asked about the social world. Levitas and Guy (1996) give government statistics as an example of these problems. They examined a number of sets of official statistics drawn from surveys, using a number of questions through which they evaluated the reports considered. These questions concerned any suppression or manipulation of data and the ways in which this might be offset by new data sets; the treatment of divisions such as class, gender and ethnicity; what is revealed about increasing or decreasing inequality; what we might conclude from the data, and what it does *not* tell us? (Levitas and Guy, 1996, p. 4).

These authors raise questions about how concepts such as 'employment', 'unemployment', 'gender' 'class' and 'ethnicity' are defined and how these definitions often distorted or made invisible the realities of living in Britain. The main conclusion of their work is that the definitions used in official statistics still produce measures which embody the interests of the state rather than of citizens. They warn that it is only with the utmost care that such data can be interpreted for democratic purposes.

There are other methodological concerns about surveys. The design is generally top down and therefore contains items of interest to the researcher (as with official statistics), which may not be seen as of relevance by the respondent. Sampling has to be carefully constructed if representativeness is to be achieved and validity maintained. Errors can occur if, for example, the sampling frame is incomplete or questions are badly worded and may be interpreted in different ways by different respondents, thus affecting reliability, or if responses are recorded incorrectly. Even careful sampling can be compromised by non-response (claims to representativeness lose credibility with a very small response rate, for example). Moreover, as we have seen, surveys tend to identify surface characteristics and are seldom capable of examining meanings in any depth. Key questions for consumers of survey research should be how selection of participants was achieved, whether they reflect the characteristics of a larger group, how many of those sampled actually took part in the study, and whether the results are valid in that they report faithfully the intentions of the respondents.

Conclusion: social surveys and social justice

There is a widespread belief, held both by the scientific research community and the public at large, that survey research is the most rigorous and scientifically sound method to achieve objectivity.

Governmental bodies frequently employ surveys to cast light on and provide answers to social problems. Researchers concerned about the scope of poverty, racism and sexism have found the survey method and other statistically based forms of research to be very suitable for their purposes. One of the most powerful aspects of these approaches is that they can put a problem on the map by showing that it is more widespread than was previously thought, because their techniques gather large quantities of numerical data that can generalize to large populations. Survey methods have been used very effectively to show that the problems that particular groups experience are not simply idiosyncratic but are indicative of widespread patterns of oppression.

The statistics produced by surveys are powerful because they are concise, and therefore easily communicated to policy makers and to the general public. They are easy to remember and comprehend (though can also be misleading). Their results can be presented in pictorial form to people who are illiterate or have little understanding of numbers (Reinharz, 1992). Survey materials can be made available for secondary analysis and critique, and alternative interpretations offered – a capacity that is much less possible in qualitative research.

One enormous advantage of representative social surveys is the capacity they offer to the researcher to generalize the findings – they can put a problem on the map by showing that it has its origins in structural causes rather than in individual inadequacy. As Oakley says of the later poverty surveys:

> what was essential here was that the poverty surveys not only yielded evidence of the *extent* of poverty, but revealed its structural regularities – its links with unemployment, wage rates and poor housing – thereby demonstrating that poverty was socially determined rather than, as some eugenists would have it, flowing from some incurable biological defect.
> (Oakley, 2000, p. 134)

Social survey research has made and continues to make an enormous contribution to social work as a way of setting practice in the context of injustice. The challenge of survey research in social work is, on the one hand, to conduct research that meets the standards of mainstream social sciences – validity, reliability, objectivity, replicability – and, on the other, to confront the rigid dichotomies between researcher and researched, and resist the process of depoliticizing research. Researchers with a concern for social justice do not resolve the contradictions between their training in both social sciences and social movements, but they do try to confront and work with the challenges this brings. The principle is always that social justice is a perspective (or a number of perspectives) not a method, and that therefore a pluralism of methods may be drawn in to its support.

We have examined a number of survey approaches in social work, some of which seem to have no such perspective underpinning them. Others show a concern with social justice but stop short of delivering relevant data. What is missing is an imaginative opening up to ways in which the questions can be explored, coupled with an ongoing critique of the methods to hand. At the same time, we have to be concerned with how we understand and use statistics resulting from surveys carried out by official sources, and keep in mind the possibility that statistics are ever vulnerable to political manipulation and interference.

main points

- Social survey research is probably the most common research approach used in social work
- Social surveys can be of people, organizations, communities or other topics such as journal articles
- The approach allows economic study of large populations through the process of sampling
- Sampling can take a number of forms
- Surveys produce concise and easily communicated statistics
- Surveys provide a platform for claiming representativeness
- Surveys are a snapshot picture rather than an in-depth examination
- Surveys can use quantitative or qualitative methods
- The exact form questions take can determine the answer given
- The design of surveys is generally 'top-down'

stop and think

- What do you think are the advantages of social surveys? Make a list.
- What is a sampling frame? Think of a topic you would be interested to study, and identify where you might locate a sampling frame.
- What is the purpose of sampling?
- What is the purpose of a pilot study?
- In what different ways might you present *descriptive* statistics?

- De Vaus, D A *Surveys in Social Research*, 4th edn (London: Routledge, 1995)
  A detailed guide for designing social survey research.
- Diamond, I and Jefferies, J *Beginning Statistics: an introduction for social scientists* (London: Sage, 2001)
  Straightforward instructions for conducting a range of different types of statistical analysis.
- Sheppard, M *Social Research in the Human Sciences* (London, Jessica Kingsley Publishers, 2004), especially Chapter 5
  This is basic text for social workers and health workers. It takes readers through the rudiments of a number of methods. Chapter 5 is good on statistical analysis.
- Somekh, B and Lewin, C (eds) *Research Methods in the Social Sciences* (London: Sage, 2005), Chapter 25
  A useful and concise chapter on social surveys.

11 Evaluation research

Introduction

Evaluation in social work is as popular as 'evidence-based practice' and 'research-mindedness', and is required increasingly in all the work of social care. This is part of a global call for value for money in an ever-changing world. Evaluation in the twenty-first century is receiving close attention internationally, and rapidly moving global conditions have introduced different actors into the evaluation arena. Chelimsky and Shadish (1997) brought together a collection of papers discussing different perspectives, methods and uses of evaluation across the world, leading them to characterize its purposes as threefold:

- evaluation for accountability (e.g. the measurement of results or efficiency);
- evaluation for development (e.g. the provision of evaluative help to strengthen institutions);
- evaluation for knowledge (e.g. the acquisition of a more profound understanding in some specific area or field. (p. 10)

Each of these three purposes takes on more or less significance according to the setting, the motivation of stakeholders and the political climate in which it takes place. Evaluation in social work meets all three of these characteristics and has become an essential feature of practice, given the external pressure on programmes to be accountable and to produce evidence of effectiveness and value for money, and the internal urge to boost confidence in the profession by demonstrating and publicizing its successes. The principle of evaluation is now enshrined in legislation covering social care, children's services, health, education and all other public services activities. As highlighted in Chapter 1, all activities have been opened up to review, appraisal, audit quality assurance, audit rating – the monitoring and evaluation process touches all. Lishman (1998) gives a number of reasons why evaluation skills should be an integral dimension of practice:

> Evaluation examines our effectiveness and can help us improve it, can increase our accountability to users and clients, develops our knowledge and identifies gaps in knowledge, and helps us develop new models of practice and service delivery. (p. 101)

Lishman's list covers two main areas – the evaluation and improvement of individual professional performance, and the appropriateness of services offered by an agency. This suggests models of practice along the lines of Everitt et al.'s (1992) 'research-minded' practitioner-evaluator, or Fuller and Petch's (1995) 'practitioner-researcher'. It might also suggest the external 'expert-evaluator' who remains distant from the action. Here the practitioner's role is limited to providing data.

There are different approaches to evaluation and a variety of views as to whether evaluation is research or whether it is a different animal altogether. Patton (1997) argues that programme evaluation differs fundamentally from research in its purpose for data collection. He says, 'research aims to produce knowledge and truth. Useful evaluation supports action' (p. 24). This betrays a narrow view of research within a realist paradigm, but Patton's point about evaluation is well made in terms of its pragmatic goal to inform decisions, clarify options and identify improvements that might be made in an intervention.

Evaluation is unequivocally value-laden and political because it sets out to make judgements about the worth or merit of a programme, innovation, project, service or practice. It is primarily interested in identifying problem areas, seeking relevant solutions and producing direct answers. To do this it requires criteria as to what is 'good', 'successful', 'effective', and so on, all of which can be defined in different ways and are thus open to a range of understandings. There are no methods that are specifically associated with evaluation research, and it uses the range of approaches that are considered in this text and in other books on research methods. Nevertheless there is evidence of frustration among social workers about the ability of traditional quantitative methods to engage with complexity, individuality and meaning (Felton 2005). Beyond this, it has also been pointed out by Shaw (1998) that social work evaluation has failed to address questions of social justice in its concern with 'effectiveness'. This dimension needs to be part of any appraisal of evaluation approaches.

Origins of evaluation research

Evaluation came to prominence in the USA in the 1960s, when it was used by government to monitor budgets and management processes, and was followed by a variety of models in European countries, culminating in its extensive use as a tool for controlling budgets in the European Union. In UK social work, as observed by Shaw (1996), evaluation has become a key instrument in the languages of 'cost-effectiveness, service user satisfaction, empowerment, management by effectiveness, quality, service contracts, partnership, staff supervision, financial decentralization and targeted measurement' (p. 19). Its early manifestations concentrated on experimental research designs (see Chapter 3), moving to models that shifted the focus from a knowledge-driven to a use-led approach (Weiss, 1987), or what Patton (1997) calls 'utilization-focused' evaluation. These models are all located in a realist paradigm. As might be expected, other authors hold radically different views of evaluation, such as Guba and Lincoln's (1989) 'fourth generation evaluation', within a constructivist paradigm. Pawson and Tilley (1997) comment that this more naturalistic approach brought a valuable corrective to perspectives that were obsessed with behavioural outcomes. However, it is interesting to note the revival of experimental design for evaluation (discussed in Chapter 1) and the re-emphasis on individual behaviour and on 'what works', given that this is the same language as used in the 1960s, which then fell out of favour because it 'failed to deliver the goods in terms of cumulative, productive findings' (Robson, 2000, p. 29).

Principles of evaluation research

At one level, evaluation concerns the comparison of an object of interest against a standard of acceptability (Green and Kreuter, 1991), and Rootman et al. (2006, p. 26) suggest that evaluation is the 'systematic examination and assessment of features of a programme or other intervention in order to produce knowledge that different stakeholders can use for a variety of purposes'. Patton (1997) says

> Program evaluation is the systematic collection of information about the activities, characteristics and outcomes of programs to make judgements about the program, improve program effectiveness and/or inform decisions about future programming. (p. 23)

The definition offered by Weiss (1998) offers what is probably the most comprehensive:

> Evaluation is the *systematic assessment* of the *operation* and/or the *outcomes* of a program or policy, compared to a set of

> *explicit* or *implicit standards,* as a means of contributing to the
> *improvement* of the program or policy. (p. 4, emphasis original)

This contains all the ingredients that are important to examine in any discussion of evaluation research, and will be addressed here as the chapter progresses.

There are numerous definitions such as these in the literature on evaluation, and there is wide consideration of the purposes, the goals and the types pf evaluation, but few address the principles that should govern it. An exception to this is a report of the World Health Organization (WHO), which set out guidelines for the evaluation of health promotion projects. The four core features of evaluation should be:

- *participation* and involvement of all those with a legitimate interest in the initiative
- a *variety of disciplines* involved in the evaluation, along with a broad range of information-gathering procedures
- *capacity-building* of individuals, communities and organizations should be a feature of evaluation
- *appropriate* evaluation, designed to accommodate complex interventions and their long-term impact (Rootman et al., 2006, pp. 4–5)

One of the important aspects of the WHO report is its broad view of what constitutes evidence for evaluation. Indeed it suggests that 'the use of randomized control trials to evaluate initiatives is inappropriate, misleading and unnecessarily expensive in some cases' (p. 6). This opens up the way for more imaginative quantitative approaches and for qualitative approaches.

In social work Shaw and Shaw (1997) have also attempted to draw together principles to inform evaluation practice. Based on their research with social workers, they argue that an informed evaluation of practice cannot afford to ignore the existing realities of practice: 'we need to work from the bottom up, grounding our model of evaluating in practitioners' own accounts, rather than superimposing an ideal model from the top down which will necessarily lack meaning in the context of everyday social work practice' (p. 862). The five dimensions they offer are geared to practitioners evaluating their own practice. I have adapted them for application to a more general approach to evaluation:

- Evaluation must start from the knowledge of practitioners. Much of what informs practice is unspoken and unarticulated. Actions are full of meanings that are not readily available. The effort for evaluation is to learn how to facilitate practitioners to talk about things that are seldom expressed.

- There is a need for a cultivation of reflexive evaluation – the ability to examine what one is saying at the same time as saying it. This entails the evaluator helping practitioners to 'bend back' on action to recognize the knowledge that informs it.
- Evaluation will rest on plausible and falsifiable evidence – it is plausible if it makes sense of all the available information in a coherent manner, while remaining open to the possibility of new forms of interpretation.
- Evaluating will be for and with the service user – 'for' as to its purpose and 'with' as to its process. Service user knowledge, intentions and motives are all crucial to understanding why an intervention works or does not work. Service users are not passive objects to whom things are done, their co-operation and their choice are what make the difference between success and failure. The chances of co-operation are enhanced if service users are active participants in the process.
- The methodology of evaluation will have at its core qualitative research methods 'translated' for practice. Here Shaw and Shaw argue that qualitative methods have major implications for evaluating the *process* of intervention, thus shifting the focus from *outcomes* (see below for a discussion of process and outcome evaluation). The suggestion is that process deserves much greater attention, and potentially holds answers to the 'how' and 'why' questions that elude quantitative methods.

The Shaw and Shaw approach is food for thought to take us beyond a view of social work (and other health and welfare professions) as technically driven, bureaucratic occupations, and recognizes that ideas, values, motivations and beliefs about individuals and society inform the actions of both them and their clients. Any evaluation approaches that do not or cannot take account of these can neither touch the complexity of human interaction towards change, nor can they address questions of morality and social justice that still remain at the heart of intervention in people's lives.

Some of the key features of evaluation research that make it distinctive are:

- it is applied – it deals with real-life situations that require attention;
- it is practical – it is concerned with the detail of specific practices;
- it is action-oriented – it looks for immediate solutions;
- it is political – it is linked to policy and political decisions.

These are all factors that will appeal to both practitioners and policy makers who look for quick answers to pressing questions (although policy makers do not always take account of the results of evaluation, as discussed by Humphries, 2004b).

Doing an evaluation

Facing the possibility of conducting an evaluation can be a daunting task, and the first step is to get one's bearings in terms of the parameters or boundaries of the task. It is unlikely that any evaluation will answer all the possible questions one could ask, and in negotiation with stakeholders the priorities can be identified. Shadish et al. (1991) set out five fundamental elements of evaluation that the evaluators will need to establish at an early stage. According to them, an evaluation:

1. is usually based on defining the object of inquiry;
2. should define the range of acceptable standards;
3. should reflect the evaluator's thinking about the conditions necessary to produce knowledge (what counts as evidence and what is it to be compared with?);
4. usually reflects how evaluation information can be used and the objectives it helps to pursue;
5. should identify the approaches and practices evaluators follow.

These underline the importance of being clear about what actually is to be studied, the objectives of the evaluation; having a sense of what standard is acceptable as a measurement of effectiveness; what kinds of knowledge are relevant and what methods are appropriate to access it; how the evaluation will be used; being clear about the nature of the relationship between evaluators and the programmes evaluated. Evaluations are normative in that they start from a sense of what programmes *should* have achieved, and they set out to measure whether indeed the standard has been achieved. Pawson and Tilley (1997) are explicit about the political implications of this: 'here lies the great promise of evaluation: it purports to offer the universal means with which to measure "worth" and "value". Evaluation, in short, confers the power to justify decisions' (p. xii). Shaw (1996, p. 184) adds another political dimension to this, asserting that 'it must be a means of empowerment and social change'. This position is uncontroversial in practice and policy debates, and is incorporated into official discourses about health, social care and education. Evaluation is therefore a political activity designed to aid the allocation of resources, and the decisions made in relation to the points above exclude some questions in favour of others. In determining how things should be, the question arises as to whose objectives are being served and to what political ends.

Stakeholders

This leads to the issue of the range of groups who might have an interest in evaluation, and the extent to which they are affected by or can affect the evaluation. Robson (2000, p. 16) offers a list of the key players:

- *Policy makers*, who are responsible for taking decisions about the setting up, continuation, closure or expansion of programmes or services. They are only likely to take account of any evaluation if they consider that it focuses on issues they feel are important.
- *Sponsors*, who fund and may help to set up a programme or service. Their involvement in the evaluation can vary from a 'hands-off' approach to determining how the evaluation should be carried out.
- *Management*, responsible for managing the programme. Involving management and taking note of their interests is important for issues of access to relevant data and towards effective implementation of any recommendations.
- *Staff or practitioners*, responsible for carrying out the programme or running the service. They may be anxious about the implications of any evaluation for them.
- *Clients or participants*, often those with most at stake. Their voice often goes unheard, but their involvement may be crucial. They may also be represented by relevant organizations.
- *Evaluators*, who have an interest in carrying out a good-quality evaluation. This can only happen when all other stakeholders are actively involved. They all need to be taken along to facilitate co-operation and utilization of the results.
- *Interested others*, such as neighbours to a project, or those associated with another similar project, for example, might be significant.

Robson points out that the evaluator has a responsibility to all of these groups, since people are more likely to accept and use information and to implement changes when they both have a stake in and are personally involved in the decision-making processes.

Formative and summative evaluation

Evaluation may be formative or summative, and it may focus on *outcomes* or on *process*. These need some explanation. Formative evaluation is concerned with the project in process, and has an objective of identifying how it might be improved. Summative evaluation examines its previous performance and makes a judgement as to its worth. Sarantakos (2005) sums this up by saying that formative evaluation asks, ' "What can be done to make this programme work?"; summative evaluation asks, "Is the programme good enough to continue?" ' (p. 324). The differences he sets out between formative and summative evaluation are shown in Table 11.1.

The concept of formative and summative evaluation suggests a model of research loosely (or not so loosely) based on experimental

Table 11.1 Formative and summative evaluation: a comparison

Formative evaluation	Summative evaluation
1. Asks: how can the program be improved?	1. Asks: should the programme be continued or terminated?
2. Is done by participants, managers and other interested people	2. Is done by policy planners and/or fund providers
3. Involves both process and outcome evaluation	3. Involves both process and outcome evaluation
4. Offers feedback aimed at improving the program	4. Assesses overall effectiveness of the program in question
5. Uses quantitative and/or qualitative methods	5. Uses quantitative methods and produces data that facilitate detailed assessment
6. Researchers are involved, interactive and compassionate	6. Researchers are passive, independent, uninvolved

Source: S Sarantakos, *Social Research*, 2005, 3rd edn. Reproduced with permission of Palgrave Macmillan.

methods, discussed in Chapter 3. Further, the separation of these two forms of evaluation is a rather false division, since it is always desirable to have information about how to improve a programme or service. These concepts are convenient for evaluators in deciding where to focus their interest, and have nothing to do with the programme itself. Their usefulness is in helping to delineate the boundaries of the evaluation.

Outcome and process evaluation

Like formative and summative evaluation, in some ways discussion of outcome and process evaluation is another false division, since the two are intertwined. *Outcome* evaluation refers to effectiveness – did the after-school club succeed in improving school attendance? This is a cause-effect model (measure the variable in which one is interested before the administration of 'treatment' and again afterwards in an attempt to gauge the cause of any change), where the criterion for measurement would be attendance at school before and after the project. Outcome evaluation tends to be based on quantitative methods, and experimental styles of investigation are widely used in social work and social care. The question that arises here is the same as in other similar research with human beings – how can we be sure that the after-school club was the cause of any change in attendance? And if the programme does 'work', will it transfer to other settings? Pawson and Tilley (1997) comment that programmes work for some people in some circumstances and not for others. There may be outcomes that deviate from the intended objectives, such as the lads in the after-school project getting together as a soccer team (and doing that instead of attending school!). It is difficult to account for unintended outcomes in this type of outcome study, and it is unlikely to be feasible in small-scale research. Nevertheless, variations on the experiment are used on a daily, informal basis. In higher education, for instance, examinations and essays are taken as outcome evidence as to whether teaching has been effective. The basis of outcome evaluation is the extent to which the programme being evaluated has clear objectives in the first place, and the methods used to evaluate this are appropriate to these objectives (an outcome of a programme for men who are violent towards their partners would be a reduction in violent incidents). In some cases, getting reliable evidence is still problematic.

To answer the question of when might you use an experimental design, Robson lists a number of methodological reasons, but his most telling one is 'if your sponsor and/or other audiences you wish to influence, are positively inclined to experimental approaches and the quantitative statistical findings they generate' (2000, p. 60). Outcome evaluation is therefore the most likely choice in what Robson calls *stakeholder* evaluation, where the sponsors have paid for it, and management and staff are judged by the success or failure of a programme. Those who are targeted in the programme may have been coerced or may have volunteered for it, and these conditions may affect their motivation to succeed in it. Their role in determining its objectives and its content, and perhaps the interests they are able to invest in it, will be less to the fore than those of the major stakeholders. This raises questions of ethics and power, and the extent to which any user-led approach is possible within such an evaluation approach.

Process evaluation is employed when the actual running of the programme is the focus of interest. The question here is whether the initiative is 'on target' to meet the objectives, is doing what was intended, and what might be done to keep it on track. This may be the main research interest, but the description is a rather static one. In effect, process evaluation has an interest in the dynamic interaction among participants, and the effect this has on the direction of the programme. Robson suggests a number of questions a process analysis might ask:

- How are clients brought into the program?
- What happens to them when involved with the program?
- Are clients' needs being met?
- How do staff and clients interact?
- How is the program perceived by staff and clients?

- What is the day-to-day reality of the program?
- What are the patterns of activity (including both formal and informal, unanticipated activities)?
- Is the program changing? If so, how? (Robson, 2000, p. 63)

These are useful questions, and the methods suggested by them indicate largely qualitative methods, including interviewing, participant observation and analysis of documents and records (see Chapter 9). From the collection of such data one can begin to see the process of implementation – settings, who benefits and who does not, variability amongst staff, use of resources, and so on. Complex relationships can be grasped through this approach, and the meanings of events to different actors involved may become clearer. At the same time, quantitative data is not excluded. The size of the group, gender distribution, variety of ethnicities, attendance patterns, frequency and length of sessions all can add to an understanding of the impact of the programme.

This approach implies a more collaborative attitude than that discussed earlier (though of course qualitative approaches are as open to being imposed on research subjects as other approaches). In its attempt to understand 'what is going on' it engages all participants – staff and members – in giving their perspectives and in having a say. Such participation has the potential for a more holistic picture of a project to emerge. Robson's (2000) view of *participatory* evaluation is rather different from the principles I discussed in Chapter 4. In his model a major evaluative role is given to practitioners, but not to service users. He describes a joint responsibility between evaluator and practitioners, with practitioners having a role in deciding what is important, in collecting data and in interpreting results. He quotes research to make the point that this 'jointness' gives a necessarily active role to practitioners while still helping to maintain the rigour which is also necessary. In social work writers such as Adams (1990) Shaw (1996) and Beresford (2000) have called for more control by users of both practice and evaluation. Shaw, for example, offers a different model of participatory evaluation, arguing for the importance of service users to feel and to be part of the process. Drawing on feminist and Third World perspectives on 'voice', he argues for a model that includes oppressed people in the process of problem identification, project implementation and evaluation: 'the focus is on collective inquiry about concrete problems, mutual collaboration and action for change' (Shaw, 1996, p. 121). Shaw acknowledges the problems of achieving authentic participation, but believes it can open up sources of knowledge not available by other means. Indeed he suggests that participatory evaluation offers a 'sharply uncomfortable perspective on social work practice, especially when applied to community interventions' (p. 121).

Elsewhere Shaw advocates a model of evaluation that is based on critical theory (see Chapter 7). In this model problems are conceptualized within their social, political and cultural context. It is different from critical research and is critical *evaluation* because it examines the contradictions of practice (Shaw, 1998). It therefore goes beyond 'participatory' evaluation and is undertaken explicitly for political purposes. Robson (2000) sees this as bringing people to an emancipatory understanding of the context in which they operate so that they are able to question the value of policies, practices and programmes themselves, asking whether these are a mechanism of managerial control rather than ways of striving for equality and social justice. It has an action orientation, with a view to transforming organizational practices. Robson sees problems with this model, but Shaw is clear that evaluation must not only be about measuring effectiveness of practice but should also be empowering and effect change in society and in individual lives.

The reflective practitioner

In this discussion of different approaches to evaluation, the focus has been on programmes, projects, initiatives that are community-based and involve change for or in service users. A common model of evaluation is that where the goal is the improvement of individual professional practice – Schön's notion of the 'reflective practitioner' that was discussed in Chapter 5. This entails developing the necessary skills and experience to carry out an evaluation of one's own practice. Gould (1999) offers a model of the reflective practitioner based on action-learning cycles which can be repeated as long as is feasible. Gould's stages are:

1. Concrete experience – the immersion of the practitioner is the situation as it presents itself, the lived reality of the service user, and the shared seeking of a definition of the problem.
2. Reflective observation or reflection-on-action becomes the dominant mode of inquiry. This might include dialogue with various key people, such as colleagues from other professions who may be involved in the situation, within supervision, internal mental reflection or formal meetings such as case conferences.
3. A preliminary definition of the problem emerges, suggesting forms of action that might be appropriate to take.
4. The insights gained through reflection-on-action are translated into new prescriptions for action and are tested out in practice. This leads back into concrete experience (phase 1) and further. review. (p. 71)

The advantages of this model are that it allows for definitions of problems and intervention strategies to be revised and changed if necessary, rather than a fixed once-and-for-all view of individual problems. It encourages practitioners to evaluate their work as it happens, at a very basic and simple level. It emphasizes a team approach and, where appropriate, a multi-agency approach so that different stakeholder perspectives on 'need' are included. However Gould's model is a rather individualistic one that does not take account of, for example, organizational constraints on definitions of need, or the politics and power involved in assessing different stakeholder interests. These dimensions are crucial to making sense of social problems in the real world, and need to be accounted for in any notion of 'the reflective practitioner'.

Examples of evaluation in social work and social care

The evaluation of social work and social care practice is part of the wider thrust of professions towards evidence-based practice, and an increasing number of examples is becoming available. As indicated earlier, the dominant model of evaluation is based on experimental or quasi-experimental designs, and is concerned largely with outcome measurement. These designs are limited in their scope:

> Quantitative evaluations, outcome-oriented measures of accountability, are typically bereft of the intensity, subtlety, particularity, ethical judgement and relevance that potentially characterize evaluation born of ethnography. (Shaw, 1999, p. 1)

I have therefore chosen examples that demonstrate this complexity, and which have lessons for evaluation practice that are much wider than the specific projects involved.

Community health in the Western Isles

Linda McKie was an external evaluator for this project, based on five of the Western Isles of Scotland. I have chosen it because of her detailed and frank description of the evaluation experience, and because it is an excellent example of the process of reflexivity on the part of the evaluator. The project being evaluated aimed to involve local communities in defining their health needs, in considering how they might be met and in deciding on priorities for action (McKie, 2002). A major aim was to gain as much involvement of the island communities as was possible. The project had a steering committee consisting of representatives of the health authorities that had funded it. It had a project co-ordinator and a part-time administrator. Evaluation was built in from the start (an example of process evaluation, although, as will become clear, this is not a separate activity from outcome evaluation), and its overall aim was to 'provide a critical assessment of the work, management structure and organization of the project'. As well as being a process and outcome evaluation, it was also formative and summative, employing an action research approach (see Chapter 5). As a result the process and outcomes of the project were examined on an ongoing basis, and the evaluation team gave regular feedback to stakeholders. Qualitative methods were used: focus groups, semi-structured interviews and questionnaires comprising open-ended questions. Small-area census data were also used to provide a socio-economic profile of island life. McKie writes:

> Participants in the project were encouraged to take an active involvement in the monitoring, reflection and resultant change processes. Drafts of data analysis were returned to many respondents and data regularly discussed with the project advisory and partners groups. In addition, project participants were encouraged to record activities, interviewing each other, making videos of activities and taking photographs, and sharing this material with the evaluation team. (p. 270)

In these ways it is apparent that much effort was put into making this a genuinely participatory evaluation. However, it emerged during the evaluation that the health project itself had not been set up with such care. When money became available from the health authority, the initiative had to be set up with great speed, giving no time for proper consultation with local people about either the content of the project or the nature of the evaluation. This had repercussions for the evaluators, who met some resentment, resistance and suspicion that the project was being run by outsiders, an instance of how events outwith the control of the researchers can impact on the work they are trying to do. McKie offers other examples of power dynamics entailed in the project and the attempt to evaluate it:

- Previous experiences of community development projects – other projects had 'come and gone' over the years. This was seen as just another one.
- Local politics – a community hospital in one of the islands was being considered for closure, creating a sense of alienation from decision-making
- Economic concerns – growing unemployment in the islands led some people to question the need for a health project instead of economic regeneration work.

- Diversity in and between islands – there are religious and cultural differences between the islands. Also tensions exist between those coming for work and local families.
- Patterns of island life – island life is organized around the weather, and the spring and summer period when the evaluator had planned to do her work was the busiest time of the year for local people. She had to adapt her plans accordingly.

These factors led to an expressed view that both the project and the evaluation were being imposed on the communities without much understanding of their island lives, and that this was unlikely to promote participation in either the project or the research.

A number of lessons can be drawn from this. The first is that an evaluation cannot free itself from perceptions of the programme being evaluated. The politics of the project itself will affect attitudes to the evaluation, and the evaluators are inevitably caught up in the issues of power that operate. It may be necessary to spend a great deal of time persuading people that their contribution will be taken seriously. A second point concerns the importance for evaluators of informing themselves of the context within which a project operates. An evaluation cannot take place in a vacuum, without reference to all those cultural, geographical and even meteorological factors that impinge on it.

There were also a number of issues that arose about the role of the evaluator, including local people's perception of her association with the steering group, as a kind of spy who would carry information from 'insiders' to powerful 'outsiders'. On the other hand, the steering group were concerned that McKie was too involved in local matters and thus less objective than was desirable. McKie says she was never able to overcome these contradictory perceptions. She did feel however that she had some things going for her – her Irish nationality and experience of working in island communities and her identity as a woman and as a mother gave her other avenues through which to relate to some project participants, and a degree of co-operation was achieved.

The conclusions McKie draws from this experience are, first, that an involvement and commitment to evaluation must be established in the design stage of a project and must be regularly reviewed. A profile of communities and localities is imperative to an understanding of contextual factors. Those targeted need to be consulted prior to the start, and any evaluation should ensure that it is situated in local socio-economic and political debates. It is also important to recognize the reality of evaluators having 'power over' project participants, and to be transparent about sharing data. Moreover, McKie emphasizes the need for creating a dialogue between participants, funders and project facilitators, and draws attention to the fact that the responsibilities and the ethical issues resulting from these relationships can be highly problematic and stressful.

A crying child

A very different evaluation approach is described by Bloom (1999), based on experimental methods, in the form of a single-system design. This is evaluation that is focused on only one system, such as an individual, a family, an organization, and so on. The system described by Bloom is the case of an 11-year-old girl, S.H. who was reported to be having difficulty settling into a new school. She cried a lot, both at home and at school, was unable to sleep and refused to go to school. The social worker's intervention consisted of a plan to enhance S.H.'s importance in the school combined with frequent counselling which involved both the social worker and relevant teachers. It was reported that within four weeks of the start of this intervention, crying had ceased at home and at school. Here the social worker was also the evaluator of her own practice – the practitioner-researcher. The intervention was based on a cognitive-behavioural approach, a common feature of evidence-based practice, where immediate behaviour is the unit of interest, not its causes or antecedents. The behaviour to be targeted was the child's crying, and no other problems were mentioned. The practitioner/evaluator set up the evaluation by engaging both the form teacher and S.H. in measuring the frequency and the timing of crying. She then plotted this on a graph to estimate the baseline rate of crying every week. After week four of charting the behaviour, counselling took place every day, both at school and at home. Charting continued to see if any changes took place over the intervention period. Crying stopped at home during the seventh week and at school during the eighth week. The practitioner/evaluator checked back with teachers eight weeks later and was told that there had been no crying in the post-study period. The behaviour change appeared to be persistent and stable. A statistical analysis for significance was not carried out because the outcomes were so distinct as not to need further support.

This is a very basic procedure, and the steps involved were:

1. Target events to be changed – which could include strengths to be increased as well as problems to be decreased.
2. Administer clear interventions – so as to be able to know what is associated with a positive change situation, and to be able to replicate the method.
3. Monitor consistently and objectively over time so as to be able to compare the reference point (baseline) with the changes after intervention. (Bloom, 1999, p. 201)

This is a relatively uncomplicated procedure for evaluation, though it has to be said that the definition of the problem, the means of appropriate intervention and the changes (if any) that take place are seldom as straightforward to identify. As we know, the real world is much more messy and complex than as depicted in the case of S.H., and in any case, it can never be certain that the intervention was the cause of the change. As Bloom himself points out, S.H.'s grandfather might have bribed her to stop crying and attend school. Or she might have stopped crying without the intervention, as she settled into the school. In addition, we are not given any detail of the content of the 'counselling' or 'enhancing S.H.'s importance in the school'. These are vague statements that make replication impossible.

Moreover, by its very nature the approach described by Bloom does not take account of why the child cried so much and went so reluctantly to school. It is reasonable to assume, given the information we have, that it was simply a case of adjusting to a new school since a strategy of confidence-building seemed to help, but it is risky not to explore other reasons for her distress. Bloom takes a rather technical view of this. He says of S.H.'s case,

> Even though only one target has been identified, it is obvious that this behaviour creates tensions for the whole family, as well as the girl and the school system. Peers are likely to know what is happening, and this may affect the girl's chances of making friends and participating in a positive youth culture . . . *The trick is to be able to pick out the critical target for intervention, the one by which a number of other factors stand or fall.* (Bloom, 1999, p. 207, my emphasis)

This invokes injunctions in ethical codes which imply that it is possible when dealing with human beings to isolate some aspects of life from others, as in laboratory conditions. The reality is much messier than this.

However, an interesting dimension of this case study is that clearly the child had been involved in the process from the start. She appears to have willingly agreed to record and report on incidents of crying, and Bloom suggests she was actively involved in the evaluation – a partner in the process. Her collection of information gave her access to feedback on how she was performing and thus gave her some control over the experiment and the evaluation. It was also important in maintaining her achievements.

This suggests that participation and some measure of control are empowering, regardless of the evaluation approach (though some designs are more compatible with this aim than are others). Single-system designs offer a systematic way of monitoring and evaluating

practice, though they do suffer from the problems ⸻
tal designs in that one can never be certain that tl
caused by the 'treatment', and they tell us little
factors of human experience that concern social w
of myriad other influences that affect us all in com
dictory ways.

Drawbacks of evaluation research

It is a daunting task to set out the drawbacks of evaluation research. After all, evaluation is always a 'good thing' to meet the demands of accountability, quality, cost benefits, and so on. Perhaps a more appropriate response is that the drawbacks are embodied in the research designs, and all those we have discussed in this book have inherent flaws. However another drawback of evaluation in the context of modern social policy is that its criteria are not concerned only with the quality of services. They are politically set, their operation is tightly controlled by managerial processes and evaluation priorities are explicit about outcomes, with what counts as evidence generally narrowly defined along the lines of observable phenomena (Shaw 1996). Yet the agendas that underpin evaluations frequently remain invisible in apparently 'objective' research designs. Part of this control is the demand for definitive answers to social problems, even though, as with all research, evaluation seldom offers unambiguous ways forward for social programmes. In appraising reports of evaluation research it is as well to remember Patton's list of sources of political influence:

- The fact that people are involved in evaluation means that the values, perceptions and politics of everyone (scientists, decision-makers, funders, programme staff) impinge on the process from start to finish.
- The fact that evaluation requires classifying and categorizing results inevitably in data being filtered.
- The fact that empirical data undergird evaluation raises the need for interpretation. Interpretation is only partly logical and deductive: it is also value laden and perspective dependent.
- The fact that actions and decisions follow from evaluation makes it political.
- The fact that programmes and organizations are involved raises questions of power, status and resources. Evaluation affects the allocation of these. One of the weapons employed in organizational conflicts is evaluative information and judgements.
- The fact that information is involved in evaluation makes it political. Information leads to knowledge; knowledge reduces

tainty; reduction of uncertainty facilitates action; action is
essary to the accumulation of power. (Patton, 1997, p. 343)
re it is recognized that evaluators need to foster a political sophisti-
cation and to remember that evaluations are used in direct proportion to their power-enhancing capability. That is, their results will be
adopted by those who calculate that their position will be strength-
ened by them, and discarded if they do not. For this reason, if for no
other, a model of evaluation that places power in the hands of those
most affected by decisions that result from it should be a goal of
those sensitized to issues of equity.

Conclusion: evaluation research and social justice

Shaw (1999) takes up the discussion of whether 'partisanship' or any
commitment to social justice should have any part in evaluation
research. He cites a number of writers who advocate that social work
evaluation should be informed by a concern for justice (though he
acknowledges that they hold different philosophies of justice).
Humphries (2004b) calls for a taking of sides in evaluation and
research, arguing, as I have here, that all research is inevitably political and that

> research that attempts solely to measure the impact of
> interventions . . . is not value-free. Rather it has taken the side
> of whatever values have inspired the interventions it
> uncritically evaluates'. (p. 114)

This is not to argue for lack of rigour or reflexivity in evaluation. It is
to argue that the evaluator needs to be clear about her/his own moral
groundings and will not be swayed by factions rather than principles.

Evaluation in social work is currently overwhelmingly concerned
with outcomes, mainly in relation to individual behavioural change,
and there is a demand for evaluations to deliver answers to what
works to achieve this. Yet it is not necessary to create a binary division between outcome and process. Social work and social care programmes form complex packages that develop in interaction with
their context, and it is appropriate that evaluations are widened to
take this into account. In this way social problems such as poverty,
sexism and racism can become issues to include in any assessment of
intervention. Questions for evaluation should include concern about
the programme's relevance to what it sets out to change and the tar-
geting of other factors, as well as its responsiveness to environmental
conditions.

Another way to approach this distinction is between terminal goals
and instrumental objectives (Rokeach, 1983). The terminal goal of

social work (not of course uncontested) is presumably that people and communities gain reasonable control over their environment, their resources and their relationships. Instrumental objectives are short-term or intermediate, and may be seen as attainments on the journey to terminal goals, such as acquiring comfortable and decent housing, or stabilizing mental health status, or achieving refugee status, or the satisfactory placement of children with adoptive parents. Evaluation does not always have to concern itself with outcomes. It can be about an overall judgement of a programme, it can be aimed at producing information to improve a programme, it can be geared to examining unexpected outcomes or it can be interested in the quality of interpersonal care offered in particular settings. The nature of social work requires a variety of evaluation techniques. We need to challenge intervention strategies organized around behavioural and cognitive methods as the exemplar of good practice, and its measurement in quantifiable terms as the gold standard of evaluation. We also need to resist the pressure for certainty and search for a model of evaluation that is 'exploratory rather than confirmatory, building . . . from the practitioners' own accounts rather than superimposing an ideal model and testing for conformity' (Elks and Kirkhart, 1993, p. 555). Finally, we need to see evaluation not just as social science methods applied to the study of interventions, but also as a democratic process that pursues self-determination and opportunity for those who are without either.

main points

- Evaluation research is carried out to promote accountability, to examine effectiveness, to identify gaps and to develop knowledge

- Evaluation research is value-laden because it makes judgements about the worth or merit of a programme or practice

- It is research that is applied, practical, action-oriented and political

- A number of different stakeholders usually have an interest in evaluations

- The literature describes evaluation as formative and summative, and as process and outcome

- Evaluations within organizations are politically set, and what counts as evidence is often narrowly defined

- Results of evaluations are used where they enhance power for some groups, and discarded where they do not

- Why is evaluation of practice or programmes important? Write down as many reasons you can think of.
- What are the implications of the idea that evaluation is value-laden?
- What do you understand to be the differences between process and outcome evaluation?
- Why is it important to be aware of the interests of all stakeholders in an evaluation? Make a list of the potential stakeholders who might be associated with a project.

taking it further

- Robson, C *Small-Scale Evaluation* (London: Sage, 2000)
  A clear and detailed guide to conducting evaluations.
- Unau, Y A, Gabor, P A and Grinnell, R M *Evaluation in Social Work* (New York: Oxford University Press, 2006)
  Mainly targeted at readers in the USA, but it is up to date and is relevant for research practice elsewhere.
- Weiss, C H *Evaluation*, 2nd edn (Upper Saddle River, NJ: Prentice Hall, 1998)
  A detailed toolkit and discussion of issues and problems in evaluation from one of the best writers on the subject.
- The journals *Evaluation* and *Journal of Evaluation Review* both offer articles representing a variety of approaches and discussion of evaluation.

12 Conclusion

Introduction

Research and evaluation skills have become a central part of the repertoire of social work and social care workers, and courses on methods are now included in the social work curriculum. Practitioners are required to collect statistics for use by others in an organization, they are expected to evaluate their own practice and they are encouraged to initiate their own primary research towards post-qualifying development. Student assessment includes a dissertation where choices of research methods and students' understanding of them must be made explicit. Whichever of these activities is demanded, it is important not only to have grasped the methodologies, but also to be able and willing to make informed critique of them, asking questions not only about their appropriateness to answer the research questions but also about the philosophical assumptions that underpin them, the ethics that inform them and the part they have to play in any aim of a more just society. Roger Fuller (1999, p. 82) sees as amongst the components of 'research-mindedness':

- an awareness of the scope and limitations of research;
- an ability to read critically the claims that emerge from research studies;
- an ability to read critically the policy changes that purport to be based on research studies;
- a sympathetic attitude toward research that may be conducted in a practitioner's own work setting.

Although Fuller has confined his discussion to research not involving practitioners directly and is not explicit about social justice (and moreover may express this differently), his vision of the practitioner who is able to read policy initiatives critically embodies some of the elements necessary for just research. It is this attitude that I have aimed to foster in the construction of this book.

Choosing methods that are 'fit for purpose'

Most authors on research methods emphasize the importance of choosing the methods that are most suited to the questions at hand, what Denscombe (2003) calls 'horses for courses' (p. 3). They also list other practical questions that the potential researcher needs to consider, such as the time available to carry out the study; its scope and the feasibility of completing it within the timescale; the resources available, such as costs, administrative support, design of instruments, and so on; the kinds of questions requiring an answer – 'how' and 'why' questions suggest different methods from 'what' and 'how many', and so on.

Even then, having made a choice, there is seldom a cookbook recipe that can be applied directly to all situations. Creativity, imagination and innovation form part of the researcher's skills, along with an ability to make the methods suit the purpose rather than making the research questions fit into the methods.

Yin (1994, p. 6) has set out a table for deciding on the appropriateness of different strategies for different situations, intended to help researchers make decisions about methods. This is reproduced in Table 12.1.

Yin's table does not cover all the methods discussed in this book, but it does offer a formula for making choices about them, and it does insist that researchers be clear about the kinds of questions they want to ask. What the literature seldom acknowledges is that research is more than a technical exercise, and has political and ethical dimensions that require consideration at every stage, from formulating the research questions to disseminating the results. The reflexive social work researcher will examine the origins of research questions; will consider the kinds of knowledge she views as important or legitimate,

Table 12.1 Relevant situations for different research strategies

Strategy	Form of research question	Requires control over behavioural events?	Focuses on contemporary events?
Experiment	How, why	Yes	Yes
Survey	Who, what, where, how many, how much	No	Yes
Archival analysis	Who, what, where, how many, how much	No	Yes/no
History	How, why	No	No
Case study	How, why	No	Yes

Source: R K Yin, *Case Study Research*, 1994. Reprinted by permission of Sage.

and the knowledge that is excluded and regarded as unimportant; will ask what stakeholder interests are served by the research and how the choice of methods is influenced by this. After all, as Everitt et al. (1992, p. 17) argue, 'If the fundamental purpose of social welfare is the pursuit of justice and equality, then practitioners have a professional responsibility to be alert to the ways in which power operates through ways of knowing.' In Chapter 3 they set out a possible value base for practice and research, paraphrased here as: the need to reject negative labels and treating people as objects to be studied; acceptance that people have a right to be heard and to control their lives; a reflection in practice and research that issues of oppression, social policy, the environment and the economy are major contributory forces in people's problems; acknowledgement of individual and collective knowledge as legitimate; using democratic and participatory methods of working and research; building into methods a challenge to oppression, whether by reason of 'race', gender, sexual orientation, class, (dis)ability or any other form of social differentiation used to support notions of superiority and inferiority. In a similar but perhaps more specific vein, Temple and Moran (2006, Appendix), conducting research alongside refugees, formulated guidelines submitted to ESRC for conducting research that is democratic and participatory. They say that good practice in research projects:

- recognizes that people may see the world differently, and uses methods that draw out different ways of seeing, interpreting and acting on the world;
- clearly states the aims and intended uses of the research;
- ensures adherence to confidentiality;
- uses appropriate methods as determined by participants' preferences;
- articulates an understanding that the use of different methods can position those involved in power relationships (e.g. using unnecessary technical jargon);
- uses methods that draw out different ways of seeing;
- specifies the consequences that methodologies can have on those who do – or do not – have a voice in the research.

Of course there are often organizational and other limitations on some of these aspects, but Temple and Moran emphasize in all respects that researchers should endeavour to be transparent and proactive in consultation, particularly about the extent to which it is intended that participants will be involved in and have some control over the shape and direction of the project.

There is no reason why social work and social care and student researchers should not grasp the principles and rules for conducting their own small-scale research projects, especially if they are guided by ethical practice that is embedded in a concept of social justice. After all, this is what social work practice purports to embrace. Moreover, it is imperative that service users be included as co-researchers, creating and having acknowledged their own knowledge, 'controlling what happens to them as is their right as citizens' (Dominelli, 2005, p. 207).

Most of the research methods and strategies discussed in this book lend themselves to a research focus that takes justice as its organizing theme. As I have argued elsewhere, it is 'the attitude of mind, the desire to make the invisible visible, the urge to centre issues of justice, equality and empowerment that constitutes the radical potential of social work research' (Humphries, 2005, p. 292).

Rediscovering research methodologies for social justice

There is increasing unease in social work about practice and research that does not conform to the vision of 'helping people' that brought many into the profession. Questions are being asked about how appropriate values can be recovered that will help in resisting the residual, technocratic and oppressive functions of much of practice and research (Jones et al., 2004). There is also a continuing and lively debate about the appropriateness of the dominant version of 'evidence-based practice' in social work research. There have been calls for a shift in the focus of research to set its sights on policies, institutional practices and structures, and on their impact on individual lives, as much as on what works to change individual behaviour.

How might we relate this concern to the task of researching social work? One answer to the question about appropriate methodologies, as I hope has been made clear in this book, is that many methodologies have the potential to expose inequality and to make available people's ways of knowing. What we need is a more critical and ethical approach to *all* kinds of methodology. But there is another level at which we need to understand the push for knowledge:

> the social experiment . . . is part of an adversary process . . . the adversaries are contending for power, not truth . . . and deep down, that is what many of us are contending for too. (Aaron, 1978, p. 275)

The urge to power holds true not only for social experimenting but also for all research, and indeed for all human endeavour. We would do well to remember that all science is an ideological representation, a social practice and product, where research questions, descriptions and explanations are shaped by 'the interests, desires and values promoted by such practices' (Harding, 1991, p. 15). The quote from Aaron helps us understand and explain arguments about qualitative and quantitative methods, and the paradigm wars, and the reasons why governments and institutions commission research which is framed to give the 'right' answers and which is ignored if the answers are 'wrong'. Oakley (2000) points out that the definition of ways of knowing has constantly been interlaced with who is doing the defining, and about how the patterning of all of this has followed certain fundamental divisions existing in the wider culture. She says:

> some ways of knowing have traditionally occupied spaces on the edge of the dominant vision, the same kinds of spaces as are filled by the lives and experiences of the socially marginalized, including women. Thus, neither methods nor methodology can be understood, *except* in the context of gendered social relations. (p. 4)

One might also add class, 'race' and other social divisions to Oakley's focus on gender. One of the purposes of social work research should be to bring those ways of knowing in from the cold, from margin to centre (hooks, 1984).

What an understanding of this might mean is that quantitative researchers envisage a practice beyond one where all that matters are larger sample sizes, adequately concealed sampling and competently executed statistical tests, behavioural-cognitive outcomes, and approaches that push people where they do not want to go. Often what people want to know and to contribute to is about those social forces that perpetuate their poverty, that result in violence towards them and that restrict their opportunities for a better life. Similarly, qualitative researchers may require more humility, caution, openness and accountability in their urge to make marginalized voices heard (see Oakley, 2000).

What is legitimate in social work research is a concern for those in the real world who continue to be disadvantaged and oppressed, and who are on the receiving end of problems for which there *is* resolution, given the political will. The invisibility and enforced silence of such groups are what make it imperative for social work researchers to attempt to pursue an ethical practice in examining the conditions and policies that lead to this marginalization.

Social work researchers need to take sides consciously, not with 'movements' *per se*, but in embracing particular ethical values towards a more just society. Values provide a series of principles from which we can try to deduce goals and then develop policies. Values help us to clarify 'what we believe to be right or wrong, permissible and impermissible' (Weeks, 1993, p. 190). Surely such values must include an opposition to injustice and a commitment to alleviating and even preventing suffering? They lead us to oppose social and institutional arrangements that accommodate themselves complacently to policies and practices that are manifestly wrong:

> Research that is concerned to expose and challenge inequalities is entirely compatible with these values. Research that attempts to measure solely the impact of interventions, regardless of their relationship to the social context, is not value free. Rather it has taken the side of whatever values have inspired the intervention it uncritically 'evaluates'.
> (Humphries, 2004b, p. 114)

This means that the research-minded practitioner who is informed by a critical reflexivity will ask questions about what is being required of the research process, and whose interests are reflected in it. Nor will she take sides in the sense of privileging the voices of 'the oppressed' without interrogating all perspectives. The ultimate goal may be to democratize ways of knowing, so that the knowledge of marginalized groups will attain similar status to that of scientific 'knowers'. *Then the focus can more legitimately be on choosing the right methods for the research question.* But the power dynamics will not evaporate, and there will always exist a potential debate as to the nature of social problems and research questions. A notion of social justice may help to define the parameters of the question more effectively.

main points

- The choice of research methods should be appropriate to the research questions to be addressed
- Most methodologies can accommodate an examination of social structures and make available people's ways of knowing
- 'Taking sides' in research is a legitimate choice, based on values that aim to alleviate or prevent injustice and suffering

stop and think

- What kinds of questions might you ask yourself in choosing methods appropriate to social work research problems?
- In your view, are some methods more compatible with an ethical approach informed by social justice than are others? If yes, make a list of these methods, jotting down reasons for your choice.
- What do you think is meant by 'taking sides' as a researcher?

■ D'Cruz, H and Jones, M *Social Work Research: ethical and political contexts* (London: Sage, 2004), Chapter 3
This is an accessible text that takes ethics informed by commitment to social justice as its organizing principle to explore a number of dimensions of research practice.

taking it further

References

Aaron, H J *Politics and the Professors: the Great Society in perspective* (Washington, DC: Brookings Institution, 1978)

Adams, R *Self Help, Social Work and Empowerment* (London: Macmillan, 1990)

Alston, M and Bowles, W *Research for Social Workers* (St Leonards, NSW, Aust: Allen and Unwin, 1998)

Atkinson, P, Coffey, A, Delamont, S, Lofland, J and Lofland, L (eds) *Handbook of Ethnography* (London: Sage, 2001)

Atweh, B, Kemmis, S and Weeks, P *Action Research in Practice: partnership for social justice in education* (London: Routledge, 1998)

Audi, R (ed.) *The Cambridge Dictionary of Philosophy* (Cambridge University Press: Cambridge, 1995)

Audit Commission, *Misspent Youth* (London: Audit Commission, 1996)

Baldwin, M 'Day care on the move: learning from a participatory action research project at a day centre for people with learning difficulties' *BJSW*, 27 (6) (1997) 951–58

Baldwin, M 'Working together, learning together: cooperative inquiry in the development of complex practice by teams of social workers', in P Reason and H Bradbury (eds) *Handbook of Action Research* (London: Sage, 2001) 287–93

Barnes, C and Mercer, G *Doing Disability Research* (Leeds: Disability Press, 1997)

Becker, H S 'Becoming a marihuana user' *American Journal of Sociology*, 59 (1953) 41–45

BASW (British Association of Social Workers), *Code of Ethics* (Birmingham: BASW, 2004)

Becker, H *Outsiders: studies in the sociology of deviance* (New York: Free Press, 1963)

Bell, J *Doing Your Research Project: a guide for first-time researchers in education and social science*, 2nd edn (Buckingham: Open University Press, 1993)

Benhabib, S *Situating the Self: gender, community and postmodernism in contemporary ethics* (Cambridge: Polity Press, 1992)

Bennett, T 'The effectiveness of a police-initiated fear-reducing strategy' *British Journal of Criminology*, 31, (1991) 1–14

Benson, D and Hughes, J A *The Perspective of Ethnomethodology* (London: Longman, 1983)

Beresford, P 'Service users' knowledge and social work theory: collaboration or conflict?' *BJSW*, 30 (4) (2000) 489–503

Beresford P and Croft, S 'Service users and practitioners united: the key component for social work reform' *BJSW*, 34 (1) (2004) 53–68

Beresford, P and Turner, M *It's Our Welfare: report of the Citizen Commission on the future of the welfare state* (London, National Institute for Social Work, 1997)

Bernard, C *Constructing Lived Experiences: representations of black mothers in child sexual abuse discourses* (Aldershot: Ashgate, 2001)

BJSW (British Journal of Social Work) Special Issue, *Social Work and Social Justice, BJSW* 32 (6) (Oxford: Oxford University Press, 2002)

Bloom, M 'Single-system evaluation', in I Shaw and J Lishman (eds) *Evaluation and Social Work Practice* (London: Sage, 1999)

Blumer, H *Symbolic Interactionism: perspective and method* (Englewood Cliffs, NJ: Prentice-Hall, 1969)

Boruch, R F 'On common contentions about randomized field experiments', in R F Boruch and H W Riechen (eds) *Experimental Testing of Public Policy* (Boulder, CO: Westview Press, 1975)

Boruch, R F *Randomized Experiments for Planning and Evaluation* (Thousand Oaks, CA: Sage, 1997)

Bourgois, P *In Search of Respect: selling crack in El Barrio* (Cambridge: Cambridge University Press, 1995)

Bourgois, P 'Respect at work: "going legit"', in S Taylor (ed.) *Ethnographic Research: a reader* (London, Sage, 2002) 15–35

Bradbury, H and Reason, P 'Action Research: an opportunity for revitalizing research purpose and practices' *Qualitative Social Work*, 2 (2) (2003) 155–75

Brewer, C and Lait, J *Can Social Work Survive?* (London: Temple Smith, 1980)

Briskman, L and Noble, C 'Social work ethics: embracing diversity?' in B Pease and J Fook (eds) *Transforming Social Work Practice* (London: Routledge, 1999)

Brown, B, Crawford, P and Hicks, C, *Evidence-Based Research: dilemmas and debates in health care* (Maidenhead: Open University/McGraw-Hill Education, 2003)

Bryman, A *Quantity and Quality in Social Research* (London: Macmillan, 1988)

Bulmer, M (ed.) *Social Research Ethics* (New York: Holmes and Meier, 1982)

Butler, I 'A code of ethics for social work and social care research', *BJSW*, 32 (2002) 239–48

Butler, I and Drakeford, M 'Which Blair Project? Communitarianism, social authoritarianism and social work' *Journal of Social Work*, 1 (1) (2001) 7–19

Butler, I and Pugh, R (2004) 'The politics of social work research', in R Lovelock, K Lyons and J Powell (eds) *Reflecting on Social Work – Discipline and Profession* (Aldershot: Ashgate, 2004) 55–71

Cameron, D, Frazer, E, Harvey, P, Rampton, M B H and Richardson, K *Researching Language: issues of power and method* (London: Routledge, 1992)

Carabine, J 'Unmarried motherhood 1830–1990: a genealogical analysis', in M Weatherell, S Taylor and S J Yates (eds) *Discourse as Data: a guide for analysis* (London: Sage, 2001) 267–310

Cealey Harrison, W and Hood-Williams, J 'More varieties than Heinz: social categories and sociality in Humphries, Hammersley and beyond' *Sociological Research Online*, 3 (1) (March 1998)

Chambers, R *Rural Appraisal: rapid, relaxed and participatory*, Discussion Paper 311 (London: Institute of Development Studies, 1992)

Chambers, R *Whose Reality Counts? Putting the First Last* (London: IT Publications, 1997)

Charon, J M *Symbolic Interactionism: an introduction, an interpretation, an integration* (Englewood-Cliffs, NJ: Prentice-Hall, 1992)

Chelimsky, E and Shadish, W R (eds) *Evaluation for the 21st Century* (Thousand Oaks, CA: Sage, 1997)

Cicourel, A *The Social Organisation of Juvenile Justice* (New York: Wiley, 1976)

Clarke, A *Situational Analyses: grounded theory after the postmodern turn* (Thousand Oaks, CA: Sage, 2004)

Cohen, L, Manion, L and Morrison, K *Research Methods in Education*, 5th edn (London and New York: RoutledgeFalmer, 2000)

Connolly, W *The Terms of Political Discourse* (Princeton, NJ: Princeton University Press, 1983)

Cooke, B and Kotari, U (eds) *Participation, the New Tyranny?* (London: Zed Books, 2001)

Corbin, J and Holt, N L 'Grounded Theory', in B Somekh and C Lewin (eds) *Research Methods in the Social Sciences* (London: Sage, 2005) 49–52

Cornwall, A and Jewkes, R 'What is participatory research?' *Social Science and Medicine*, 41 (12) (1995) 1667–76

Craig, G 'Poverty, social work and social justice' *BJSW*, 32 (6) (2002) 669–82

Cree, V *From Public Streets to Private Lives* (Aldershot: Avebury, 1995)

David, M and Sutton, C *Social Research: the basics* (London: Sage, 2004)

Davies, R M and Kelly, E 'The social worker, the client and the social anthropologist' *BJSW*, 6 (2) (1976) 213–31

Davis, A and Horobin, G (eds) *Medical Encounters: the experience of illness and treatment* (London: Croom Helm, 1977)

D'Cruz, H and Jones, M *Social Work Research: ethical and political contexts* (London: Sage, 2004)

de Koning, K and Martin, M *Participatory Research in Health: issues and experiences* (London: Zed Books, 1996)

Denscombe, M *The Good Research Guide for Small-Scale Social Research Projects*, 2nd edn (Maidenhead: Open University Press, 2003)

Denzin, N K *The Research Act in Sociology: a theoretical introduction to sociological methods* (Butterworths: London, 1970)

Denzin, N K *Interpretive Ethnography: ethnographic practices for the 21st century* (London: Sage, 1997)

Denzin, N K and Lincoln, Y S (eds) *Handbook of Qualitative Research* (Thousand Oaks, CA: Sage, 1994)

Dockery, G 'Participatory research: whose roles, whose responsibilities?', in C Truman, D M Mertens and B Humphries (eds) *Research and Inequality* (London: UCL Press, 2000) 95–110

DOH (Department of Health) *The Research Governance Framework for Health and Social Care: implementation plan for social care* (London: DoH, 2004)

Dominelli, L *Sociology for Social Work* (London: Macmillan, 1999)

Dominelli, L *Feminist Social Work Theory and Practice* (Basingstoke: Palgrave Macmillan, 2002)

Dominelli, L 'Social work research: contested knowledge for practice', in R Adams, L Dominelli and M Payne (eds) *Social Work Futures* (Basingstoke: Palgrave Macmillan, 2005)

Du Bois, B 'Passionate scholarship: notes on values, knowing and method in feminist social science', in G Bowles and R Duelli Klein (eds) *Theories of Women's Studies* (London: Routledge, 1983)

Duvell, F and Jordan, B *How Low Can You Go? Dilemmas of social work with asylum seekers in London* (Exeter: Department of Social Work, Exeter University, 2000)

Elks, M and Kirkhart, K 'Evaluating effectiveness from the practitioner's perspective *Social Work*, 38 (5) (1993) 554–63

Elliott, J *Action Research for Educational Change* (Milton Keynes: Open University Press, 1991)

Elliott, J *The Curriculum Experiment: meeting the challenge of social change* (Buckingham: Open University Press, 1998)

Elliott, J 'School-based curriculum development and action research in the UK', in S Hollingsworth (ed.) *International Action Research: a casebook for educational reform* (London: Falmer Press, 2001)

ESRC (Economic and Social Research Council) *Programme on Research Methods* (London: ESRC, 2001)

Evans, C and Fisher, M (1999) 'Collaborative evaluation with service users: moving towards user-controlled research', in I Shaw and J Lishman (eds) *Evaluation and Social Work Practice* (London: Sage, 1999)

Everitt, A, Hardiker, P, Littlewood, J and Mullender, A *Applied Research for Better Practice* (London: Macmillan, 1992)

Fairclough, N *Critical Discourse Analysis: the critical study of language* (London: Longman, 1995)

Fairclough, N *New Labour, New Language?* (London: Routledge, 2000)

Fairclough, N 'The discourse of New Labour: Critical Discourse Analysis', in M Weatherell, S Taylor and S J Yates (eds) *Discourse Theory and Practice: a reader* (London: Sage, 2001) 229–66

Fawcett, B 'Researching disability: meanings, interpretations and analysis', in B Fawcett et al. (eds) *Research and Practice in Social Work* (London: Routledge, 2000)

Fawcett, B, Featherstone, B, Fook, J and Rossiter, A (eds) *Practice and Research in Social Work: postmodern feminist perspectives* (London: Routledge, 2000)

Felton, K 'Meaning-based quality-of-life measurement: a way forward in conceptualizing and measuring client outcomes?' *BJSW*, 35 (2) (2005) 221–36

Ferguson, I and Barclay, A *Seeking Peace of Mind: the mental health needs of asylum seekers in Glasgow* (Stirling: University of Stirling, 2002)

Ferguson, I and Lavalette, M 'Beyond power discourse: alienation and social work' *BJSW*, 34 (3) (2004) 297–312

Finch J '"It's great to have someone to talk to": the ethics and politics of interviewing women', in C Bell and H Roberts (eds) *Social Researching: politics, problems, practice* (London: Routledge, 1984)

Fine, M and Weis, L 'Writing the "wrongs" of fieldwork: confronting our own research/writing dilemmas in urban ethnographies', in G Shacklock and J Smyth (eds) *Being Reflexive in Critical Educational and Social Research* (London: Falmer Press, 1998) 13–35

Fook, J 'Deconstructing and reconstructing professional expertise', in B Fawcett, B Featherstone, J Fook and A Rossiter (eds) *Practice and Research in Social Work: postmodern feminist perspectives* (London: Routledge, 2000)

Fook, J *Social Work: critical theory and practice* (London: Sage, 2002)

Foucault, M *The Archaeology of Knowledge* (London: Tavistock, 1972)

Foucault, M *Power/Knowledge* (Brighton: Harvester, 1980)

Foucault, M *History of Sexuality, Vol. 1* (London: Penguin, 1981)

Foucault, M *The Foucault Reader*, edited by Paul Rabinow (New York: Pantheon, 1984)

Foucault, M 'Technologies of the self', in L H Martin, H Gutman and P H Hutton (eds) *Technologies of the Self* (London: Tavistock, 1988)

Fowler, F J *Survey Research Methods*, 3rd edn (London: Sage, 2002)

Franklin, A and Sloper, P 'Participation of disabled children and young people in decision making within social services departments: a survey of current and recent activities in England' *BJSW*, 36 (5) (2006) 723–42

Fraser, N *Unruly Practices: power, discourse and gender in contemporary social theory* (Polity Press: Cambridge, 1989)

Fraser, N *Justice Interruptus: critical reflections on the 'postsocialist' condition* (Routledge: New York, 1997)

Freed, A O 'Interviewing through an interpreter' *Social Work*, July/August (1988) 315–19

Freire, P *Pedagogy of the Oppressed* (London: Penguin, 1972)

Friedson, E *The Profession of Medicine* (New York: Dodd, Mead and Co, 1970)

Fuller, R 'Practitioner research: towards reflexive practice?', in M Potocky-Tripodi and T Tripodi (eds) *New Directions for Social Work Practice Research* (Washington, DC: NASW Press, 1999)

Fuller, R and Petch, A *Practitioner Research* (Buckingham: Open University Press, 1995)

Garfinkel, H *Studies in Ethnomethodology* (Englewood-Cliffs, NJ: Prentice-Hall, 1967)

Gaventa, J 'The powerful, the powerless and the experts: knowledge struggles in an information age', in P Park, M Brydon-Miller, B Hall and T Jackson (eds) *Voices of Change: participatory research in the USA and Canada* (Westport, CT: Bergin and Harvey, 1993) 21–40

Gendron, S 'Transformative alliance between qualitative and quantitative approaches in health promotion research', in I Rootman et al. (eds) *Evaluation in Health Promotion: principles and perspectives, Part 2, Perspectives* (Geneva: WHO, 2001) 107–21

Geoghegan, M and Powell, F 'Community development, partnership governance and dilemmas of professionalization: profiling and assessing the case of Ireland' *BJSW*, 36 (5) (2006) 845–62

Giddens, A *Sociology: a brief but critical introduction* (Orlando, FL: Harcourt Brace Jovanovich, 1982)

Giddens, A 'Structuration theory and sociological analysis', in J Clark, C Modgil and S Modgil (eds) *Anthony Giddens; consensus and controversy* (London: Falmer, 1990) 297–315

Gillman, M 'Empowering professionals in higher education?', in B Humphries (ed.) *Critical Perspectives on Empowerment* (Birmingham: Venture Press, 1996)

Glaser, B *Basics of Grounded Theory Analysis* (Mill Valley, CA: Sociology Press, 1992)

Glaser, B and Strauss, A *The Discovery of Grounded Theory* (Chicago: Aldine, 1967)

Goldberg, M *Helping the Aged: a field experiment in social work* (London: Allen and Unwin, 1970)

Gomm, R *Social Research Methodology: a critical introduction* (Basingstoke: Palgrave Macmillan, 2004)

Gould, N 'Qualitative practice evaluation', in I Shaw and J Lishman (eds) *Evaluation and Social Work Practice* (London: Sage, 1999)

Graham, H (ed.) *Understanding Health Inequalities* (Maidenhead: Open University Press, 2000)

Green, L W and Kreuter, M W *Health Promotion Planning: an educational and environmental approach*, 2nd edn (Mountain View, CA: Mayfield, 1991)

Greene, J C, Kreider, H and Mayer, E 'Combining qualitative and quantitative methods in social inquiry', in B Somekh and C Lewin (eds) *Research Methods in the Social Sciences* (London: Sage, 2005)

Grundy, S 'Three modes of action research', in S Kemmis and R McTaggart (eds) *The Action Research Reader*, 3rd edn (Geelong, Victoria, Australia: Deakin University Press, 1990)

Guba, E G (ed.) *The Paradigm Dialog* (Thousand Oaks, CA: Sage, 1990)

Guba, E G and Lincoln, Y *Fourth Generation Evaluation* (Newbury Park, CA: Sage, 1989)

Habermas, J *The Theory of Communicative Action, Vol. 2, Lifeworld and System: a critique of functionalist reason*, translated by T McCarthy (Boston: Beacon, 1987)

Hague, G, Mullender, A and Aris, R *Is Anyone Listening? Accountability and Women Survivors of Domestic Violence* (London: Routledge, 2003)

Hall, B *Notes on the Development of the Concept of Participatory Research in an International Context* (Toronto: International Council for Adult Education, 1977)

Hall, B 'Participatory research, popular knowledge and power: a personal reflection' *Convergence*, 3 (1981) 6–19

Hall, B 'Introduction', in P Park, M Brydon-Miller, B Hall and T Jackson (eds) *Voices of Change: participatory research in the United States and Canada* (Westport, CT: Bergin and Harvey, 1993)

Hall, S 'The meaning of New Times', in S Hall and M Jacques (eds) *New Times: the changing face of politics in the 1990s* (London: Lawrence and Wishart, 1989) 116–34

Hall, S 'Foucault: power, knowledge and discourse', in M Weatherell, S Taylor and S J Yates (eds) *Discourse Theory and Practice: a reader* (London: Sage, 2001) 72–81

Hammersley, M *What's Wrong With Ethnography* (London: Routledge, 1995)

Hammersley, M 'A reply to Humphries' *Sociological Research Online*, 2 (4) (December, 1997)

Hammersley, M 'Varieties of social research: a typology' *International Journal of Social Science Methodology*, 3 (3) (2000) 221–29

Hammersley, M and Atkinson, P *Ethnography: principles in practice*, 2nd edn (London: Routledge, 1995)

Hardiker, P 'Social work ideologies in the probation service', *BJSW*, 7 (2) (1977) 131–54

Harding, S *The Science Question in Feminism* (New York: Cornell University Press, 1986)

Harding, S *Feminism and Methodology: social science issues* (Milton Keynes: Open University Press, 1987)

Harding, S *Whose Science? Whose Knowledge?* (Buckingham: Open University Press, 1991)

Hart, E and Bond, M *Action Research for Health and Social Care: a guide to practice* (Buckingham: Open University Press, 1995)

Harvey, L *Critical Social Research* (London: Unwin Hyman, 1990)

Harvey, L and Macdonald, M *Doing Sociology: a practical introduction* (Basingstoke: Macmillan, 1993)

Hayes, D and Humphries, B 'Negotiating contentious research topics', in B Broad (ed.) *The Politics of Social Work Research and Evaluation* (Birmingham: Venture Press, 1999)

Hayes, D and Humphries, B (eds) *Social Work, Immigration and Asylum* (London: Jessica Kingsley Publishers, 2004)

Heritage, J 'Conversational analysis and institutional talk: analysing data', in D Silverman (ed.) *Qualitative Research: theory, method and practice* (London: Sage, 1997)

Hicks, S 'Genealogy's desire: practices of kinship amongst lesbian and gay foster-carers and adopters' *BJSW*, 36 (5) (2006) 761–76

hooks, b *Feminist Theory from Margin to Center* (Boston: South End Press, 1984)

House, E, *Evaluating with Validity* (Beverley Hills, CA: Sage, 1980)

Howarth, D *Discourse* (Buckingham: Open University Press, 2000)

Humphreys, L *Tearoom Trade* (Chicago: Aldine, 1970)

Humphries, B, *Only Connect: lone parents and volunteers* (Edinburgh: Guild of Service, 1976)

Humphries, B 'Empowerment and social research: elements for an analytic framework', in B Humphries and C Truman (eds) *Rethinking Social Research* (Aldershot: Avebury, 1994) 185–202

Humphries, B 'From critical thought to emancipatory action: contradictory research goals?' *Sociological Research Online*, 2 (1) (March 1997)

Humphries, B 'The baby and the bathwater: Hammersley, Cealey Harrison and Hood-Williams and the emancipatory research debate' *Sociological Research Online*, 3 (1) (March 1998)

Humphries, B 'Feminist evaluation', in I Shaw and J Lishman (eds) *Evaluation and Social Work Practice* (London: Sage, 1999)

Humphries, B 'From welfare to authoritarianism: the role of social work in immigration controls', in S Cohen, B Humphries and E Mynott (eds) *From Immigration Controls to Welfare Controls* (London: Routledge, 2002)

Humphries, B 'What else counts as evidence in evidence-based social work?' *Social Work Education* , 22 (1) (2003) 81–91

Humphries, B 'An unacceptable role for social work: implementing immigration controls' *BJSW*, 34 (1) (2004a) 93–108

Humphries, B 'Taking sides: social work research as a moral and political activity', in R Lovelock, K Lyons and J Powell (eds) *Reflecting on Social Work: discipline and practice* (Aldershot: Ashgate, 2004b)

Humphries, B 'From margin to centre: shifting the emphasis of social work research', in R Adams, L Dominelli and M Payne (eds) *Social Work Futures* (Basingstoke: Palgrave Macmillan, 2005)

Humphries, B 'Research mindedness', in M Lymbery and K Postle (eds) *Social Work: a companion for learning* (London: Sage, 2007)

Humphries, B and Martin, M 'Disrupting ethics in social research', in B Humphries (ed.), *Research in Social Care and Social Welfare* (London: Jessica Kingsley Publishers, 2000)

Humphries, E M *The Ideologies of Social Workers and Volunteers: and the effect of these on services offered to clients of social work departments*, unpublished PhD thesis (Edinburgh: University of Edinburgh, 1983)

IFSW/IASSW (International Federation of Social Workers/International Association of Schools of Social Work) *Ethics in Social Work: statement of principles* (Bern, Switzerland: IFSW/IASSW, 2005)

Jones A 'Family life and the pursuit of immigration controls', in S Cohen, B Humphries and E Mynott (eds) *From Immigration Controls to Welfare Controls* (London: Routledge, 2002)

Jones, C 'Voices from the front line: state social workers and New Labour' *BJSW*, 31 (4) (2001) 547–62

Jones, C, Ferguson, I, Lavalette, M and Penketh, L, *Social Work and Social Justice: a manifesto for a new engaged practice* (www.liverpool.ac.uk/sspsw/manifesto) (2004)

Jones, J H *Bad Blood* (New York: Free Press, 1981)

Jordan, B with Jordan, C *Social Work and the Third Way* (London: Sage, 2000)

Kellor, F *Experimental Sociology* (New York: Macmillan, 1901)

Kelly, L *Surviving Sexual Violence* (Cambridge: Polity Press, 1988)

Kelly, L, Regan, L and Burton, S 'Defending the indefensible? Quantitative methods and feminist research', in J Holland, M Blair and S Sheldon (eds) *Debates and Issues in Feminist Research and Pedagogy* (Clevedon: Multilingual Matters, 1995) 235–47

Kemmis, S, 'Action research in retrospect and prospect', in S Kemmis and R McTaggart (eds) *The Action Research Reader*, 3rd edn (Geelong, Victoria, Australia: Deakin University Press, 1990)

Kemmis, S and McTaggart, R (eds) *The Action Research Planner* 3rd edn (Geelong, Victoria, Australia: Deakin University Press, 1988)

Kirk, S A (ed.) *Social Work Research Methods: building knowledge for practice* (Washington, DC: National Association of Social Workers, 1999)

Kirkpatrick, S A 'Social science research under siege: scarcity or conspiracy?' *Social Science Quarterly* 64 (4) (1984) 705–17

Kitzinger, C and Frith, H 'Just say no? The use of Conversation Analysis in developing a feminist perspective on sexual refusal', in M Weatherell, S Taylor and S J Yates (eds) *Discourse as Data: A Guide for Analysis* (London: Sage, 2001) 167–85

Krug G and Hepworth J 'Poststructuralism, qualitative methodology and public health research methods as a legitimation strategy for knowledge' *Critical Public Health*, 7 (1 and 2) (1997) 50–60

Land, H and Hudson, S 'Methodological considerations in surveying Latina AIDS caregivers: issues of sampling and measurement', in S A Kirk (ed.) *Social Work Research Methods: building knowledge for practice* (Washington, DC: National Association of Social Workers, 1999) 456–75

Lather, P 'Issues of validity in openly ideological research: between a rock and a soft place' *Interchange*, 17 (1986) 63–84

Lather, P *Getting Smart* (New York: Routledge, 1991)

Lather, P 'Fertile obsession: validity after poststructuralism' *Sociological Quarterly*, 34 (1993) 673–94

Lavalette, M and Mooney, G *Class Struggle and Social Welfare* (London: Routledge, 2000)

Leonard, P *Postmodern Welfare: reconstructing an emancipatory project* (London: Sage, 1997)

Levitas, R and Guy, W (eds) *Interpreting Official Statistics* (London, Routledge, 1996)

Lewin, C 'Elementary quantitative methods', in B Somekh and C Lewin (eds) *Research Methods in the Social Sciences* (London: Sage, 2005) 215–25

Lewin, K *Resolving Social Conflict: selected papers on group dynamics* (New York: Harper, 1948)

Lincoln, Y and Guba, E G *Naturalistic Inquiry* (Beverley Hills, CA: Sage, 1985)

Lishman, J 'Personal and professional development', in R Adams, L Dominelli and M Payne (eds) *Social Work: themes, issues and critical debates* (London: Macmillan, 1998) 89–103

Macdonald, G *Effective Intervention for Child Abuse and Neglect* (London: Wiley, 2001)

Macdonald, G and Roberts, H *What Works in the Early Years?* (Ilford: Barnardo's, 1995)

McKie, L 'Engagement and evaluation in qualitative inquiry', in T May (ed.) *Qualitative Research in Action* (London: Sage, 2002)

McLaughlin, K 'From ridicule to institutionalisation: anti-oppression, the state and social work' *Critical Social Policy*, 25 (3) (2005) 283–305

McQueen, D V and Anderson, L M 'What counts as evidence: issues and debates', in I Rootman et al. (eds) *Evaluation in Health Promotion: principles and perspectives* (Geneva: WHO Regional Publications European Series, 2001) 63–81

Maguire, P *Doing Participatory Research: a feminist approach* (Amherst, MA: Center for International Education, 1987)

Maguire, P 'Proposing a more feminist participatory research: knowing and being embraced openly', in K de Koning and M Martin (eds) *Participatory Research in Health* (London: Zed Books, 1996) 27–39

Mark, R *Research Made Simple: a handbook for social workers* (London: Sage, 1996)

Martin, M 'Developing a feminist participatory framework: evaluating the process', in B Humphries and C Truman (eds) *Rethinking Social Research* (Aldershot: Avebury, 1994) 123–45

Martin, M 'Issues of power in the participatory research process', in K de Koning and M Martin (eds) *Participatory Research in Health: issues and experiences* (London: Zed Books, 1996)

Martin, M *Participatory Research: an educational process*, unpublished PhD thesis (Manchester: University of Manchester, 1999)

Mayhew, H *London Labour and the London Poor, Vol. 1: The London Street-Folk* (London: George Woodfall and Son, 1851)

Metcalfe, F and Humphreys, C 'Fostering action research and action research in fostering' *Qualitative Social Work*, 1 (4) (2002) 435–50

Mienczakowski, J 'Ethnography in the form of theatre with emancipatory intentions', in C Truman, D M Mertens and B Humphries (eds) *Research and Inequality* (London: UCL Press, 2000)

Morgan, S 'Documentary and text analysis: uncovering meaning in a worked example', in B Humphries (ed.) *Research in Social Work and Social Welfare: issues and debates for practice* (London: Jessica Kingsley Publishers, 2000)

Morrison, K L *Marx, Durkheim, Weber: formations of modern social thought* (Thousand Oaks, CA: Sage, 1995)

Morrow, R A *Critical Theory and Methodology* (Thousand Oaks, CA: Sage, 1994)

Mort, F *Dangerous Sexualities: medico-moral politics in England since 1830* (London: Routledge and Kegan Paul, 1987)

Mosse, D, '"People's knowledge", participation and patronage: operations and representations in rural development', in B Cooke and U Kotari (eds) *Participation, the New Tyranny?* (London: Zed Books, 2001) 16–35

Mullender, A and Hague, G 'Giving a voice to women survivors of domestic violence through recognition as a service user group' *BJSW*, 35 (8) (2005) 1321–42

NACRO, *Grow Up and Be Responsible* (London: National Association for the Care and Resettlement of Offenders, 2001)

Newman, T, Moseley, A, Tierney, S and Ellis, A *Evidence-based Social Work* (Lyme Regis: Russell House Publishing, 2005)

Oakley, A *Experiments in Knowing: gender and method in the social sciences* (Cambridge: Polity Press, 2000)

O'Brien, J and Lyle, C *A Framework for Accomplishment* (Decatur, GA: Responsive Systems Associates, 1987)

Ong, B N, Humphris, G, Annet, H and Rifkin, S 'Rapid appraisal in an urban setting, and example from the developed world', *Social Science and Medicine*, 32 (8) (1991) 909–15

Onyett, S *Case Management in Mental Health* (London: Chapman and Hall, 1992)

Orme, J 'Social work: gender and justice' *BJSW*, 32 (6) (2002) 799–814

Park, P 'What is participatory research? A theoretical and methodological perspective', in P Park, M Brydon-Miller, B Hall and T Jackson (eds) *Voices of Change: participatory research in the USA and Canada* (Westport, CT: Bergin and Harvey, 1993) 1–20

Park, P, Brydon-Miller, M, Hall, B and Jackson, T (eds) *Voices of Change: participatory research in the USA and Canada* (Westport, CT: Bergin and Harvey, 1993)

Parker, H J *View From the Boys: a sociology of downtown adolescents* (London: David and Charles, 1974)

Patton, M Q *Utilization-Focused Evaluation: the new century text* (Thousand Oaks, CA: Sage, 1997)

Patton, M Q *Qualitative Research and Evaluation Methods*, 3rd edn (Thousand Oaks CA: Sage, 2002)

Pawson, R and Tilley, N *Realistic Evaluation* (London: Sage, 1997)

Payne, G and Payne, J *Key Concepts in Social Research* (London: Sage, 2004)

Pease, B and Fook J (eds) *Transforming Social Work: postmodern critical perspectives* (London: Routledge, 1999)

Pitcairn, K 'Exploring ways of giving a voice to people with learning disabilities, in B Humphries and C Truman (eds) *Rethinking Social Research* (Aldershot: Avebury, 1994) 59–81

Platt, J ' "Case study" in American methodological thought' *Current Sociology*, 40 (1992) 17–48

Platt, J 'Cases of cases . . . of cases', in C C Ragin and H Becker (eds) *What is a Case? Exploring the Foundations of Social Inquiry* (New York: Cambridge University Press, 1992)

Plummer, K (ed.) *Symbolic Interactionism: volumes 1 and 2* (Aldershot: Edward Elgar, 1991)

Plummer, K (ed.) *Modern Homosexualities: fragments of lesbian and gay experience* (London: Routledge, 1992)

Plummer, K *Telling Sexual Stories: power, change and social worlds* (London: Routledge, 1995)

Polit-O'Hara, D and Hungler, B *Nursing Research: principles and methods* (5th edn) (Philadelphia: Lippincott, 1995)

Potts, M K 'Social support and depression among older adults living alone', in S A Kirk (ed.) *Social Work Research Methods: building knowledge for practice* (Washington, DC: National Association of Social Work, 1999) 194–212

QAA (Quality Assurance Agency) *Benchmark Statement for Social Policy and Social Administration and Social Work* (Gloucester: QAA for Higher Education, 2000)

Ragin, C C and Becker, H S (eds) *What is a Case? Exploring the Foundations of Social Inquiry* (New York: Cambridge University Press, 1992)

Ramsbotham, Sir D *Report of the Fourth Inspection of HMYOT and RC Feltham* (London: HM Inspector of Prisons, Home Office, 2001)

Reason, P *Participation in Human Inquiry* (London: Sage, 1994)

Reason, P and Bradbury, H (eds) *Handbook of Action Research: participative inquiry and practice* (London: Sage, 2001)

Reid, W J and Smith, A *Research in Social Work* (New York: Columbia University Press, 1989)

Reinharz, S *On Becoming a Social Scientist* (New Brunswick, NJ: Transaction Books, 1984)

Reinharz, S *Feminist Methods in Social Research* (New York: Oxford University Press, 1992)

Robson, C *Small Scale Evaluation* (London: Sage, 2000)

Rokeach, M 'A values approach to the prevention and reduction of drug abuse', in T J Glynn et al. (eds) *Preventing Adolescent Drug Abuse: intervention strategies* (Rockville, MD: US Department of Health and Human Services, 1983) 172–94

Rootman, I, Goodstadt, M, Hyndman, B, McQueen, D V, Potum, L, Springett, J and Ziglio, E (eds) *Evaluation in Health Promotion, Principles and Perspectives* (Geneva: WHO Regional Publications European Series, 2006)

Rose, H *Love, Power and Knowledge* (Cambridge: Polity Press, 1994)

Rossiter, A, Prilleltensky, I and Walsh-Bowers, R 'A postmodern perspective on professional ethics', in B Fawcett, B Featherstone, J Fook and A Rossiter (eds) *Practice and Research in Social Work: postmodern perspectives* (London: Routledge, 2000)

Rowntree, B S *Poverty and Progress: a second social survey of York* (London: Longman's, Green and Co, 1941)

Royse, D R *Research Methods in Social Work*, 4th edn (Pacific Grove, CA and London: Brooks Cole–Thomson Learning, 2003)

Rutter, J *Refugee Children in the UK* (Maidenhead: Open University Press, 2006)

Sackett, D L, Richardson, W S, Rosenberg, W and Haynes, R B *Evidence-Based Medicine: how to practice and to teach EBP* (New York: Churchill Livingstone, 1997)

Sarantakos, S *Social Research*, 3rd edn (Basingstoke: Palgrave Macmillan, 2005)

Schön D A *The Reflective Practitioner* (San Francisco: Jossey-Boss, 1983)

Schön, D A *Educating the Reflective Practitioner* (San Francisco: Jossey-Boss, 1987)

Schostak, J F *Understanding, Designing and Conducting Qualitative Research in Education* (Buckingham: Open University Press, 2002)

Schutt, R K *Investigating the Social World: the process and practice of research* (Thousand Oaks, CA: Pine Forge Press, 1996)

Schutz, A, *The Phenomenology of the Social World*, translated by G Walsh and F Lehnert (Evanston, IL: Northwestern University Press, 1969)

Shadish, W R, Cook, T D and Leviton, L C *Foundations of Program Evaluation* (Thousand Oaks, CA: Sage, 1991)

Shaw, I *Evaluating in Practice* (Aldershot: Arena, 1996)

Shaw, I *Be Your Own Evaluator: a guide to reflective and enabling evaluation* (Wrexham: Prospects, 1997)

Shaw I *Evaluating for Social Justice*, paper presented at World Congress of IFSW and IASSW, Jerusalem, July 1998

Shaw, I *Qualitative Evaluation* (London: Sage, 1999)

Shaw, I 'Ethics in qualitative research and evaluation' *Journal of Social Work*, 3 (1) (2003) 9–29

Shaw, I and Lishman, J (eds) *Evaluation and Social Work Practice* (London: Sage, 1999)

Shaw, I and Shaw, A 'Keeping social work honest: evaluating as profession and practice' *BJSW*, 27 (6) (1997) 847–69

Sheldon, B 'The validity of evidence-based practice in social work: a reply to Stephen Webb' *BJSW*, 31 (5) (2001) 801–9

Sheppard, M *Appraising and Using Social Research in the Human Services: an introduction for social work and health professionals* (London: Jessica Kingsley Publishers, 2004)

Smith, G *Social Need: policy, practice and research* (London: Routledge, 1980)

Somekh, B and Lewin, C (eds) *Research Methods in the Social Sciences* (London: Sage, 2005)

Stake, R E *The Art of Case Study Research* (Thousand Oaks, CA: Sage, 1995)

Stake, R E 'Case studies', in N Denzin and Y Lincoln (eds) *Strategies of Qualitative Inquiry* (London: Sage, 1998)

Stanley, L 'Feminist praxis and the academic mode of production: an editorial introduction', in L Stanley (ed.) *Feminist Praxis* (London: Routledge, 1990) 3–19

Stapf, K H 'Laboruntersuchungen', in E Roth (ed.) *Sozialwissenschaftliche Methoden* (Wien: R Olenbourg Verlag, 1995)

Stark, S and Torrance, H 'Case study', in B Somekh and C Lewin (eds) *Research Methods in the Social Sciences* (London: Sage, 2005)

Strauss, A and Corbin, J *Basics of Qualitative Research*, 2nd edn (Thousand Oaks, CA: Sage, 1998)

Sudnow, D *Passing On* (Englewood Cliffs, NJ: Prentice-Hall, 1967)

Tandon, R 'The historical roots and contemporary tendencies in participatory research: implications for health care' in K de Koning and M Martin (eds) *Participatory Research in Health: issues and experiences* (London: Zed Books, 1996) 19–26

Taylor, S 'Locating and conducting Discourse Analytic Research', in M Weatherell, S Taylor and S J Yates (eds) *Discourse as Data: a guide for analysis* (London: Sage, 2001) 5–48

Taylor, S 'Researching the social: an introduction to ethnographic research', in S Taylor (ed.) *Ethnographic Research: a reader* (London: Sage, 2002) 1–12

Temple, B and Edwards, R 'Limited exchanges: approaches to involving people who do not speak English in research and service development', in B Temple and R Moran (eds) *Doing Research with Refugees* (Bristol: Policy Press, 2006)

Temple, B and Moran, R (eds) *Doing Research with Refugees* (Bristol: Policy Press, 2006)

Titmuss, R 'Foreword', in M Goldberg *Helping the Aged* (London: Allen and Unwin, 1970)

Townsend, P and Davidson, N (eds) *Inequalities in Health. The Black Report: the health divide* (London: Penguin, 1988)

Townsend, P, Phillimore, P and Beattie, A *Health and Deprivation: inequality and the North* (London: Routledge, 1988)

Trinh, T M-ha *Woman, Native, Other: writing postcoloniality and feminism* (Bloomington, IND: Indiana University Press, 1989)

Truman, C 'User involvement in large scale research: bridging the gap between service users and service providers?', in B Broad (ed.) *The Politics of Social Work Research and Evaluation* (Birmingham: Venture Press, 1999)

Truman, C 'New social movements and social research', in C Truman, D M Mertens and B Humphries (eds) *Research and Inequality* (London: UCL Press, 2000)

Truman, C 'Ethics and the ruling relations of research production' *Sociological Research Online*, 8 (1), 2003 <http://www.socresonline.org.uk/8/1/truman.html>

Truman, C and Humphries, B 'Rethinking social research: research in an unequal world', in B Humphries and C Truman (eds) *Rethinking Social Research* (Aldershot: Avebury, 1994)

Tuck, V *Links between Social Deprivation and Harm to Children: a study of parenting in social deprivation*, unpublished PhD thesis (Open University, UK, 1995)

Tuck, V 'Socio-economic factors: a neglected dimension in harm to children', in J Batsleer and B Humphries (eds) *Welfare, Exclusion and Political Agency* (London: Routledge, 2000)

Tuhiwai Smith, L *Decolonizing Methodologies: research and indigenous peoples* (London and New York: Zed Books, 1999)

Turner, S P *The Search for a Methodology of Social Science* (Dordrecht: Reidel, 1986)

Van Dijk, T 'Principles of critical discourse analysis' *Discourse and Society*, 4 (1993) 249–85

Vanstone, M 'Behavioural and cognitive interventions', in I Shaw and J Lishman (eds) *Evaluation and Social Work Practice* (London: Sage, 1999) 219–34

Walshe, K and Rundall, T G 'Evidence-based management: from theory to practice in health care' *Millbank Quarterly*, 79 (3) (2001) 429–57

Walter, I, Nutley, S, Percy-Smith, J, McNeish, D and Frost, S *Promoting the Use of Research in Social Care Practice, SCIE Knowledge Review, 7* (Bristol: Policy Press, 2004)

Weatherell, M, Taylor, S and Yates, S J (eds), *Discourse as Data: a guide for analysis* (London: Sage, 2001a)

Weatherell, M, Taylor, S and Yates, S J (eds) *Discourse Theory and Practice: a reader*, London, Sage, 2001b)

Webb, S A 'Some considerations on the validity of evidence-based practice in social work', *BJSW*, 31 (1) (2001) 57–79

Weber, M *The Methodology of the Social Sciences*, translated and edited by E A Shils and H A Finch (New York: Free Press, 1949)

Weber, M *Basic Concepts in Sociology* (London: Peter Owen, 1969)

Weeks, J 'Rediscovering values', in J Squires (ed.) *Principled Positions* (London: Lawrence and Wishart, 1993)

Weiss, C H 'Using research in the policy process: potential and constraints' *Policy Studies Journal*, 4 (1976) 224–28

Weiss, C H 'The circuitry of enlightenment' *Knowledge, Creation, Diffusion, Utilization*, 8 (1987) 274–81

Weiss, C H 'Policy Research: data, ideas or argument?', in Wagner, P, Weiss, C H, Wittrock, B and Wollman, H (eds) *Social Sciences and Modern States: national experiences and theoretical crossroads* (Cambridge: Cambridge University Press, 1991)

Weiss, C H *Evaluation* 2nd edn (Upper Saddle River, NJ: Prentice Hall, 1998)

Welbourn, A 'Rapid rural appraisal, gender and health – alternative ways of listening to needs' *ids bulletin*, 23 (1) (1992) 8–18

Weyts, A, Morpeth, L and Bullock, R 'Department of Health Research Overviews – Past, Present and Future: an evaluation of the dissemination of the Blue Book, "Child Protection: Messages from Research"' *Child and Family Social Work*, 2 (2000) 215–23

Whyte, W F *Street Corner Society: the social structure of an Italian slum* (Chicago: University of Chicago Press, 1981)

Whyte, W F (ed.) *Participatory Action Research* (Newbury Park, CA: Sage, 1991)

Wilkins, P 'Storytelling as research', in B Humphries (ed.) *Research in Social Care and Social Welfare* (London: Jessica Kingsley Publishers, 2000) 144–53

Williams, C and Soydan, H 'When and how does ethnicity matter? A cross-national study of social work responses to ethnicity in child protection cases' *BJSW*, 35 (6) (2005) 901–20

Williams, F 'Principles of recognition and respect in welfare', in G Lewis, S Gewirtz and J Clarke (eds) *Rethinking Social Policy* (London: Sage, 2000) 338–52

Wodak, R, de Cillia, R, Reisigl, M and Liebhart, K *The Discursive Construction of Identity* (Edinburgh: Edinburgh University Press, 1999)

Wodak, R and Meyer, M *Methods of Critical Discourse Analysis* (London: Sage, 2001)

Wooffitt, R 'Researching psychic practitioners: conversational analysis', in M Weatherell, S Taylor and S J Yates (eds) *Discourse as Data: a guide for analysis* (London: Sage, 2001)

Yar, M 'Beyond Nancy Fraser's "perspectival dualism", *Economy and Society*, 30 (3) (2001) 288–303

Yin, R K *Case Study Research: design and methods*, 2nd edn (Thousand Oaks, CA: Sage, 1994)

Young, I M *Justice and the Politics of Difference* (Princeton, NJ: Princeton University Press, 1990)

Internet resources

Research in social work and social care

Department of Health research governance, http://www.doh.gov.uk/research/rd3/nhsrandd/researchgovernance/ethics/ethics.htm

BASW Code of Ethics, www.basw.co.uk
IASSW Ethics in Social Work: statement of principles, www.iassw-aiets.org
AASW (Australian Association of Social Workers): www.aasw.asn.au
These are codes of ethics from social work professional organizations, that set out distinctive guidelines for research in social work.

JUC/SWEC Theorising Social Work Research seminar series
http://www.elsc.org.uk/socialcareresource/twsrindex.htm
Papers from a series of seminars designed to promote the development of research in social work.

Social Care Institute for Excellence (SCIE): www.scie-socialcareonline.org.uk
Contains many resources on good practice, including articles on evaluations undertaken, research design and related topics in social care

Inter-Centre Network for Evaluation of Social Work Practice: www.intsoceval.org
An international network of researchers engaged in a wide range of evaluation studies.

General

British Sociological Association Code of Ethics: http://www.britsoc.org.uk/about.ethic.html

INTUTE: Social Sciences, http://www.intute.ac.uk/socialsciences.html
A database of web resources for research tools and methods

www.sosig.ac.uk/
An online catalogue of hundreds of high quality internet resources.

Discourse Analysis Online Journal: http://extra.shu.ac.uk/daol/index.html
Provides a wide range of articles and approaches to discourse analytic research

Ethnography Journal: www.sagepub.co.uk/journal.aspx?pid=105533
The main international journal dedicated to ethnographic research

Action Research: http://scu.edu.au/schools/gcm/ar/arhome.html
A comprehensive site with access to *Action Research International* Journal, resource papers, booklists, extracts from dissertations and other materials.

Sarantakos, http://www.palgrave.com/sociology/sarantakos
A companion website to Sarantakos (2005) with further information and exercises based on a range of methods

Index

cognitive-behavioural approach, 46, 183

Cohen, L, 28, 72, 75, 78, 84

community, 64, 65
  care assessment, 81–8
  development, 181
  health, 180–3

consent, forms, 81–3
  informed, 22

contradiction, 105

control, 41–4
  group, 37

convenience, 38

conversation analysis (CA), 122–3

Cooke, B, 66

Corbin, J, 144

Cornwall, A, 50, 60, 65

covert methods, 135

Craig, G, 24–5

Crawford, P, 44

Cree, V, 129, 141–2

crisis, 105

critical conversations, 79
  dialectical, 107
  discourse analysis (CDA), 123–4, 131–2
  pluralism, 107
  theory, 104, 179

Croft, S, 16

cultural bias, 160

David, M, 89, 94, 157

Davidson, N, 153

Davies, R M, 135

Davis, A, 135

deception, 23

decision making, 163–4

deconstructive textual analysis, 117

de Koning, K, 52

Denscombe, M, 1, 190

Denzin, N K, 14, 136, 144–7, 149
  (DELTA), 54, 61

dialogue, dialectic, 75

disability, 104

discourse analysis, 129
  analytic research, 121–2
  counter, 130

Dockery, G, 52

DoH, 19

domestic abuse, 88
  survivors, 114

domination, 106

Dominelli, L, 2, 109, 192

Drakeford, M, 12

Du Bois, B, 34

Economic and Social Research
  Council (ESRC), 20, 191

education, 52, 53–4

Edwards, R, 29

elderly people, 39

Elks, M, 187

Elliott, J, 29, 71

emancipation, 105, 179

emancipatory mode, 72–4

empiricism, 36

empowerment, 67, 78

epistemology, 13

ethical research, 19

ethics, 44–5
  codes of, 20
  situated, 27

ethnicity, 161–2

ethnographic, ethnography, 89, 134, 142, 147–9
  crises in, 145–7

ethnomethodology, 139

evaluate, evaluation, 72, 74
  for accountability, 169
  for development, 169
  for knowledge, 169
  formative, 175
  fourth generation, 171
  outcome, 173–6
  participatory, 178
  process, 173–6
  reflexive, 173
  summative, 176, 181
  utilization-focused evaluation, 171

Evans, C, 57

Everitt, A, 3, 170, 191

evidence-based practice, 4–7

existential sociology, 136

experimental group, 37

experiments, 33

external influences, 16

interpretive communities, 140
    sociology, 135
interview, interviews, 89, 92–4, 110
interviewer effect, 42
intimacy, 25

Jewkes, R, 50, 60, 65
Jones, C, 31, 192
Jones, J H, 34
Jones, M, 109
Jordan, B, 31, 47
Jordan, C, 47

Keider, H, 8
Kelly, E, 135
Kelly, L, 109, 161
Kemmis, S, 70, 71, 74, 83
kinship, 95
Kirk, S A, 151,158
Kirkhart, K, 187
Kirkpatrick, S A, 33
Kitzinger, C, 123
knowledge, nature of, 63
Kotari, U, 66
Kreider, H, 95
Kreuter, M W, 171
Krug, G, 34

Lait, J, 39
Land, H, 160
language, 127, 131
Lather, P, 147, 149
Lavalette, M, 31
legitimation, crisis in, 146
Leonard, P, 108
Levitas, R, 165
Lewin, C, 28, 69, 154, 155, 157
Lincoln, Y, 144
Lishman, J, 169–70
Lyle, C, 55–8

Macdonald, G, 40, 46
Macdonald, M, 155–6, 157
Maguire, P, 52, 65
Manion, L, 28, 72, 75, 78, 84
Mark, R, 1
Martin, M, 21, 52, 64, 65
Marxism, 104, 130

Max-Con-Min rule, 37
Mayer, E, 8, 95
Mayhew, H, 152
McKie, L, 180–3
McLaughlin, K, 31
McTaggart, R, 70, 71, 74, 78
measurement, 154
mental health, 109–12
Mercer, G, 51, 57
Metcalfe, F, 78–81
methodological questions, 62–6
methodology, 13
Mienczakowski, J, 53, 61
Mooney, G, 31
Moran, R, 191
Morgan, S, 128–9
Morpeth, L, 78
Morrison, K L, 28, 72, 75, 78, 84
Morrow, R A, 105, 107
Mort, F, 152
Mosse, D, 66, 67
motherhood, unmarried, 130
mothers, 162–3
    black, 116–17
Mullender, A, 109, 114–16

narrative methods, 139–40
National Association for the Care
        and Resettlement of Offenders
        (NACRO), 47
National Occupational Standards, 2
natural, naturalistic methods, 89,
        134, 138
need, assessment of, 142–3
New Deal for Lone Parents, 130
New Labour policy, 126–7
Newman, T, 5
Noble, C, 19, 27
non-reactive techniques, 138

Oakley, A, 4, 9, 11, 152, 166, 193
objective, objectivity, 36, 62, 69, 153
objectivist tradition, 136
O'Brien, J, 55–8
observation, non-participant, 114
Office for National Statistics, 112
Ong, B N, 61
ontology, 13